PEARCE GENEALOGY

BEING THE

RECORD OF THE POSTERITY OF RICHARD PEARCE

AN EARLY INHABITANT OF

PORTSMOUTH, IN RHODE ISLAND,

WHO CAME FROM ENGLAND, AND WHOSE GENEALOGY IS TRACED BACK TO 972

WITH

AN INTRODUCTION OF THE MALE DESCENDANTS OF JOSCELINE DE LOUVAINE, THE SECOND HOUSE OF PERCY, EARLS OF NORTHUMBERLAND, BARONS PERCY AND TERRITORIAL LORDS OF ALNWICK, WARKWORTH AND PRUDHOE CASTLES IN THE COUNTY OF NORTHUMBERLAND, ENGLAND,

BY

COL. FREDERICK C. PIERCE,

Author of Peirce History, Pierce Genealogy, etc. Member of the British Harlequin and other historical societies.

1888
ROCKFORD
ILLINOIS

Notice

In many older books, foxing (or discoloration) occurs and, in some instances, print lightens with wear and age. Reprinted books, such as this, often duplicate these flaws, notwithstanding efforts to reduce or eliminate them. The pages of this reprint have been digitally enhanced and, where possible, the flaws eliminated in order to provide clarity of content and a pleasant reading experience.

Pearce Genealogy: Being the Record of the Posterity of Richard Pearce an Early Inhabitant of Portsmouth, in Rhode Island, Who Came from England, and Whose Genealogy is Traced Back to 972

Originally published
Albany, N. Y.
1888

Reprinted by:

Janaway Publishing, Inc.
732 Kelsey Ct.
Santa Maria, California 93454
(805) 925-1038
www.janawaygenealogy.com

2014

ISBN: 978-1-59641-289-7

Made in the United States of America

TO

HON. RICHARD J. OGLESBY

GOVERNOR OF THE

STATE OF ILLINOIS

FOR WHOM THE AUTHOR OF THIS VOLUME ENTERTAINS THE HIGHEST PERSONAL ESTEEM

THIS WORK IS

MOST RESPECTFULLY DEDICATED

BY HIS FRIEND

THE AUTHOR.

"Concerning this nepular history, then; is it a human invention, or is it a Divine record? Is it 'a tale told by an idiot signifying nothing,' or is it a plan of infinite imagination signifying immortality?"

Prof. BENJAMIN PEIRCE,

of Harvard University.

AUTHOR'S PREFACE.

For the past fifteen years the undersigned has been at work on the Pearce (however spelled) genealogy. First a genealogical record of the posterity of John Pers, of Watertown, 1630, my ancestor, was published. Then followed a record of the descendants of Sergt. Thomas Peirce, of Charleston. While collecting material for these families much valuable data was obtained for the present work and another volume, the posterity of Capt. Michael Peirce, soon to be issued. The task of compiling the present work has been much more arduous than that of either the two other books. A vast amount of correspondence has been conducted with persons bearing the name, and with others, descendants of Pearces. Rhode Island town records have been examined, as have the wills and inventories of estates of deceased members of the family, all involving an untold amount of labor. The work of compiling was prolonged on account of business which could not be neglected, and nearly all of the work upon this volume has been done during evenings after other duties had been finished.

My thanks are especially due to the Duke of Northumberland, Judge James O. Pierce, of Minneapolis, Mrs. A. R. Howland, of Westport, Mass., and the many others who rendered valuable aid and assistance. Very truly,

FRED. C. PIERCE.

ROCKFORD, ILL., Dec. 1, 1887.

The name of Pearse is a common one in England, being undoubtedly derived from the baptismal name, Peter or Pirse, or Pierse, as it was called after the Conquest and while French was still the court language, and has been variously called or written Pieres, Pierse, Pierce, Pearce, Piers, Peires, Peirce, Peirse, Pearse, Peers, and families of the same name settled in the counties of Gloucester, Kent, Devon, Norfolk, Bedford, Somerset, Suffolk, England.

Percy—Piercy—Percey—Pierce—Pearce, etc.—Local. The renowned family of Northumberland, England, derived their name from Percy Forest, in the province of Maen, Normandy, whence they came, which signifies a stony place, from *pierre*. It may signify a hunting place, from *pirsen*, Teutonic, to hunt; *percer*, French, to penetrate, to force one's way.

—[Arthur's Etymological Dictionary of Christian Names, 1857.]

The following are the different ways the name is spelled in several countries:

English.	French.	Swedish.	Danish	Dutch.	Italian.	Spanish.	Portuguese,
Peter.	Pierre.	Per.	Pedeo.	Pieter.	Pietro.	Pedro.	Pedro.
Piers.	Pierrot.			Piet.	Pier.		Pedrinho.
Pierce.	Perrin.				Piero.		
	Peire.				Pietruccio.		

[From History of Christian Names, England, 1863.]

THE ENGLISH BRANCH.

The name of Percy, often tragic, but always honorable, is more interwoven than any other with the early minstrelsy and romance of England. The family which it denoted never perhaps exercised over the destinies of England the mighty power which, during the Wars of the Roses, was wielded by a junior branch of their Northern rivals, the Nevills,* but peculiar instancesrendered it far more the favorite of the bards. The proximity of the Percies to the border involved them in continual hostility; which being often carried on with petty forces, and consisting of making or repelling a foray, was rather in the nature of a private feud than a national war; and hence their heroes were the more capable of being individualized with dramatic effect. This family was also fortunate, in the vicinity, on the opposite border, of a house so powerful as to rival its own sovereign princes. The Douglass it was glorious to overcome—by the Douglass it was not disgraceful to be vanquished. Thus the Percies became the theme of the minstrels of two nations; and national prejudice would lead those of each to extol the prowess of their family, whether they

"Make the story
The triumph of the foe to tell,"

or that of their own countrymen to cover their country's shame to enhance its glory.

In taking a survey of the house of Percy, we shall hastily pass over the pristine patriarchs of the race, as Manfred, the Dane,† and

"Brave Galfred," who "to Normandy
With vent'rous Rolla came;
And, from his Norman castles won.
Assumed the Percy name,"‡

and descend in their pedigree to Agnes de Perci, the heiress of this lofty line which had been enriched, by the conquest of England

---

*See Local Historian's Table Book, Traditional Div., vol. 2, pp. 63–5, and also Bulwer's novel of "The Last of the Barons," where the character of the heads of this branch are drawn with fidelity, as well as eloquence.

†Born about 972. He was a Danish chieftain. See Burke's Heraldry.

‡The Hermit of Warkworth.

and the favor of its kings, with vast possessions in Yorkshire* and Lincolnshire. She became the bride of Josceline de Louvaine, brother of Adeliza, second queen to the first Henry of England, and younger son of Godfrey, Count of Lorraine and Bruxells, and reigning duke of Brabant.† Yet the proud condition was imposed on the Flemish prince, on his accepting the Norman alliance, that he should relinquish either his own name or coat of arms in favor of that of his bride. He decided the option by assuming the name of Percy; and the ancient royal arms of Brabant are at this day borne the first of the eight hundred and ninety-two quarterings of the Percy shield.‡

The wealth which Josceline thus acquired by marriage received an accession by the grant of the honor of Petworth, in Sussex, which was bestowed on him by the queen, his sister. This was a part of the earldom of Arundel; the estates of which had reverted to the crown in consequence of the rebellion of a former earl, and were settled on the queen in dower. She, after the death of the king, her husband, married William de Albini, who thus obtained the earldom matrimonial of Arundel; and of him Josceline held Petworth by the Knights' service of being his castellan, and, during siege, defending his castle of Arundel for forty days.§

The grandson and eventful heir of this marriage, William de Perci, third territorial lord of Petworth—whose mother was Isabel de Bruce of Skelton, daughter of the elder branch of that family, which afterwards gave kings to Scotland—had two wives. His second wife was Ellen de Baliol, who brought to her husband, Dalton, in the bishoprick of Durham, since called Dalton—Percy,‖ and this was not improbably the first English possession acquired by

---

*Of the Yorkshire possessions of this family, Topcliff in the North riding, and Spofford in the West riding, became their chief residences.—Dugdale's Baronage, vol. 1, p, 270. In the deanery of Craven, in the West riding of Yorkshire, the Percies held, from the era of the conquest, an extensive domain called the Percy fee; where, however, they had no residence. In the time of Henry VIII, it passed from them to the Cliffords, in consequence of a marriage. —See Whitaker's Craven.

†"They sung how Agnes, beauteous heir,
The queen's own brother wed—
Lord Josceline, sprung from Charlemagne,
In princely Brabant bred." —Hermit of Warkworth.

There is a printed pedigree tracing the descent of Agnes de Perci up to Manfred; and that of Josceline de Louvaine up, through Gerberga, daughter and heiress of Charles, Duke of Lorraine, to Charlemagne, and, in the male line, to the ancient dukes of Hainault.

‡Not more famous in arms than distinguished for its alliances, the house of Percy stands pre-eminent for the number and rank of the families which are represented by the present Duke of Northumberland, whose banner consequently exhibits an assemblage of nearly nine hundred armorial ensigns, among which are those of King Henry the Seventh, of several younger branches of the blood-royal, of the sovereign houses of France, Castile, Leon and Scotland, and of the ducal houses of Normandy and Brittany, forming a galaxy of heraldic honors altogether unparalled.—Quarterly Review, No. cxliii, May, 1848, p. 170.

§Dallway's Sussex, vol. ii, p. 268. Miss Strickland's Lives of the Queens of England.

‖"In 1870 Henry, Lord Percy, sold this manor to Sir John Nevill of Raby," Lord Nevill.—Surtees' Dur., vol. iii, p. 98.

the house of Percy, north of the Tees.* The male issue was by this second marriage; and the son and heir, Henry de Percy, wedded Eleanor, daughter of John Plantagenet, Earl of Warren and Surrey, descended from a base-born son of Godfrey Plantagenet, Count of Anjou, the second husband of Maud of England, Empress of Germany.

On the early death of two elder sons, his youngest son, Henry de Percy, succeeded to the family inheritance of wealth and honors. From youth to age he was a warrior. He was one of the victors in the battle of Dunbar; and was highly distinguished throughout the Scottish wars† during the reign of King Edward the First; and he is alleged to have been rewarded by the victorious English monarch with the Scotch Earldom of Carrick, which Robert the Bruce (afterwards king of Scotland) was declared to have forfeited by slaying the Red Comyn in the church at Dumfries.‡ In 1299, seven years previously to this he had received a writ of summons to the House of Lords, by which the barony in fee of Percy was created. It was he who acquired Alnwick§ in the county of Northumberland, which has, to the present day, been transmitted to his descendents. He also obtained the Lordship of Corbridge,|| in Northumberland, by

"Ere Percy,—liv'd there many an English knight—
Before brave Douglas,—many a Scottish wight,
Who undistinguish'd lie without a name,
Now having lost the heralds of their fame."

"*Cheviot, a poetical fragment,*" *belonging to the beginning of the last century, edited by John Adamson, Esq., of Newcastle,* 1817.

†He was, in the 25, Edward I (1297), sent to Scotland in command of some forces of his uncle, Earl of Warren, who was general of all the armies north of the Trent.—Dugdale's Baronage, vol. 1, p. 272.

‡Ibid, vol. i, p. 273.

§Alnwick, at the time of the Conquest, belonged to William Tyron, a Saxon baron, who was slain in the battle of Hastings. His daughter and his possessions were conferred by the conqueror on his follower, Ivo de Fesco; whose daughter and heiress carried it to her husband, Eustace Fitz-John. Descended from them was William de Vescey, the last of a line of feudal barons; who, on the death of his only legitimate son, in the Welsh wars, granted to King Edward I. some lands in Ireland, that his natural son, William de Kildare, might be allowed to suceeed him in the Northumberland property; and, upon his death, appointed Anthony Beck, the most princely of the bishops of Durham, trustee for his son, then a minor. The bishop, offended, as has been alleged, at the language which this son had been reported to have used respecting him, appropriated the property to his own use, and eventually sold it to Henry, Lord Percy, by a deed dated 1309, signed by some of the principal persons of the time, and confirmed by King Edward II., the next year; and Lord Percy, in order to perfect his title, took the precaution to obtain a re-lease from Sir Gilbert de Aiton, a collateral relative, but right heir to William de Visci. Anthony Beck appears to have appropriated this barony to himself for many years before he sold it; so that Lord Percy must have profited by, rather than promoted, the alleged fraud, which has affixed so deep a stain on the otherwise lofty character of the prelate.—*Beauties of England and Wales. vol. xii, part* 1, *by the Rev. J. Hodgson. Gough's Camden's Britannia, Dugdale's Baronage.* It has been asserted that the deed of feofment from de Vescy to the bishop still exists: and it has been argued that, because in this no express trusts appear, there could have been no implied ones.—*Description of Alnwick Castle, published by W. Davison, at Alnwick, ed. of* 1823.

||Here the descendants of Lord Percy for centuries kept a court in princely state; so that the poet, though a laureate, scarcely exaggerates when, in allu-

purchase: and in the 5, Edward II., received the governorship of the then royal castle of Bamborough. He died in 1315, leaving by his wife, the Lady Eleanor Fitz-Alan, a son, Henry, Second Baron Percy of Alnwick, born 1299.

This baron appears to have been one of the most fortunate, as well as one of the most gallant and able of his race. During his minority he received an accession to his family property, in a grant of the Northumbrian fees belonging to Patrick de Dunbar, the Scotch Earl of Dunbar and March, who had rebelled against Edward II. He afterwards, in 1326, with Queen Isabella, Prince Edward and some of the barons, participated in the successful attempt to suppress by force the influence of the Spencers: and on the young prince succeeding to the crown as Edward III., the Percy received from him the custody of the castle of Skipton, in Yorkshire, and a grant of the castle and barony of Warkworth, in Northumberland. As he was a favorite of King Edward III., who supported the claims of Edward Baliol to the throne of Scotland, he received from the latter large grants, in that country, of the forfeited estates of the partisans of David Bruce, the rival claimant to that crown. In 1346 he was one of the chiefs in council of those forces that gave battle to the Scots at Nevill's Cross, and took their king, David Bruce, prisoner.* The Douglas was in the army of the vanquished; and thus early may that rivalry in arms of these two great border names be presumed to have commenced. His wife was Idonea de Clifford, daughter of Robert, Lord Clifford, whose race had such high ancestral title to beauty;† and by her he had a numerous offspring: of which Thomas de Percy was made Bishop of Norwich at the early age of twenty-two: Matilda de Percy married John, Lord Nevill, of Raby, and was mother of the first Earl of Westmoreland: and Henry de Percy, his eldest son, succeeded his father as third Lord Percy of Alnwick, 1351–2. Lord Percy (third) had, in 1346, during his father's life, accompanied Edward III. in the expedition to France, which, on the 26th of August, was crowned by the victory of Cressy: and afterwards held high employments. He married the Lady Mary Plantagenet, ‡daughter of Henry, Earl of Lancaster, grandson of King Henry III., when his bride was aged fourteen years only. And dying in 1362, at

---

sion to the state in which the future Earl of Northumberland had lived, he speaks of the

> "Barons and those knyghtes bold,
> And other gentlemen with hym entertayned
> In fee, as menyall men of his household
> Whom he as lord worshiply maintayned."
> [Skelton's Elegy on the Death of the 4th Earl of Northumberland.

Dugdale's Baronage, vol. i, p. 273.

*See Local Historian's Table Book, Historical Div., vol. i. p. 120.

†From his family, at an earlier period, sprung the Fair Rosamond ("*Rosa mundi, non Rosamunda*") of King Henry II., whose skin, according to tradition, was so delicate that Queen Eleanor saw, through her "crystal" throat, the poisoned wine trickling, which she had administered.

‡She was the sister of Henry Plantegenet, Duke of Lancaster, whose daughter and heiress was first wife to her third cousin, John of Gaunt, who, in consequence of this alliance, was, by his father, Edward III., created Duke of Lancaster.

the age of forty-six, left her two sons, Henry, created Earl of Northumberland, and father of Hotspur; and Thomas, created Earl of Worcester, names which the drama has vied with history in rendering illustrious.

The near alliance of the two brothers by blood to the reigning family, and the stirring times in which they lived, ensured them the opportunity of distinction, while their own ability and enterprise urged them to profit by it. Both served with honor in the French wars of Edward III.; both long enjoyed the favor of his weak successor, Richard II., and by him were elevated to their earldoms; both deserted his falling fortunes, and combined to place the able and domineering Henry of Bolingbroke on his throne; and both, unable to endure the severe sway with which he wielded the rod of empire they had placed in his hand,* endeavored by open war to depose him, and perished in the bold attempt. The details of the lives of these eminent men would be the history of a great part of the three reigns in which they flourished, and it can here be only attempted to notice slightly a few of the more prominent events in which they bore a part.

In the tenth year of the reign of Richard II. (1387) Worcester, then only Sir Thomas Percy, was appointed admiral of the English fleet sent to Spain to attempt, in behalf of John of Gaunt, the seizure of the kingdoms of Castile and Leon, to which he had laid claim in right of his second marriage to Constance of Castile. Five years later he was sent to Paris to conclude a final peace with Charles VI., and there, as Froisart relates, the French monarch "made a dinner to the English knightes, and caused Syr Thomas Percy to sytte at his borde, and called hym cosyn, by reason of Northumberlande's bloud."† In the meantime Northumberland, then Lord Percy, had, together with John of Gaunt, been conspicuous as a protector of John Wickliffe,‡ the early religious reformer; and had held the high office of Marshal of England at the coronation of Richard. It was then that he was raised to his earldom—an accession of honor which we shall find to have been the forerunner of a long series of brilliant calamities to himself and his descendants.

While Worcester remained single, Northumberland was twice married; and by his first wife, Margaret Nevill, sister of the first Earl of Westmoreland, was father of an eldest son,§ Henry,

*Thus, previously to the open rupture, Worcester is represented as haughtily reminding King Henry of the services of his family:

"Our house, my sovereign liege, little deserves
The scourge of greatness to be used on it;
And the same greatness to which our hands
Have help to make so portly."

[Henry IV, part 1, page 3.

†The wife of Henry III, from whose second son, Crouchback, the mother of Northumberland and Worcester was descended, was a French princess; and through her was, probably, their most recent alliance to the reigning house of France. We may here observe that the style of address used in those days, by the courtesy of the kings to their higher nobility, seems to have been handed down from a period when the connections acknowledged by it were generally a matter of fact.

‡Hume's History of England, ch. xvii.

§Hotspur was born 30th May, 1364 (Dallaway's Sussex, vol. ii, p. 272) more than twenty years before Prince Henry of Wales, who was born in 1387,; so called from his noble bearing and restless energy of character, "Prince Hotspur* of the North,"—a name which must ever shine forth the brightest of English chivalry,† if the united efforts of ballad writer, the dramatist, and the historian, can preserve any name from oblivion. His second wife, sister and heiress of Anthony, Lord Lucy, bore him no children; yet conveyed to him all her broad lands, on the easy condition that he and his heirs male should incorporate the arms of Lucy into the Percy shield.

In the twelfth year of King Richard, Hotspur avenged the capture of his banner before Newcastle-on-Tyne, in the life's blood of the Douglas at Otterburn;‡ though there is no historical authority for the statement of the ballad that the antagonist leaders having on this occasion§ personally encountered each other, the English chief with his own hand slew his opponent,‖ and for thus bedeck-

---

that Shakspere has taken the license of a poet in representing them of the same standing, and making King Henry exclaim:—

"Oh, that it could be proved
That some night tripping fairy had exchanged
In cradle-clothes our children, where they lay;
And called mine—Percy, his—Plantagenet!"
[Henry IV, Part 1, Act 1, Scene 1.

According to Mr. Tyler's view, in his life of Henry of Monmouth, Shakspere has taken another liberty with historic truth in misrepresenting the early character of the Prince of Wales.

*"Sir Henry Percy received his *soubriquet* of Hotspur from the Scots with whom he was engaged in perpetual forays and battles. He was first armed when the castle of Berwick was taken by the Scots, in 1378, when he was fourteen years old; and from that time till the battle of Holmedon, *his spur was never cold.* Historical illustrations to the first part of Henry IV. in the Pictorial Shakspere. Another explanation of this, literally, *nom de guerre*, varying somewhat from the former, is that he "was called by the French and Scots Harre Hatesporre, because, in the silence of the night, and while others reposed in sleep, he would labor indefatigably against his enemy, as if *heating* his spurs, which we call Hatesporre."—Knighton, p. 2696. But, perhaps, the daring and impetuous character, which this surname implies, may be better understood by calling in aid, as an illustration, a couplet from our modern chivalrous poet, Walter Scott:—

"Let Stanley charge, with *spur of fire*,
With Chester charge, and Lancashire."
[The Battle (Canto VI,) in Marmion.

†"Among a grove, the very straightest plant."
[Part 2, Henry IV, Act 1, Scene 1.

‡See the account of the battle in the Local Historian's Table Book, Historical Div., vol. i, p. 137. The field of this conflict, lying between the burn Otter and the river Reed, is marked by a pillar called "Battle Stone," and sometimes, though improperly, "Percy's Cross." The Douglas who fell here was James, second Earl of Douglas.

§The bare fact of a personal encounter having taken place between Percy and the Douglas was probably engrafted by the ballad writer into the battle of Otterburn from the skirmish before Newcastle; for "there," says Froissart, "fought hand to hand the Douglas and Sir Henry Percy; and by force of arms the Earl won Sir Henry's person."

‖"The Percy was a man of strenghth,
I tell you in thys stounde;
He smote the Douglas at the sworde's length,
That he felle to the grouynde.

"The sworde was scharpe and sore can byte,
I tell you in sertayne.
To the harte he cowde hym smyte;—
Thus was the Douglas slayne."
[Ancient Ballad of the Battle of Otterboarne, Percy's Reliques.

There is a modern ballad on the same subject in the Local Historian's Table Book, Legendary Div., vol. i, p. 266.

ing the knighthood of the middle ages with the *spolia opima* of classic antiquity. The battle does not appear to have terminated in favor of the English ; for Hotspur and his brother, Sir Ralph Percy, were left prisoners with the enemy. The tragic incidents of this encounter, with the aggravation of the death instead of the capture of the Percy, seem to have been transferred by the ballad-writers to the perhaps imaginary battle-field of Chevy Chase ; or rather both battles are thus treated as one.

> "This was the houtynge off the Cheviat ;
> That tear begane this spurne ;
> Old men that knowen the grounde well yenoughe,
> Call it the battell of Otterburn.
>
> "At Otterburn began this spurne
> Upon a monnyday ;
> Ther was the dougghti Douglas slean,
> The Persi never went away."*

On the landing in Yorkshire of Henry of Bolingbroke—

> "Sick in the world's regard, wretched and low,
> A poor unminded outlaw sneaking home"—†

the great family triumvirate of the Percies supported him with all their power, whether or not they then believed—as they afterwards alleged—

> "That he did nothing purpose 'gainst the state,
> Nor claim no fartherer than his now fall'n right,
> The seat of Gaunt, dukedom of Lancaster."‡

Be this as it may, the debt of gratitude for a crown was too heavy for the sovereign in full to pay, and too clear for the subject in aught to abate. Under such circumstances the favors the Percies received they would regard as instalments of their dues, while those that were denied would seem the infliction of injuries. To these obvious ingredients of dissatisfaction others were shortly added. Owen Glendower, claiming§ to be descended from the ancient princes of Wales, had then lately prevailed upon the Welsh again to renounce their allegiance to England, and had carried off, to the fastnesses of his own country, Sir Edward Mortimer,‖ the brother-in-law of Hotspur, as a prisoner of war. On Hotspur's application to King Henry for permission to ransom his connection from captivity, he is said to have been answered that "Mortimer had gone of his own choice to Glendower ; and, therefore, *no loyal subject* could wish him back."¶ Shortly after-

---

*The more ancient version of Chevy Chase.

†Part 1, Henry IV, Act 4, Scene 3.

‡Part 1, Henry IV, Act 5, Scene 1.

§Such as take an interest in the claim of "the irregular and wild Glendower" to a royal descent are referred to an elaborate pedigree of him under the heading of Hughes of Gwerclas, in the 2nd ed. of Burke's Commoners.

‖His sister, the wife of Hotspur and the "gentle Kate" of Shakspere, was in fact called Elizabeth. See a note appended to the will of her father, Edmond de Mortimer, Earl of March, in Sir Harris Nicolas' *Testamenta Vetusta*, p. 112. In this will, which is dated 1 May, 1380, he bequeaths to "our dear Son, Monsr. Henry Percy," a small nonche, in the form of the body of a stag and the head of an eagle.

¶A glance forward over the pages of history will suffice to shew what strong reason the Lancastrian princes must have had for attempting to depress the family of Mortimer. The daughter and heiress of Lionel Plantagenet, Duke of Clarence, elder brother of their ancester, John of Gaunt, married Edward

wards, on the return of the Scots from a destructive inroad they had made into Northumberland, they were intercepted and vanquished by the Earl and his son Hotspur at Hamildon* hill, near Wooler and Archibald, third Earl of Douglas, their general, together with other great nobles, was taken prisoner. King Henry, however, being anxious to use the captives as a means of obtaining an advantageous peace with Scotland, forbad the Percies to treat for their ransom. This prohibition the Percies conceived to infringe on what was their due by the laws of war; and they resisted it accordingly. In the end Douglas obtained his liberty by coalescing with Northumberland and Mortimer by espousing the daughter of Glendower. And the Percies destined, like a branch of the Nevill'st† in a subsequent stage of history, to subvert the dynasty they had been so instrumental in raising; and formed, for that purpose, a confederacy with the Scotch and Welch chieftain to place the young Earl of March on the throne. When the war was ready to break out, Northumberland was siezed with an illness at Berwick; and Hotspur, taking command of the forces in his stead, and, accompanied by Douglas, marched towards Shrewsbury to join Glendower. His uncle, Worcester, the king's lieutenant, in South Wales, revolted and joined him with reinforcements. Glendower had not yet come up, when Henry, with what power he could muster, hastened to encounter the insurgents—and on the 21st of July, 1403, mid the conflicting cries of "St. George" and "Esperence, Percy,"‡ began the battle of Shrewsbury. Here the honorable rivalry of the Percy and the Douglas, fighting for once on the same side, developed itself in prodigies of valor. At length Hotspur fell by an arrow from a nameless hand: and with him fell the confidence of the rebels; for

> "That earth, that bore him dead,
> Bore not alive so stout a gentleman." §

Mortimer, Earl of March; and had transmitted to her descendents the lawful right of the crown, on the extinction, in the person of Richard II., of the issue of the eldest brother, the Black Prince. The representative of the house of Mortimer was then Edward, Earl of March; who may be presumed to have only been restrained by his boyhood from pressing his undeniable claim to the throne. Sir Edward Mortimer was his uncle, and, as such, the legitimate guardian of his interests. The young earl, indeed, died without issue; but left a sister and heiress, Ann Mortimer, who married Richard Plantagenet, Duke of York, to whom she was first cousin, twice removed; and their godson, under the name of Edward IV., received in her right that crown from the line of Lancaster, from which it had been so long usurped.

*See Table Book, Hist. Div., vol. i, p. 145. The battle fought here forms the groundwork of Walter Scott's drama of "Halidon Hill," in which the scene of action is transferred from Homildon to the earlier battle-field of Halidon. There is a ballad on the subject of this battle fought here, at page 152 of Bell's "Rhymes of Northern Bards."

†See Table Book, Traditional Div., vol. ii, p. 64.

‡"*Esperence en Dieu*" is still the motto of the Percy; of which, in relation to this motto, it has been eloquently said: "At one moment the provincial monarch of unmeasured lands, the lord of impregnable fortresses, and the chief of countless vassels—the next the tenant of a prison, from which there was seldom any other escape than death. The vicissitudes of fortune taught them the instability of all human greatness, and that the only sure trust is '*Esperence en Dieu.*'"—Quarterly Review, No. cxliii

§This exclamation over his body is by Shakspere placed in the mouth of his generous enemy, Henry, Prince of Wales.—Part 1, Hen. IV., Act 5, Scene 4.

The rout was now general: Douglas and Worcester were taken prisoners, and the latter was beheaded.¶

After the suppression of the rebellion, the king became formally reconciled to Northumberland,* and "at the request of the commons, commanded the Earl of Northumberland and Ralph Nevill, Earl of Westmoreland" [who in the late insurrection had remained firm to the Lancastrian cause] "in token of perfect amity to kiss each other it open parliament."† But the wounds that rankled in Northumberland's breast were only superficially cured. He secretly connived at the insurrection headed by Mowbray and Archbishop Scrope, and after the suppression of ‡ that, being pursued by the king into Northumberland, he fled into Scotland, taking with him his grandson, the young Henry Percy, the only son of Hotspur and the hope of the house. Thence, in 1407, the earl, together with Lord Bardolf, his companion in exile, returned to Northumberland and his ancient tenantry and retainers flocked to the standard of their banished lord. He published a proclamation that he came to relieve the nation from their tyranny and august oppression, and advanced with his forces as far south as Karnesborough, in Yorkshire, but was defeated and slain§ at Branham Moor, in that county, by Sir Thomas Rokeby, sheriff; and his head, white with age, was forwarded by the victor, as a trophy, to London.‖

Henry Percy, the second earl, succeeded, on the death of his grandfather, to an inheritance of confiscated estates and attainted titles. But the Scots, in whose care the old man had left him, showed their generosity in bringing him up as kindly as if he had not been the whelp of the lion breed which had been the defence of the English, and the terror of the Scottish border. And he is said never to have forgotton his obligations to that nation.

In the early part of the reign of King Henry V., while young Percy was still in exile, a conspiracy was formed, by the Earl of Cambridge, to bring him back to Scotland, together with the imposter, Thomas de Trumpyngton, who, from a remarkable similarity of appearance, was enabled to personate the deceased king, Richard II., and, with their aid, to raise an insurrection. The plot was discovered; and the Earl of Cambridge paid by his life the penalty of treason. Immediately after this the name of Henry de Percy Knt. appears in the list of the retinue of Henry V., in his voyage on that expedition which led to the victory of Agincourt; though it is not enrolled in the list of its losses; and therefore the

---

And here we may observe that there is no more authority for Shakspere's account that Hotspur died by the sword of the Prince of Wales, than there was for that of the ballad that Douglas died by the sword of Hotspur.

¶ Buried at St. Peter's church, Shrewsbury.

*In Brydges' Collins, vol. ii, p. 262, it is stated that it was not thought advisable to proceed with much harshness against this earl, "lest all the north should revolt to the Scots"—so much more powerful in those times were the ties which bound the retainer to his immediate lord than those which united him to his king.

†Brydges' Collin's Peerage, vol. ii, p. 263.

‡For the mode of its suppression see Table Book, Legendary Div., vol. ii, pp. 58–9.

§February 29, 1408.

‖On the tragical end of this earl there is a quaint old poem, which is given in the Table Book, Traditional Div., vol. i, p. 130.

party designated by it may be presumed to have been either wounded at the previous siege of Harfleur or left there in garrison. It seems improbable that this person* was the young representative of the family, as the accounts we have of the latter state that he was afterwards sent for by the king from Scotland; and, therefore, we presume that he was then remaining there. However, he, in the early part of the reign of Henry V., was restored to his family lands and honors by the young monarch, whose cousin, the Lady Eleanor Nevill, he had married; and who was moved towards him by the intercesion of his aunt, the Countess of Westmoreland, daughter of John of Gaunt, as well as by the merits and misfortunes of the northern chieftain. And for thus much of its facts, the beautiful ballad of the "Hermit of Warkworth,"† of which the Percy and his bride are the hero and heroine, has its warrant in history. Nor had the house of Lancaster reason to repent of its kindness to the exile,‡ for, as his grandfather and father had died fighting for its subversion, he and four of his sons fell fighting in its defence.

"In the third year of King Henry VI. he, for the better confirmation of the dignity of Earl of Northumberland, obtained a charter of creation thereunto, with the yearly fee of £20, '*nomine comitis*,' out of the profits of that county."§ About eleven years later a battle, rather of a private than a national character, is alleged to have taken place between this Earl of Northumberland and Earl William Douglas, of Angus, at Pepperden, near the Cheviot Hills.‖ This, as it was consequent upon an incursion

* This Sir Thomas Percy appears likely to have been the son of Sir Thomas Percy, a younger brother of Hotspur; and, if so, he would stand in the relation of first cousin to the personage now under notice in the text. He would, in all probability, have been in that gay cavalcade, whose advance to the place of embarcation is thus described by Drayton with so much of the glow of chivalry:—

"The nobler youth, the common rank above,
On their curveting coursers mounted fair,
One wore his mistress' garter; one her glove;
And he a lock of his dear Lady's hair;
And he her colours, whom he most did love—
There was not one but did some favour wear
And each one took it on his happy steed
To make it famous by some knightly deed." [Battle of Agincourt.

The line of Sir Thomas Percy is mentioned in Collins' Peerage, vol. ii. of the supplement, p. 684. It may be remarked here that the article on the Northumberland title in Collins' Peerage, which evinces an intimate acquaintance with the papers of the family, is alleged, in Sir Egerton Brydges' Restituta, vol. iii, p. 520, to have been drawn up by Dr. Thomas Percy, the Bishop of Dromore.

†See pp. 70–1, Collins' Peerage.

‡Hume, in chapter xxi of his History of England, speaking of the Earls of Northumberland and Westmoreland, says: "the whole north of England, the most warlike part of the kingdom, was, by means of these two potent noblemen, engaged warmly in the interests of Lancaster."

§Collins' Peerage.

‖Ridpath, in his Border History, p. 401, quoting a passage from Hollinshead's Chronicles, which states that, on the part of the English, were slain there "Henrie of Cliddesdale, John Oglile, and Richard Persie, with fifteen hundred other of Gentlemen and commons, of which gentlemen forty were knights," adds that the Percy had, on this occasion, been met "in his own territories at a place called Pepperden-on-Brammish, not far from the mountains of Cheviot." The fall here of Richard Percy (probably a cadet of the Northumberland family) may well have suggested the slaughter of the Percy to the writer of Chevy Chase.

made by the English earl into Scotland, is suggested in Brydges' edition of Collins' Peerage, to have afforded the outline of the ballad of Chevy Chase* of which the old version moved the stout heart of Sir Philip Sidney more than the sound of a trumpet,† while the Homeric spirit of the more modern version has received the highest eulogium from the critical Addison.‡

On the breaking out of the war of the roses,§ in 1455, this Earl, who had been appointed constable of England by Henry VI., was slain fighting near the king at the battle of St. Albans,‖ and was buried in the abbey there. Before passing to the sons of this earl, it should be observed that his martial habits had not led him to forget the interests of literature; since he is commemorated amongst the benefactors of Oxford, for having at University college there founded three fellowships for those born in the diocese of Durham, Carlisle, or York.

Of the younger children, Thomas Percy was created Lord Egremont—a title taken from a property in Cumberland possessed by the earl, his father. He fell in 1460 in the defeat at Northamp-

---

* The battle of Chevy Chase, however, is alleged in the ballads to have led to that of Homildon. The older version says:—

> "As our noble Kyng made his a-vowe,
> Lyke a noble prince of renowen,
> For the deth of the Lord Perse
> He dyd the battle of Hombyll-down;"

and that we have already seen took place two reigns previously. Under all circumstances, then, the most probable conclusion seems to be, that, in the time of this or the previous Earl of Northumberland, the Percy had violated the laws of the borders by crossing to Scotland to hunt without the leave of the Scottish warden; and that the Douglas had, in consequence attacked him; and that between the hunting party of the one and a body of the retainers of the other a conflict had arisen among the Cheviot hills, too unimportant to be recorded by historians; but which the bards have amplified and embellished by incorporating into it, besides some imaginary details, all the most striking incidents of the border wars of that age. In the Chorographia, printed originally in 1649, and, at page 41 of the edition of 1813, it is stated: "These Cheviot hills are most famous for the hunting of the Earle of Northumberland; at the hunting, the Earle Douglas of Scotland, who met him with his forces and engaged one the other, where was great bickering and skirmishes, to the losse of many men; where both Earles fought valiently, called to this day Cheviot Chase." And oral tradition of the battle may be presumed to have descended to the period at which this was first printed.

† Sir Philip Sidney's Defence of Poetry.

‡ Spectator, Nos. 70, 74.

§ Perhaps the reader will have no objection to be here reminded of the occasion to which Shakspere assigns the selection of these party badges. At a meeting of some great lords in the Temple Garden, Richard Plantagenet, afterwards Duke of York, exclaims:—

> "In dumb significance proclaime your thoughts—
> Let him, that is a true-born gentleman,
> And stands upon the honour of his birth,
> If he suppose that I have pleaded truth,
> From off this brier pluck a white rose with me."

To which John Beaufort, Earl of Somerset, in behalf of his own near kindred of the house of Lancaster, answers:—

> "Let him that is no coward, nor no flatterer,
> But dare maintain the party of the truth,
> Pluck a red rose from off this thorn with me.'
> Henry VI, Part, 1 Act 2, Scene 4.

‖ 23 May, 1455. Born, 1394.

ton, fighting for the house of Lancaster; and left a son, John, who seems probably to have been deterred by the poverty entailed on the partisans of the vanquished, from assuming his father's title *

Sir Ralph Percy was seneschal of his father's court at Alnwick; and Percy's cross, on the battle-field of Hedgeley moor, still attests the gallantry and death of him who would not seek his own safety by flight, at the expense of "the bird in his bosom"—his royalty to his king he acknowledged.* He transmitted a line of descendants,† some of the earlier of whom appear to have been pensioned, and employed by their opulent cousins, the Earls of Northumberland.‡

Sir Richard Percy fell at Towton field, fighting, like his father and brother, on the side of Lancaster, in 1464.

William Percy, an ecclesiastic, was made Chancellor of the University of Cambridge and Bishop of Carlisle, and died 1462.

---

* Brydges' Collins, vol. ii, p. 281.

* See Table Book, Historical Div., vol. i., pp. 161–2.

† The reader, weary of the gleam of this unbroken line of mailed barons, may long to find the family history diversified and adorned by the soft diffusive light of literature. If so, he will rejoice to see one, who has contributed so successfully to ballad literature as the author of the "Hermit of Warkworth," and who has done so much to revive the taste for it as the edition of "The Reliques of Ancient Poetry," appended here, as a descendant, to a race which has produced so many ballad heroes.

Dr. Thomas Percy, the distinguished Bishop of Dromore, was born at Bridgnorth, in Shropshire, in 1728, and died in 1811. He was descended from the Percies of Worcester, of which city his great great grandfather, Thomas Percy, was mayor in 1662: (See a printed pedigree inserted in the copy of Nash's Worcestershire, in the King's library in the British Museum, between pp. 94 and 95 of the second volume; and also p. 318 of the same volume). This Thomas Percy was the son of Richard Percy (Nash's Worcestershire, vol. ii, p 121), and Richard, through his father, John, and his grandfather, Thomas Percy, was the great grandson of John Percy, of Worcester, who had settled there about the year 1520. From the coincidence of name and date, and from the correspondence of the arms and tradition in the families in Northumberland and Worcester, it has been stated that this John Percy, of Worcester, was identical with John Percy who had been seated just before at Newton-on-the-Sea, in Northumberland; and who, it has been alleged, had been obliged in the reign of Henry VIII—a period most disastrous to the house of Percy—to fly from that neighborhood, in consequence of some deed of violence. (From him to the children of the Bishop of Dromore, the pedigree and its proofs are given complete in some fly sheets inserted between pp. 318 and 319 in the second volume of Nash's Worcestershire, in the king's library in the British Museum, and the library of the Dean and Chapter of Durham.) John Percy, of Newton-on-the-Sea, was, according to Brydges 'Collins, brother of Peter Percy and the son of Sir Ralph Percy of the text..

Before bidding adieu to the Bishop of Dromore, whose "attention to poetry has given grace and splendour to his studies of antiquity," it may be mentioned that Boswell has declared that he himself has examined the proofs of his descent from the Northumberland Percies, and that, "both as a lawyer accustomed to the consideration of evidence, and as a genealogist versed in the study of pedigrees, he is fully satisfied."—*Boswell's Life of Johnson.*

‡ To the cadets of their house the Earls ot Northumberland appear to have exhibited great kindness; in so much so that in Brydges' Collins, vol. ii., p. 288, it is remarked a member of this particular branch, that he "is not found to have enjoyed any office or emolument of any kind under his kinsman, the Earl of Northumberland; contrary to the usual practice of this great family, whose offices of dignity or profit appear to have been given with a preference to the inferior members of their noble house." The high blood of ancient chivalry could afford to acknowledge a poor relation!

The eldest surviving son, Henry Percy, became third earl at his father's death. He had previously married Eleanor Poynings the heiress to the baronies in fee of Poynings, Fitz-Payne and Bryan, and had been summoned to the House of Lords in her right as Baron Poynings. This alliance is said to have been obtained for him by his great uncle, the wily Cardinal Beaufort.* Yet, in days when the beauty and heiress was the prize of the tournament, and when natural guardians willingly resigned the persons and the broad lands of their fair charges into the hands of those who proved by their prowess they were best enabled to defend both, it would hardly require the diplomacy of churchmen to obtain for the Percy an advantageous alliance.

He had during his father's life been retained, at a fixed allowance, by Henry VI., to defend the town of Berwick and the east marches towards Scotland: and, on his father's death, he was permitted, in reward for his services there, to succeed at once to his inheritance, exempted from the feudal burden of reliefs. He is the Earl of Northumberland who forms one of the characters in the third part of Shakspere's King Henry VI. In the wars of the roses his fortunes fluctuated with those of the house of Lancaster. He was with the victors in the battle of Wakefield; † and fell in the defeat at Towton,‡ where, with the gallantry of his race, he in vain led on the van.

Henry Percy, his only son and heir, was but a minor at the death and subsequent attainder of his father: yet the fears of Edward IV. confined him for eight long years in the Tower; during which the Earldom of Northumberland, with its possessions, was enjoyed by one of the chiefs of the Yorkist party, John Nevill, brother of Warwick, the kingmaker. The Percy was at length, however, restored by this king to his freedom,§ his honors, and his possessions, in order thus to diminish the power of his predecessor, whose fidelity was no longer trusted; and Nevill‖ received in compensation

---

* Brydges' Collins. It will be recollected that his mother was a daughter of the Earl of Westmoreland by his wife, Joan de Beaufort, the sister of the powerful and ambitious cardinal, the horrors of whose chamber still haunt us, where "he died and made no sign."—Henry VI, Part 2, Act 3, Scene 3.

† 30 Dec., 1460. See Table Book, Traditional Div., vol. ii., p. 63.

‡ 29 March, 1461. Here, too, on the same side fell his kinsman, Sir John Nevill. See Table Book, Traditional Div., vol. ii. p. 61, and also Historical Div., vol. i., p. 160.

The loss here, on the part of the vanquished, of their leaders is thus summed up (with the mistake of introducing the Earl of Westmoreland instead of his brother, Sir John Nevill) in Drayton's poem of "The Miseries of Queen Margaret:"

> "Courageous Clifford first here fell to ground,
> Into the throat with a blunt arrow struck:
> Here Westmoreland receiv'd his deadly wound:
> Here died the stout Northumberland, that stuck
> Still to his sovereign; Wells and Dacres found
> That they had lighted on King Henry's luck:
> Trowlup and Horne, two brave commanders, dead;
> Whilst Somerset and Exeter were fled."

§ He was released from the Tower 27 October, 1469. (9 Edw.: 4).—*Rymer's Fœdera*, xi., 649.

‖ Warkworth's Chronicles of the first thirteen years of Edward IV. (printed for the Camden Society), p. 4.

the empty title of Marquis of Montague, with still more empty promises. Shortly after this, the anticipated revolt of Warwick and Montague placed the sixth Henry again on the throne. But, in the March of 1471 Edward returned from the brief exile into which he had been driven, and disembarked at Ravenspur, on the Yorkshire side of the Humber, where—an auspicious omen—Henry IV. had formerly landed. In Yorkshire the possessions and influence of the Percy were in those days overwhelming. The young earl, however, did not oppose the march of Edward and his little army through that county : and thus, by his example, discouraging the opposition of others, rendered, at a most critical period, a most important service to the house of York.* He, nevertheless, did not venture to lead his friends and retainers actually to join that standard, in fighting against which his own father and their kindred had fallen only ten years before. He wàs afterwards appointed by Edward to be warden of the east and middle marches towards Scotland : and in the twenty-second year of his reign, he was one of the chiefs in that army which, under the command of Richard Duke of Gloucester, advanced into Scotland, and took the city of Edinburgh.

On the accession of Richard to the throne, this earl was constituted lord high chamberlain of England. At the battle of Bosworth † field he was present but remained inactive; whether wavering between his recent obligations to the house of York, represented in the male line by the king, and his ancient family alliance with the line of Lancaster, represented, through the Beauforts, by Henry of Richmond ;‡ or influenced by prudence, or lethargy of character—probable results of his early confinement. Be this as it may, his conduct on this occasion satisfied the victor, and he was received into favor by the new dynasty of Tudor—a favor which, in four years, proved fatal to him ; since he was employed by the king in enforcing the collection of an unpopular tax ; and was murdered § at Cockledge, in Yorkshire, by a mob who erroneously supposed him to be the adviser of it. His countess, Maud, the daughter of William Herbert, first Earl of Pembroke, had borne him four sons and three daughters.

---

* "Grete partye of the noble men and commons in thos parties were twords th' Erle of Northumbarland, and would not stire with any lorde or noble man other than the sayde Erle or his commandment: and for soo muche as he sat still, in such wise yf the Marques" (of Montague, who, according to Lingard, was lying at Pontefract with an army sufficiently numerous to have overwhelmed the invaders) "wolde have done his besines to have assembled them in any manier of qwarell, neither for his love, whiche they bare hym non, ne for any commandment of higher authoritie, they ne wolde, in no cawse, ne qwarrell, have assisted hym."—*Historie of the arrivall of K. Edward IV. (printed for the Camden Society)*, *pp*. 6, 7.

† 24 August, 1485.

‡ His mother, Margaret, the wife of Edmund Tudor, Earl of Richmond, was daughter and heiress of John Beaufort, Duke of Somerset, and great granddaughter of John of Gaunt, Duke of Lancaster.

§ 28 April, 1489. On this tragic event Skelton has composed a poem called "An Elegy on Henry, fourth Earl of Northumberland;" which is printed in Percy's Reliques.

Of his younger sons, Sir William Percy was one of the commanders at Flodden-field, and is alleged* to have afterwards participated in the insurrection called the Pilgrimage of Grace. Alan Percy was a priest. Josceline Percy, who was employed in the management of the family estates, married Margaret Frost of Beverley, a Yorkshire heiress, and transmitted a line,† the elder branch of which continued, for a long period, to reside in the neighborhood of Beverley.

Henry Algernon‡ Percy, the eldest son, was only eleven years old when, on the death of his father, he succeeded as fifth earl of Northumberland. In 1497, the year before he came of age, he was one of the commanders of the royal forces that dispersed the Cornish rebels, who had advanced to Blackheath. Six years later the honorable office was assigned to him of conducting the Princess Margaret§ Tudor, the affianced bride of James IV., from

---

* Brydges' Collins.

† Thomas Percy, a yonnger brother of it, was, according to a system of consideration pursued by this great family towards their own cadets, appointed auditor and constable of Alnwick to the ninth Earl of Northumberland, who stood to him in the relation of second cousin once removed, and, through him, at the latter end of the reign of Queen Elizabeth, the earl had carried on some secret negotiations with James of Scotland, in order to secure the succession of that monarch. Thomas Percy was a convert to the church of Rome, though, his kinsman, the earl, was a Protestant: and it has been alleged that James with a view of rendering the Roman Catholic body propitious to his accession, made to Percy, on these occasions, flattering promises of indulgence to their faith; which, when securely seated on the throne, he disregarded. Percy, deceived himself, had been the means of deceiving others; who now looked upon him as a traitor to their cause. He appears to have been a man of turbulent character, for he had been previously connected with an insurrection; namely, that of the Earl of Essex in the time of Queen Elizabeth. He was an enthusiast in religion; and in all probability personally an injured man. Hence he was easily led to conceit, together with a few desperate persons, that gunpowder-treason plot; in the midst of the horrors resulting from which he expected to avenge his private wrongs and to re-establish his religion. On its discovery he fled to Holbeach-house, in Worcestershire; in the court-yard of which, while defending himself, he was shot, 8 November, 1605.—Nash's Worcestershire, vol. i., p. 587. Brydges' Collins, pp. 303 and 382. Lingard's History of England, vol. ix. pp. 35, 57, 12mo. Ed. The conspirator was ancestor of descendants (now in the male line extinct or lost) who for a considerable period resided at Cambridge, and on whom the male representation of the family, in England at any rate, appears eventually to have devolved. A pedigree of the Percies of Beverley and of Cambridge is given in *Collectanea Topographica et Genealogica*, vol. ii., pp. 60–3. It is there remarked that an interesting feature in this pedigree is that it contains the names of several persons who, but for the attainder of 1572, would, on the death of the eleventh earl, and the rejection of the claim of the Trunkmaker, have become Earls of Northumberland; namely:—Allan Percy, of Beverley, who died in 1692; Francis Percy, a stonecutter, of Cambridge, who died in 1717; Charles Percy, a common council man of Cambridge, who died in 1743; and the Rev. Josceline Percy, who died in 1755; but it may since have appeared somewhat questionable whether George Percy, the youngest son of the eighth earl, did not leave male descendants in America; and if he did these would have the priority.

‡ The name of Algernon—a name much cherished in the Percy family—was originally a nick-name attached to William de Percy, a companion in arms of the Conqueror; and may be rendered in modern language, "William with the Whiskers," or "*Aux Moustaches.*"—Brydges' Collins.

§ An account of her progress is given in the Table Book, Hist. Div., vol. i., pp. 175–80.

Northamptonshire to Scotland; whence her descendants were soon destined to return—her granddaughter to ascend the scaffold, her greatgrandson, the throne. In the early part of the reign of Henry VIII., he was in France with those English forces which gained, before the walls of Terouenne, the victory called "the battle of Spurs," from the vigor with which the enemy used their spurs when they should have used their swords. And he returned again to France to accompany the king to the "Field of the Cloth of Gold."* His tastes were as magnificent as befitted one of the highest nobles under the gorgeous dynasty of the Tudors:† but his expenditure exceeded the revenue of his vast estates, and entailed debt on his successor. He expired on the 19th of May, 1527; and was the first earl of Northumberland of his house that had died in his bed; so heavy was the tax to be paid for the excitement and power of feudal lordship.‡ By his wife, Catharine Spencer,§ he left three sons and two daughters.

Of his daughters, the Lady Margaret Percy is presumed to be the heroine‖ of the "Nut-brown Maid;" who, when her constancy is

---

* Rutland Papers (printed for the Camden Society) p. 30.

† This is the earl whose Household Book of Expenditure at Wresil and Lekinfield has been printed under the editorship of Dr. Thomas Percy, Bishop of Dromore. Of this earl and his family there is a notice in the preface to the Household Book, at pp. 20–24.

‡ Inclusive of Hotspur, who did not live to come to the earldom to which he was heir, five generations following had died violent deaths; and, inclusive of the Earl of Worcester, brother of the first Earl of Northumberland, five earls had died violent deaths.

If we look back to the times in which these deaths occurred, we shall find that all excepting the last, were in the wars of the disputed succession, which followed the Lancastrian usurpation—the most glorious, but the most tragic period of the Percy history. In feudal times, to the nobles themselves, indeed, clothed in impenetrable armour, from which the arrow glanced and by which the sword was turned, war had sometimes been divested of its havoc, and seemed a game in which there was little but the dignity and excitement of nominal danger: for, besides the protection of their coats of mail, they were defended in the hour of defeat by the avarice of the victor, whose interest would lead him to spare an opulent enemy in order to obtain his ransom. But at length the barons, allied by blood to each other and to each rival claimant of the crown, entered into this contest with all the bitterness of a family feud; and every injury, itself retributary, was the forerunner of a severe retribution; till the armor, which defended the vanquished from the sword of the conqueror reserved him only for the axe of his executioner; and the combatants, like Shylock in the play, preferred flesh to gold. It may be mentioned as an illustration of the peculiar bitterness with which these domestic hostilities were carried on, that, while we have observed such numbers of the Percies to have been swept away in these wars, it has fallen to our lot to notice here but one Percy, and he at best, but a cadet, who lost his life in the border warfare with the Scots during all the centuries for which the Percies were the guardians of the English frontiers.

§ Her mother was the Lady Eleanor Beaufort, daughter and co-heir of Edmond Beaufort, Duke of Somerset, the younger brother of John Beaufort, Duke of Somerset, in his descent from the latter of whom Henry VII. claimed the representation of the house of Lancaster. The Countess of Northumberland and that monarch were therefore second cousins.

‖ This is suggested with considerable ground of probability in Whitaker's History of Craven, in a note at page 229 of the first edition. The ballad of the "Nut-brown Maid" is printed in Percy's Reliques.

tried by telling her of the outlawry of her lover, entreats to be allowed to share all his privations, rather

> "than
> That he should to the grene wode go,
> Alone, a banyshed man."

Her husband, Henry Clifford, who succeeded as eleventh Baron Clifford, and was afterwards created earl of Cumberland, is recorded to have led, in his father's time, the life of an outlaw, at the head of a band of daring freebooters, levying contributions on the affrighted monks and villagers of Westmoreland and Yorkshire.

Passing on to the male descendants of the last mentioned Earl of Northumberland, we shall quickly find the executioner, after his short respite, again called in to play his part: and we shall observe, that the succession of the earldom does not for the most part devolve in the same direct line from father to son that it has hitherto done.

Of his sons, the second, Sir Thomas Percy, married Eleanor daughter and co-heir of Sir Guiscard Harbottal* of Beamish, in the county of Durham, and had a family by which the male line of the Percy was continued. In 1536 he was residing at Seamer, in Yorkshire, until the month of October, when those consecutive insurrections commenced, called "the Pilgrimage of Grace," in consequence of their having been undertaken in behalf of the monastic establishments and ceremonials of Rome: † but he then immediately repaired to his mother at Wresil castle. Here he heard that Robert Aske "the great captain" had already been at the gates, with a numerous host who shouted "thousands for a Percy." However, as he did not like the rising, he attempted to leave the neighborhood; but found himself way-laid in every direction by the insurgents, who at last, between force and entreaty, induced him to join them. After the suppression of the last of the outbreaks of this "armed pilgrimage," which was effected in the following spring, he was arraigned for treason, in consequence of his conduct on these occasions, and pleaded "not guilty;" but towards the conclusion of the trial, knowing probably that in his day conviction was a sure consequence of a state prosecution, and that his only chance of appeasing his imperious monarch lay in entire submission, he withdrew his former plea and pleaded guilty. Sentence was then given that he should be hanged, drawn and quartered, at Ty-

---

* Surtees' Durham, vol. ii., p. 225.

† Another of the professed purposes of this "pilgrimage" was "the purifying of the nobility and the expulsing all villan blood;" (Life of Henry VIII., by Lord Herbert, of Cherbury) aimed probably at the minister Thomas Cromwell, who, though the son of a fuller (according to Lingard, or a blacksmith (according to Banks), near London, was raised to the barony of Cromwell and Earldom of Essex, by the temporary favor of the king, by whom he had been employed in the confiscation of church property. A similar object was proposed by the insurgents of 1569. Such appeals to the prejudices of the people have often been responded to; for the pride of the poorer classes is generally too high to submit to the government of one sprung from their own station. By so unexpected an ally are the great principles of "degree, priority and order" upheld!

burn ; and shortly afterwards, in the June of 1537, it was accordingly executed.*

The third son of Sir Ingelram Percy † died in 1538. s. p.

---

* The compiler of this sketch owes these particulars to the kindness of the author of the memorials of the rebellion of 1569 ; whose industry and ability was later engaged in tracing for publication the singular and interesting details of " the Pilgrimage of Grace."

† Sir Ingelram Percy is commonly stated to have died with no issue, but a illegitimate daughter. From him, however, James Percy, the trunkmaker of Dublin, who in the time of Charles II. claimed the Earldom of Northumberland as heir male of the Percies, stated himself to be legitimately descended. The line of his alleged descent is given in a note to the later editions of Burke's Peerage. Some remarks on this claim are contained in Sir Egerton Brydges' *Restituta*, vol. ii. pp. 519, 528. Here it appears that the trunkmaker had at first claimed to be the great grandson of Sir Richard Percy, a younger son of the eighth earl, and had then shifted his claim, and drawn his descent from this Sir Ingelram Percy younger son of the fifth earl ; and that afterwards his excuse for having selected the former descent was, that, believing himself sprung from the Earls of Northumberland, but not knowing the precise line, he had been advised "to fix upon the wrong party as the only way to find out the right." It is certainly no disproof of the noble descent of a person in humble circumstances that he himself should not always have known the precise line of it ; or that he should have found a difficulty in tracing it. The heralds in their visitations took no account of the reduced descendants of cadets. To repair these omissions, there were no inquisitions after the death of those who had no land ; and their wills (if wills they left) were probably proved in some petty local court where they were ill preserved and where there was no index. There are few parish registers to record their births, deaths, and marriages that commence earlier than the latter end of the sixteenth century ; and the lamp of oral tradition, when held up to the night of ages, is found so dim as only to render the darkness visible. In a few generations, especially after the laws against retainers were enforced, there was apt to be as little of correspondency between the chief of a great family and its distant members, as between the gold of the head and the iron and clay of the feet of that visionary image which troubled the spirit of the Eastern monarch. As an illustration of these positions it may be mentioned that however well established the descent of Francis Percy, of Cambridge (who was by trade a stonecutter), may now be from Josceline Percy younger son of the fourth earl (see note another page), there is a letter to him from no less an authority than Sir William Dugdale, deducing his descent from Guiscard Percy, grandson of the fifth, and younger brother of the seventh and eighth earls, and a letter to him also from the trunkmaker himself acknowledging cousinship with him, and assigning him a third descent, namely from a Robert Percy, whom he calls the second son of the above mentioned Sir Ingelram Percy. Both these letters are given in Banks' *Stemmata Anglicana*, and at pp. 29–32, of the part of it forming the Appendix to vol. ii. of his Extinct Baronage.

The " Case of James Percy claimant to the Earldom of Northumberland " was printed in 1680 or 1685 in London, in folio. It is rare ; but there is a copy of it in the library of the British Museum, so that the enquirer after truth may exercise his own judgment on its allegations. This subject shall be dismissed after observing that different genealogists have formed very different estimates of their truth ; for Sir Egerton Brydges, who may have some fellow feeling for a disappointed claimant, says, at vol. iii., p. 527 of his *Restituta* :—" I confess that till I can receive the contradiction of a strong case on the other side, I cannot reflect on the statement disclosed in this publication of Percy without strong suspicions that there was a good deal of truth mingled up with his claim :" while the author of an article in the *Collectanea Topographica et Genealogica*, says, at vol., ii. pp. 57–8 :—" the claim of James Percy the trunkmaker, which was commenced in 1672, and maintained with singular pertinacity until 1689, is notorious from its remarkable circumstances ; but his statements never obtained credit from judicious enquirers."

The eldest son and successor, Henry Algernon Percy, sixth Earl of Northumberland, had, during the life of his father, been placed amongst the gentlemen of the retinue of Cardinal Wolsey, as an introduction to public life. While thus situated he became enamoured of the fair Anne Boleyn,* then maid of honor to Queen Catharine; unconscious that his rival was his sovereign. The attachment is believed to have been returned: and it has been said by some to have even led to an engagement.† But King Henry discovered it: and Wolsey was employed to break it off.‡ He, as the best expedient for parting the lovers, sent for the father of the young lord to court; and induced him to use all his parental authority in enforcing on him a marriage with another. And, in the year 1524,§ Lord Percy became the husband of the Lady Mary Talbot, daughter of George fourth Earl of Shrewsbury. The marriage was childless and unhappy, and ended in a separation. The interference of the cardinal was never forgiven either by the queen or her early admirer, and he was in time made to feel the vengeance of both—Anne undermined his hold on the king's affec-

* ANNE BOLEYN, whose tragical story, is well known, was born in the year 1507 and in her childhood accompanied Mary, the sister of Henry VIII to France, where she remained in the Court of that Queen and of her successor, the wife of Francis I. for many years. She was afterwards attached to the household of the Duchess of Alencow. Anne, to English beauty added the lively charms of foreign manner. Viscount Chateaubriand describes her as "rivalling Venus." It is most probable that she was present at the field of the cloth of gold, when Henry might have been smitten by her charms. The time of her return from France is doubtful, but it is placed in 1527 when her father was hero in an embassy to France. At that time she became a maid of honor to Queen Katherine, the wife of Henry VIII. and was receiving the addresses of Lord Percy, the eldest son of the Duke of Northumberland. If the assertion of Henry VIII. is to be credited, he had long entertained scruples concerning the lawfulness of his marriage with his brother's widow. and had attributed to the violation of God's law the premature death of all his children by Katharine, excepting the Princess Mary. The most charitable and credulous, however, abstain from thinking that the moment of his proceeding openly to annul the marriages was identical with the commencement of his addresses to Anne Boleyn, and that a similar coincidence marks the catastrophe of this unhappy woman. A letter to her in 1528 from the King alludes to his having been one whole year struck with the dart of love and her engagement with Lord Percy was at this time broken up by the intervention of Wolsey, in whose household that nobleman was brought up. After this malicious interference Anne returned to Hever, but she kept up a correspondence with Henry by letters. Some of the King's letters to her are still extant in the library of the Vatican. Although not assisted with the delicacy of expression usual in these days, they show unquestionably that Anne Boleyn was the beloved, not the mistress of the King. The crafty Cardinal having first prevailed on the Earl of Northumberland to forbid his son's marriage with Anne, succeeded in persuading Sir Thomas Boleyn to withdraw his daughter from Court. While Anne was repining in exile Henry contrived the marriage of her lover Lord Percy to the daughter of the Earl of Shrewsbury. Anne Boleyn was crowned Queen of England June 1, 1533, but was soon executed in 1536. The Earl of Northumberland soon followed the object of his juvenile affection to the grave, overwhelmed with shame and sorrow by the execution of his brother, Sir Thomas Percy, who had been involved in Aske's rebellion.

† Life of Henry VIII. by Lord Herbert of Cherbury, fol. pp. 285-6.

‡ There is a modern ballad, professing to contain the lamentation of the earl on his separation from his lady love, given in the Table Book, Legendary Div. vol. i., p. 113.

§ Lingard's History of England.

tions: and, when in 1530 he was at length arrested at Cawood castle near York, Lord Percy, who had become Earl of Northumberland,* carried the warrant.

The policy of the Tudors in depressing the power of the ancient nobility, by forwarding an act of parliament to allow the breaking of entails, and by encouraging a lavish expenditure among their barons, while they filled the places of highest civil trust and emolument with persons of inferior birth, eventually did its work in the case of this earl: and towards the close of a life, whose dawn had been brilliantly promising, the pecuniary, as well as domestic, circumstances of Northumberland must have been desperate. His necessities, but not his will it may be presumed, consented to sue Cromwell, the upstart minister, for his interest to obtain for him the captaincy of Berwick. In a letter, dated from Topcliff, 6 November, 1535, after stating that the death of Sir Thomas Clifford was expected, and that would make a vacancy, he thus proceeds:—"to whych rome, good Mr. Secretorye, I pray yow helpe me: wherby ye shall not only recover a pouer nobull man beyng in decaye, but also get your selff much wyrsheppe, that bye your meanes so pouer a man shall be recoweryd, as I am; and bynd me, my frendes, and them that shall come off me, ever (as never the lese I am most bondon affore) next the Kyng our Maister, to be tword you and all yours duryng ouer lyffes." And then he adds, what his experience,† perhaps, of the secretary may have taught him would be a still more moving appeal to his feelings:—"And, good Mr. Secretorye, I shall not fayl to gyff you a 1000 markes for the

---

* Thus in Shakspere's Henry VIII. Griffith, relating to Queen Katharine the end of Wolsey, says:

> "the stout Earl of Northumberland
> Arrested him at York, and brought him forward
> (As a man sorely tainted) to his answer." Act 5, Scene 2.

But the shade of Wolsey was shortly to be avenged; for, by a refinement of cruelty, the Earl of Northumberland was obliged to sit on the trial of Queen Anne. She was found guilty on the 15th day of May, 1536; and sentenced to "be brought to the green within the tower and there burned or beheaded, as shall please the king." On the same day, when the Lord Rocheford was brought to the bar, the Earl of Northumberland was "absent on account of sudden illness." Could this illness have arisen from the part he had been compelled to take in the sentence of the queen?

For the latter part of this note acknowledgements are again due to the kindness of the author of the "Memorials of the Rebellion of 1569."

† Cromwell as well as Northumberland, had been retained in the establishment of Wolsey, and probably both were contemporaneously in his service. Cromwell has generally been believed to have, on the fall of Wolsey, been conspicuous for "his honest behaviour in his master's cause" (*Cavendish*), and to have eventually left his service with his sanction; as the cardinal joined in the fears of his *protege* lest his fortunes should be sacrificed to his fidelity.

> "Say, Wolsey—that once trod the ways of glory,
> And sounded all the depths and shoals of honor—
> Found thee a way, out of his wreck, to rise in."
> [Henry VIII., Act 3, Scene 2.

Yet the turn given by Dr. Lingard to Cromwell's conduct is, that he "despairing of the fortunes of the fallen favorite, hastened to court." It would be well, however, if the sectarian bias of Dr. Lingard, *pace, tanti viri*, had never led him in a still less justifiable instance to foul the ashes of the distinguished dead. See the Quarterly Review, No. LXV. article 1.

sayme, bryngyng yt to pas."* Whether or not this vacancy actually did occur, and this humble suit was successful, the embarrassments of the earl cannot have been removed ; for in the following spring, he alienated to the king in fee, by a deed of bargain and sale dated the 3rd of February, 26 Henry VIII, his house of Petworth and other lands in Sussex, his lands in Hackney in Middlesex, and large estates in Lincolnshire, Pembrokshire, Carmarthenshire, and Somersetshire, &c. And this disposition of his property was, in the following spring, confirmed by Parliament.† In the same session of Parliament another act ‡ was passed, in the performance of certain covenants between the king and the earl, settling all the other lands, that belonged to the earl, upon himself and the issue of his body (of which there was none) and then upon the king "his heirs and successors for ever in augmentation and encrease of the imperial crown." In this there are clauses saving to third parties their interests in such incumbrances as had previously § been made : and a small provision is thus reserved for his brother and heir presumptive, Sir Thomas Percy (who was not yet implicated in the Pilgrimage of Grace as it took place half a year later ||), and for Henry and Thomas Percy sons of this brother.¶ The difficulties in which the earl allowed himself to be involved, and the disposition ** he was in

* State Papers published by the Record Commission, vol. v. p. 34.

† An act of Parliament (27 Henry VIII. c. 38), passed in the spring of 1536, assures and confirms these extensive territories to the king in fee simple. See Statutes of the Realm, fol. 1817, Vol. III.

‡ 27 Henry VIII. c. 47. Statutes of the Realm, fol. 1817, vol. III.

§ By sec. 17, the lands comprised in the Percy fee "equivalent in extent to half Craven," were confirmed, "in consequence of a settlement," to Henry Lord Clifford, in the event of his brother in law Northumberland dying without issue male. *Whitaker's Craven*, p. 235. 1st Ed. This territory was carried by the daughter and heiress of the fifth and last Earl of Cumberland, to her husband Richard Boyle Earl of Burlington and of Cork, and through an heiress of this family, was transferred to the house of Cavendish, in which it is now vested.

|| The session called 27 Henry VIII., in which this and the previously mentioned acts were passed, commenced 4 February 1536, and the parliament itself was dissolved, 14 April, 1536 : but the Pilgrimage of Grace commenced as late as October, 1536, which was after the first session of the new parliament, and that, meeting 8 June in the same year, is styled 28 Henry VIII.

¶ It is provided in this act (sec. 4.) that "Sir Thomas Percy, Knight, brother of the said earl and his heyrs and assigns" shall neither be prejudiced in the enjoyment of the manor of Kyldacle in Yorkshire which had been settled on him : nor (sec. 34) in an annuity of 100 marks out of the "Lordships and manors of Prowdehow, Ovyngham, Hedley, Harlow, Horseley, Kyrkewhelpyngton, Ingo, Britley, and Baresford" in Northumberland : nor in the "constableshyp of the castell of Prodehowe aforsayd with xli. yerly goyng out of the premysses for the exercysyng of the same offyce, nor also to or for the Stuardship of the seide Lorships manors Londs Tentements and other Heredytaments aforsayd with vi lb. xiiis. iiiid. sterlying to and for exercysing of the offyce ; all whiche premysses the sayd Sir Thomas Percy brother of the sayde Erle, and Thomas and Henry sonnes of the said Sir Thomas, have to them and to ther assignes for terme of ther lyves and the longest lyver of them, as by graunte of the said Erle," ——— "more pleynley appereth."

** He might, perhaps, have been the less reluctant to transfer that part of the family possessions which was to vest in the crown ; for he might entertain the hope that it would be kept together, and would, at some future period, be restored to his heirs, — a hope which the event would to a great extent have ustified.

consequence led to make of the inheritance of his ancestors have rightly acquired for him the appellation of "Henry the Unthrifty."

The earl expired together with all his accumulated titles, 30th June, 1537, about the period of the execution of his next brother and heir Sir Thomas Percy; and not improbably of a heart broken at beholding the ruin of his house. The vial devoted to wrath, too full to hold this last calamity, shivered.

It will be recollected that Sir Thomas Percy, the attainted brother of the late earl, had a family. It consisted of two sons who grew to manhood, named Thomas and Henry; besides a third son Guiscard, who is presumed to have died in infancy, and female issue. These had the mortification to see the title of Northumberland raised to a dukedom, and, together with much of the lands of their ancestors, conferred by Edward VI., on John Dudley, the father in law of the Lady Jane Grey, the ill-fated and favorite cousin once removed of the young monarch. However, the wanned crescent * of the Percies was soon again to fill its horns. Mary succeeded to the throne, and the Dudleys in their turn were attainted† for treason. The attachment of the house of Percy to the connection with Rome would ensure it the favorable consideration of the new queen. And soon (in 1557) the elder of the two brothers so confirmed her regard by putting down a rebellion at Scarborough, that she restored to him those of his family possessions‡ which had lately been held by Dudley; and created anew§ the Earldom of Northumberland‖ and the barony of Percy with other titles, with limitations in tail male to himself and similar limitations in remainder to his brother Henry, after they had passed from their family for an interval of twenty years. However, after the accession of Elizabeth, the same religious opinions entangled him in a knot of difficulties, which he attempted, like his father, to cut with the sword.

The captivity of the beautiful Queen of Scots, the heiress presumptive to the crown of England, had awakened the sympathy of

---

* The perhaps ideal origin of this badge of the Percies is represented as forming one of the themes of the minstrels of their house.

"They sung, how in the Conquerer's fleet
Lord William shipp'd his powers;
And gained a fair young Saxon bride,
With all her lands and towers.

Then journeying to the Holy Land,
There bravely fought and died
But first the *silver crescent* won
Some Paynim Soldan's pride. [Hermit of Warkworth.

† See "A Lamentable Ditty" on this subject, in the Table Book, Legendary Div., vol. i. page 91.

‡ Besides these, the Percies eventually acquired, through Dudley's attainder, Lion House, in Middlesex. Formerly a nunnery, it had been confiscated and granted to Dudley; but was restored by Mary to its ancient use. In the time of Elizabeth it was again secularized; and, though not one of the ancient Percy possessions, was at length granted by her to Henry Percy ninth Earl of Northumberland.

§ Sir Harris Nicolas' Synopsis of the Peerage, p. 483.

‖ In 1558, the newly created earl merited the continuance of her favour by commanding, together with his brother, the border cavalry which repelled at Gorindon, not far from the Duddoe Stones, a formidable band of Scotch who were ravaging the country. Ridpath's Border History, p. 590.

many of its nobility: but especially of those attached to the connection with Rome; since they hoped through her means eventually to obtain ascendence or toleration for their faith. Amongst these the Earls of Westmoreland and Northumberland had been brought to entertain* projects for her liberation.

"And woe to the mermaid's wyly tongue;
And woe to the fire was in her 'ee;
And woe for the wiching spell she flung,
That lur'd the North Star from the sky!"

It, nevertheless, does not appear that the earls were then prepared to rush into open rebellion: but, as their consultations with their friends had excited a suspicion, which their explanations had been unable to remove, a letter was, on the 13th of November, 1569, delivered to Northumberland at his Yorkshire castle of Topcliff, peremptorily requiring his immediate attendance at court. This was at night followed by a hostile clamour about the castle; arising either from the zeal of headstrong friends who wished to startle him into committing† himself to a rebellion in which their hearts were already enlisted: or the loyalty of officious enemies who, though without warrant, expected to gain credit by arresting him.‡ Alarmed for his personal safety, he immediately took horse and fled towards Alnwick: but unfortunately called, on his road, on the Earl of Westmoreland at Brancepath. And it was there determined to unfurl the banner of the five wounds of Christ against the Protestant queen. As "the Rising of the North,§" was unconcerted, its failure was generally anticipated. And hence those even who wished success to its objects, but who were sufficiently distant to escape being drawn in by its sudden vortex, were found shrinking from its standard, or marching against it. On its suppression‖ the Earls of Westmoreland and Northumberland fled into Scotland for safety. Northumberland was there treated as a prisoner; and in the June of 1572, given up by the Earl of Morton,¶ into whose power he had passed, to** Queen Elizabeth. He was

* See Sir C. Sharp's "Memorials of the Rebellion of 1569," pp. 193–6.

† Camden's Annals under the year 1569.

‡ The account written in the spring of 1572, by Leslie, Bishop of Ross, the faithful adherent of the Scottish queen, and published in "Anderson's Collections relating to Mary Queen of Scotland," vol. iii., p. 81.

§ The events connected with this rebellion have been celebrated in several ballads, as "The Rising of the North," given in the Table Book, Legendary Div., vol i., p. 43; "Jock o' the Side," page 37;" "Northumberland betrayed by the Douglas" page 51; and another on the same subject with the last at vol. ii., page 12; "An Answer to the Proclamation of the Rebels," page 113; "The Pope's Lamentation" on their defeat, page 154; "Claxton's Lament" in the "Memorials of the Rebellion," page 270.

‖ See Table Book, Historical Div., Vol. i., pp. 213–14.

¶ See Ridpath's Border History, p. 645. James Douglas, fourth Earl of Morton, was then the most powerful minister under the Scottish regent: and about six months afterwards himself attained to the regency.

** Lord Hunsdon, who in behalf of Elizabeth then received the custody of Northumberland, says of him "trewley he semes too follow hys owld humors, reddyar to talke of hawks and hownds than anything els."—Sir C. Sharpe's Memorials of the Rebellion of 1569, p. 330. Such a man, attached to the simple pleasures of a country gentleman of his day, and possessed of endearing rather than commanding qualities, was little calculated to lead with success the rebellion into which untoward circumstances had plunged him.

then conducted to York, and beheaded there in a place called the Pavement, the 22d of the following August. To crown the infamy of the transaction, his betrayer received in gold the price of blood.

Sir Walter Scott under feelings of shame and indignation, writes thus of the conduct of his countrymen :—"It was an additional and agravating circumstance, that it was a Douglas who betrayed a Percy; and when the annals of their ancestors* were considered, it was found that while they presented many acts of open hostility, many instances of close and firm alliance, they never, till now, had afforded an example of any act of treachery exercised by one family against the other."†

The seventh Earl of Northumberland had ‡ by his wife the Lady Anna Somerset, daughter of the second Earl of Worcester, a son who died in early life, and four daughters; the co-heirs of the eldest branch of the house of Percy. Of these daughters three were born previously, and one about nine months subsequently to the rebellion of their father: and they appear to have been early inured to poverty and hardship.§ The eldest daughter Elizabeth ‖ became the wife of Richard Woodroffe, of Wolley, Esq. The second, Lucy, was married to Sir Edward Stanley of Tong Castle, grandson of the third Earl of Derby.¶ The third, Jane, was espoused by Lord Henry Seymour, second son of the first Duke of Somerset, but died without issue.** And Mary,†† the youngest, born under the melan-

* A brief, but accurate account of the illustrious house of Douglas, will be found in the 2d edition of Burke's Extinct Peerage.

† Tales of my Grandfather, vol. iii., chap. 7.

‡ The Countess of Northumberland eventually found a retreat in Brussels, and is believed to have been accompanied by some cadets of the Percy family. There was a Belgian gentleman of the name of Percy resident in Brussels in 1838, who claimed to be an offshoot of the house of Northumberland, and who, not improbably, might be descended from one of these.

§ Sir C. Sharp's Memorials of the Rebellion of 1569, p. 349.

‖ Amongst the lineal heirs of the daughters of the earl mentioned above, would now lie in abeyance, were it not for the attainder of their ancester, the ancient barony by writ of Percy, with the other baronies in fee of the family: and probably the older Earldom of Northumberland also; as it is stated by Banks to have been conferred in the first year of Richard II. "*Sibi et hæredibus suis.*" For the descendants of this daughter see Banks' *Baronia Anglica Concentrata,* vol. ii., p. 369.

¶ Burke's Peerage, title Earl of Derby. Their daughter and co-heir Venetia Stanley, a lady of extraordinary beauty, but "of far purer birth than fame," became the wife of Sir Kenelm Digby, "whose name is almost synonymous with genius and eccentricity." Preface to the private memoirs of Sir Kenelm Digby. For the descendants of Venetia Stanley see introduction to ibid.

** Banks' *Bar. Ang. Con.*

†† Some writers, following Brooke, have stated that there was another sister Mary, older than this, and married to Sir Thomas Grey of Werk. Vincent however states that he made enquiries of contemporaneous members of the Percy family, and found that there were not two Maries. The mistake may probably be thus accounted for.—As the Earls of Northumberland and Westmoreland were attainted on the same occasion; and, as each left daughters only, their families might easily have been confounded with each other; and, as Katharine Nevill, a daughter of the latter earl, actually did marry Sir Thomas Grey. Such a confusion might produce this erroneous statement. There is an elaborate pedigree of Grey of Heton, Chillingham, and Wark, in

choly star that watched the ruin of her father's house, made early vows of celebacy, and eventually became founder and prioress of a convent of Benedictine nuns at Brussels.

Sir Henry Percy, the brother of the last earl, was able, spirited, ambitious and intriguing: yet something of a pervading restraint seems to have been thrown over his daring character by the strength of his affection towards his wife and children; and by his anxiety that such moderate* portion of the family possessions as had been restored should be transmitted to his own issue.† He had been privy to the plans for the liberation of Mary, formed previously to the "Rising." But, on his brother's sudden rebellion, foreseeing probably that it must be unsuccessful, and trusting that his allegiance would save the estates and titles from being again confiscated entirely from the house of Percy, he made a show of loyalty to his queen,‡ took the joint command of a force with Sir John Forster one of her captains, and is said to have even come to a skirmish with the rebels.§ After the suppression of this rebellion, his connivance at former plots became known to the court. But it is probable he found a secret friend there in the person of Cecil; the marriage of whose son to Dorothy Nevill, the daughter and co-heir of the fourth Lord Latimer and his own sister in law, he seems previously to have forwarded‖—an alliance which must have been highly advantageous to the aspiring family of the minister. However he was indicted, in the Easter term 1572, (the crime by perhaps a mild construction being treated as a contempt) "for that he with divers others, did conspire for the delivery of the Queen of Scots out of the custody of the Earl of Shrewsbury¶" and, on pleading guilty, was fined 5,000 marks; though their payment was never exacted. And the house of Percy was thus made to afford almost contemporaneously an instance both of the clemency, and of the rigour of the queen. He succeeded his brother in the estates and newly created titles, under the late entail by Queen Mary unaffected by his attainder;**

Raine's North Durham: and it may be mentioned, in confirmation of this view, that there, though the marriage with Katharine Nevill is mentioned, no notice occurs of an alliance with Mary Percy. However it may have been that, according to the fashion of an age when the inclinations of the bride elect were little connsulted, the Lady Mary Percy had in childhood been simply betrothed to Sir Thomas Grey.

* Memorials pp. 337, 355. And, for the amount of rental, at that period, of the Percy property in Northumberland, see note therein p. 83.

† Idem p. 356.

‡ Idem p. 55.

§ It may not be improbable that the skirmishes, mentioned in a letter Idem, p. 109, Hollinshed's Scotland, p. 397, and Stow's Annals, p. 664, (in the latter two of which, Sir Henry Percy is mentioned as having taken part,) allude to the same transaction, though there is a slight difference in their dates.

‖ Memorials p 352.

¶ Official memorandum from the records of the court of Queen Bench printed in Corbett's State Trials, vol. i., 1115.

** "In virtue of Philip and Mary's letters patent, May 1, 1557, granting the earldom to Thomas and the heirs male of his body, and in failure thereof to Henry with the same limitations: the latter grant being distinct from that of his elder brother, and not affected by his attainder; though it could not take place till his disease." Carte's History of England vol. iii., p. 590.

and thus became eighth Earl of Northumberland. But he was afterwards suspected of participating in a plot, charged against Sir Francis Throgmorton, to effect the liberation of the Queen of Scots by a conjoint invasion and rebellion: and was, in 1584, in consequence, sent to the tower. Here on the 21st of June, 1585, he was found shot in bed; but whether by the hands of an assassin or a suicide has been by some supposed to remain still a problem in history. However the attendant circumstances, followed by the verdict of the coroner's jury,* make it more reasonable to conclude that, anticipating a conviction, and true to his ruling passion, zeal for the prosperity† of his line, he rashly determined to take his own life, in order that, by dying unattainted, he might be able to transmit‡ to his family their interest in his estates; and, as he himself is said to have expressed it, "to balk Queen Elizabeth of their forfeiture."§

After his accession to the title, this earl had lived much at Petworth in Sussex; for the border had ceased to be the post of danger and of honor. The influence of England was then all powerful in the Scottish counsels; and in the next reign the crowns of both kingdoms were fixed on the same head; and the days of northern chivalry had drawn to a close. What remains, therefore, of the Percy descents shall be hastily glanced over. The earl had married Catharine Nevill, the daughter and co-heir of John fourth Lord Latimer, to whom had devolved a confluence of baronies by writ,‖ which remain yet in abeyance amongst the descendants of his daughters¶—By her the earl had eight sons** and three daughters

---

* Corbett's State Trials, vol. i., 1122.

† Idem.

‡ "If a traitor dies before judgment pronounced, or is killed in open rebellion, or is hanged by martial law, it works no forfeiture of his land: for he was never attainted of treason." Blackstone's Commentaries vol. iv., p. 382. And by *felo de se*, unlike the felony committed by the murder of another, the personal property alone is forfeited.

§ Carte's History of England vol. iii., p. 590.

‖ Besides, according to Banks, the co-heirship of the Earldom of Suffolk.—*See Baronia Anglica Concentrata*, vol. i.

¶ After the death of the 4th Baron Latimer, that title was claimed (Camden's Annals Sub. A. D. 1585) and, apparently, for a short time even assumed, by a male collateral relative; but, as it was a barony by writ, the daughters and their descendants as heirs general have a preference over the cousin as heir male. See *Baronia Anglica Concentrata*.

** Of these George went to Virginia, and is alleged in Brydges' Collins, vol. ii., p. 328, to have "died in March, 1632, having never been married" yet it is stated in Baronia Anglica Concentrata that in 1827 there were, amongst the landholders in Virginia, "two brothers of the name of Percy who claimed descent from the said Mr. George Percy." Two other of the sons of the eighth earl, Sir Charles and Sir Josceline Percy were involved in the Earl of Essex's insurrection; and were committed on that account to the Fleet prison; but were afterwards pardoned. It is curious to observe that in one of the Cecil papers published in Lodge's Historical Illustrations, vol. iii., p. 120, their names are spelled "Pearcy;" while the surname of the 7th Earl of Northumberland is, in the register of his burial at St. Crux, York, spelled "Pearsey;" and hence it is reasonable to presume that "John Pearsye" a gentleman usher, and "Robert Pearsey" a gentleman and household servant, to this earl, who were both confined in Durham jail for participation in the rising of the North (*Memorials* p.

Henry Percy, the eldest son was in his 22d year when, on the death of his father, he became ninth Earl of Northumberland. Three years later he seized the opportunity of gaining honorable distinction by joining as a volunteer in the expedition which destroyed the Spanish Armada. The sufferings of his family in the cause of Mary were likely to recommend him to the confidence of her son : and in the latter part of the reign of Elizabeth, whilst yet some uncertainty hung over the succession of James, he deserved the gratitude of that king and of the English and Scotch nations by forwarding by his secret counsels that auspicious event which finally produced their union. Yet, though unlike his ancestors he had embraced the doctrines of the reformation, he was suspected of a connivance in the gunpowder plot, in consequence solely of his friendship for his kinsman Thomas Percy,* his constable of Alnwick castle, who was one of the conspirators : and, in 1605, a little more than two years after the accession of James, was arrested on that ground, and, through a sentence of the court of Star chambers, was fined £20,000 and imprisoned above fifteen years in the tower. The earl however, who was much adicted to scientific pursuits, lived for some years after his release in great splendour, and died in the year 1632, on the 5th of November—the day which had brought upon him so many troubles.†

By his wife the lady Dorothy Devereux, sister of the earl of Essex, the favorite of Queen Elizabeth, he had two daughters, and two surving sons. The elder of the daughters, the Lady Dorothy, timid, affectionate and sensible, conferred and received as much happiness,‡ as this chequered state admits of, in her marriage with Robert Sidney, second Earl of Leicester : while the younger, the Lady Lucy, haughty, eccentric and intriguing, found a field for the display of her rare beauty § and talent in uniting herself to James Hay, an adventurous courtier whom the favour of James I. exalted to the Earldom of Carlisle. The younger of the sons, Henry Percy, was a gallant royalist general in the civil wars, and died unmarried ; after having been elevated to the peerage by Charles I., with the title of Baron Percy of Alnwick in 1659.

Algernon Percy the elder son, succeeding his father, became tenth Earl of Northumberland. He was a man of great consideration

129) would have been drawn by warmer ties than those of mere servitude to the standard of their unfortunate lord. In the accounts commonly given of the family of the eigth earl all the sons, except the eldest are said to have died without issue.

* See note another page.

† Banks' Extinct Baronage, vol. ii. A memoir of this earl is given in Lodge's Portraits.

‡ See extracts from her letters to her husband given in the sketch of her in Lodge's Portraits. She was mother of Algernon Sidney, celebrated as an enthusiastic republican and author of "Discourses Concerning Government," whose execution has been considered one of the judicial murders perpetrated by Lord Chief Justice Jeffreys.

§ Her beauty was such that Venus is styled, by the poet Waller, "The bright Carlisle or the court of Heaven."—*The country to my Lady of Carlisle.* There is a memoir of her in Lodge's Portraits.

with all parties. In the rupture between the king and the parliament he eventually sided with the latter; possibly taking his notions of the gratitude of princes and the justice of the Star chamber from the experience of his father. Yet he deprecated the outrageous excess committed by his own party in the execution of their sovereign. He afterwards favored the restoration; and then with even the loyalists so high was his estimation that he was appointed to fill, at the coronation of Charles II., the dignified office of lord high constable. This earl, who had resided much at Petworth, died, in the sixty-sixth year of his age, 13th Oct., 1668. He had been twice married; but his issue male, an only son, was by his second wife, the Lady Elizabeth Howard,* daughter of Theophilus second earl of Suffolk.

Josceline Percy, eleventh† and last Earl of Northumberland of his line, was twenty-four years old at the demise of the late earl his father. He was the sole hope of his noble house whose expectations were raised very high for him: nor were these doomed to be disappointed otherwise than by his premature death; which took place, 21st May, 1670, at Turin, as he was on his travels on the continent, after he had held possession of his honors a little less than two years. He had married the lady Elizabeth Wriothesley the daughter and co-heir of Thomas fourth Earl of Southampton, lord high treasurer of England: and had issue a son and two daughters. The son Henry, Lord Percy, the last heir apparent to the titles of his house died in infancy 2d of May, 1668, more than two years before his father.

After these events, the Northumberland title and territory were for a short time severed. The earldom,‡ afterwards raised to a dukedom, was conferred by Charles II., on his own illegitimate son George Fitzroy; who, however, died without issue. The territory we shall find to have centered in the heiress of the last mentioned earl of the Percy house.

The younger of the daughters, of the tenth Earl of Northumberfand, the Lady Henrietta Percy, having died whilst an infant; the elder, the Lady Elizabeth Percy, became sole heiress of her lather. She was married to Charles Seymour, known to history as the proud Duke of Somerset;§ and had a large family;‖ of which

---

* By his marriage with this lady, the earl acquired the noble residence at Charing Cross, London, which thence changing its name with its proprietors, is still enjoyed by their descendants.

† He was the eighteenth Lord of Petworth of his family. See Dallaway's Sussex, vol. ii. p. 279.

‡ Shortly previous to this creation James Percy the trunkmaker emerged from obscurity and unsuccessfully prosecuted his claim.

§ The Lady Elizabeth Percy, though very young in 1682 when this marriage took place, had already been previously married to Henry Cavendish, Earl of Ogle, the eldest son of the Duke of Newcastle, who died without issue; and had been contracted to Thomas Thynne, Esq., of Longleate, whose bright prospects procured his assassination through a rival in 1632. This tragic incident is represented in bas relief on his monument in Westminster Abbey.

‖ Of this family the only personages who had surviving issue at all were Duke Algernon, the son and successor, and a daughter, the Lady Catharine

the eldest surviving son Algernon Seymour, Duke of Somerset* by descent, and Earl of Northumberland, and of Egremont by creation, had, with a son who died young, a daughter and sole heiress, the Lady Elizabeth Seymour. This lady became the wife of Sir Hugh Smithson, a Yorkshire baronet, who in consequence of this alliance, assumed the name of Percy and obtained the Dukedom of Northumberland: and she transmitted to her grandson by this marriage, Hugh Percy, the present Duke of Northumberland, the sole lineal representation of the last four earls of the house of Percy, together with all which should accompany the living blood of his princely ancestors.

Seymour, married to Sir William Wyndham, the tory leader of the opposition to the Walpole administration in the time of George I.:—

That "Wyndham, just to freedom and the throne,
The master of our passions and his own."—Pope.

On the death of Duke Algernon without any surviving son, his dukedom of Somerset devolved on a distant cousin on his father's side; the earldom of Egremont, together with the honour of Petworth and some lands in Yorkshire passed by a peculiar patent and settlement to his nephew Sir Charles Windham, the son of the above mentioned marriage; and the earldom of Northumberland devolved according to its limitation, with the estates in Northumberland and Middlesex, on his son-in-law Sir Hugh Smithson.

* During his father's life he was styled Earl of Hartford, the second title of his family:—

"Now Percy's name no more does fill the north;
Hartford succeeds in honor, fame, and worth,
Seymour and Percy both in him unite—
He a good patriot, and a hardy knight.'.—Cheviot.

THE AMERICAN BRANCH.

From the foregoing historical sketch of the English branch of the Percies it will be seen that Peter[17] Percy* was son of Ralph[16] Percy ; he (Peter[17]) was born in 1447 and his descent is as follows from the first ancestor: Galfred[1], William[2], Alan[3], William[4], William[5], Agnes[6], Henry[7], William[8], Henry[9], Henry[10], Henry[11], Henry[12], Henry[13], Henry[14], Henry[15], Ralph[16].

Peter[17] Percy had a son Richard[18]. The father was standard bearer to Richard the Third at the battle of Bosworth Field in 1485.

Richard[18] founded Pearce Hall in York, England, where he lived and died leaving an eldest son Richard[19], Jr.

Richard[19], Jr. resided on the homestead of his father and had two sons Richard[20], Jr., b. 1590, and William[20]. It was at this time that the spelling of the name in this branch was changed from Percy to Pearce.

Richard[20] Pearce, Jr., (Richard[19]) b. 1590 ; m. in England Martha ———.

He resided in Bristol, England, and came to America in the ship "Lyons" from that place. His brother, Capt. William Pearce, was master of the ship.

Children :

1. i. Richard[21], b. 1615 ; m. Susannah Wright.
2. ii. John[21], b. ——; m. Mary ——, and Mrs. Rebecca Wheelor.
   iii. Samuel, b.
   iv. Hannah, b.
   v. Martha, b.
   vi. Sarah, b.
   vii. Wil iam, b.
   viii. Mary, b.

Capt. William[20] Pearce (Richard[19]), b. in Bristol, England about 1595 ; m. ———.

He d. July 13, 1641 (Boston Town Records). Res. Bristol, England, Boston, Mass., and Providence, Bahama Island.

---

* See note page 18,

Farmer has this :

"William Peirse, the captain of the ship 'Lyon,' wrote his name Peirse ; he was the author of the first almanack for 1639 published in North America. He was killed at Providence, one of the Bahama Islands, in 1641. Savage ii. Winthrop Index. Prince ii., Annals 69, who erroneously regards him as a member of the Boston Church, says he was ancestor of Rev. James Pierce, a well known writer and English divine, who died in 1730."

Copy of Order of Council when the troubles of Charles 1st. commenced with his Parliament. From the original books of the Privy Council :

1638. "Ordered the twentieth [of April, 1638.] Order for the Desire to passe to New England, with passengers and provisions, upon certificate, etc.: "

"Upon the humble petition of William Piers, master of the shippe called the Desire, that the Petitioner, with diverse others inhabiting in New England, did lately arryve in the Port of London, in the *said shippe being wholly built in New England*, whither the said master doth nowe desire to return in the same, and did therefore desire the leave of the board, according to his Majesties' late Proclamation, and to transport such Passengers and their necessary provisions of Howshold, as by this certificate shall be gratified according to the Tenor of his Magesties' former Proclamation. Theyr Lordships did this day give leave that the said master and shippe should retorne to New England, together with such passengers and theyr necessary provisions as is desyred and their goods to passe as formerly. Provided that the said certificats of the Passengers be first brought to the Clarke of the Council attendant, to be by him allowed, and that they doe transport noe other passingers or Provisions but such as shall be allowed."—[Charles I., Vol. 15, :41.]

1. Richard[21] Pearce (Richard[20], Richard[19],) b. 1615 in England ; m. in Portsmouth, R. I., in 1642, Susannah Wright, who was born in 1620. He died in Portsmouth in 1678 and she was deceased at that time.

Richard Pearse was at Portsmouth as early as 1654, when he was a witness to a deed of 12 acres of land and a house purchased of William James by Henry Piercy.

Jan. 14, 1657, he was a witness to a deed. June 8, 1657, he was chosen surveyor of marks of all "Cattell that goe" from this town.

June 11, 1658, he was a witness to a will. May 18, 1658, he was admitted Freeman of the Colony from Portsmouth.

Nov. 16, 1666, he purchased 2 acres 7 rods of land of Jacob Cole ; 1669 he purchased of Joseph Parker 14 acres of land in Portsmouth.

He married, probably in 1642, Susannah, daughter of George Wright of Newport, who was probably of Salem, 1637, Newport, 1648, and who in 1649 stabbed one Walter Lettice, as John Winthrop, Jr., received a letter to this effect from Roger Williams.

His will was drawn April 23, 1677, and was proved in Portsmouth Oct. 28, 1678. His son Richard was executor and he calls him his "eledest son."

RICHARD PEARCE'S WILL.

The following is an exact copy of Richard Pearce's will, on record at Portsmouth, R. I. It is as follows:

To all Christian people whome these presents may concerne Know yee that I Richard Pearce through the mercye of God being perfect in mind and memory but not well in bodye For the preventing further trouble amongst my children make this my last will and Testament as followeth—

Imprimis—I do will and bequeath unto my eldest sonne Richard Pearce my now dwelling House and land and fencing, orchard and swamps, house and out houses with all appurtenances thereunto belonging, I also give unto my eledest son Richard one pair of Oxen with a cart and wheels, with the bed and bedding that I myself lodge in with the Plough and tackeling thereunto belonging, with all the goods and Furniture belonging to the said house whatsoever.

My will is to give unto my sonn John Pearce, one shilling in silver and unto my sonn Giles Pearce one shilling in silver and unto my sonn William Pearce one shilling in silver and unto my sonn James Pearce one shilling in silver and unto my sonn George Pearce one shilling in silver and unto my sonn Jeremiah Pearce one shilling in silver and unto my foure daughters one shilling apeece in silver, to be paid within six months after my decease if demanded by the elder of them and unto the younger when they come to full age according to law. Also my will is that my sonn Richard take care, and see this my will performed and him I doe ordaine constitute and make my whole and sole executor to see this my will in all things performed and fulfilled according to the true interest and meaning of the same.

In witness thereunto I have set to my hand this two and twenty daye of April in the year of our lord God, one thousand six hundred and seventy-seven.

RICHARD PEARCE. [SEAL.]

Signed and sealed in presence of
John Heath
John Hurd
The E L I S A mark of *Elizabeth Heath*

The above written will was according to law proved before us of the Town Council of Portsmouth, R. I., the twenty-eighth of October, 1678.

John Albro Assistants.
Wm. Cadman
Latham Clarke
William Wodell
Peleg Tripp
Jacob Mott

Town Clerk's office, Portsmouth, R. I., April 20, 1882.—I hereby certify that the foregoing copy of will is a true extract from the Records in this office.

PHILIP B. CHASE,
Town Clerk.

Richard's children were :

1.+ i. RICHARD, b. Oct. 3, 1643 ; m. Experience ———.

ii. MARTHA, b. Sept. 13, 1645 ; m. Mahershallalhashboz Dyer of Portsmouth, born about 1643 ; d. 1670. He was the son of William and Catharine Dyer of England, Boston, Portsmouth and Newport. March 22, 1661, he signed certain articles relative to Westerly lands. She d. s. p. Feb. 24, 1744.

2.+ iii. JOHN, b. Sept. 8, 1647 ; m. Mary Tallman.

3. iv. GILES, b. July 22, 1651 ; m. Elizabeth Hall.

v. SUSANNAH, b. Nov. 22, 1652 ; m. Dec. 4, 1673, George Brownell, b. 1646. She d. Dec. 24, 1743. Ch.—Susanna, b. Jan. 25, 1676 ; m. John Reed of Freetown, who was town clerk there for thirty-five years ; Sarah, b. June 14, 1681 ; Mary, b. Dec. 8, 1683 ; m. William Hall ; Martha, b. Feb. 18, 1686 ; m. Samuel Forman ; Thomas, b. June 1, 1688 ; Joseph, b. Dec. 5, 1690, m. Ruth Cornell ; he was a representative to the General Court for six years ; Wait, b. Oct. 3, 1693 ; m. Joshua Sandford ; Stephen, b. Dec. 3, 1695, m. Martha Earle. George, d. April 20, 1718, in Portsmouth. In 1699–1702 he was deputy ; 1706-7-8-9-10-11 an assistant ; 1708, April, he was appointed on the committee in regard to vacant lands in Narragansett. His will is proved May 12, 1718, with wife Susannah executor. His inventory was £961 5s 10d. George was the eldest son of Thomas and Ann (———) Brownell, who was in Pourtsmouth as early as 1647.

vi. MARY, b. May 6, 1654, m. 1678 Thomas Brownell, Jr., b. 1650. Ch.—Thomas, b. Feb. 16, 1679; John, b. Feb. 21, 1682 ; George, b. Jan. 19, 1685 ; Jeremiah, b. Oct. 10, 1689 ; Mary, b. Mar. 22, 1692 ; Charles, b. Dec. 23, 1694, d. 1694 ; Thomas, d. May 18, 1732. She d. May 4, 1736 in Portsmouth, R. I.

Thomas Brownell, Jr., was the son of Thomas and Ann (———) Brownell of Portsmouth. His will was proved June 20, 1732; wife Mary and son Thomas executors. His inventory was £1,807. Mary's will was presented for probate June 9, 1735 and proved Nov. 19, 1736. Her brother George was executor. She gives her brother George a mare by his paying to her son John £8. Her inventory was £175 12s 4d.

vii. JEREMIAH b. Nov. 17, 1656. He res. in Narragansett or South Kingston, R. I.

viii. ISAAC, b. Dec. 1658. He res. in Newport, R. I.

4. ix. SAMUEL, b. Dec. 22, 1664; m. ——— ———.

5. +. GEORGE, b. July 10, 1662; m. Alice Hart and Temperance Kirby.

2. JOHN[21] PEARCE (Richard[20], Richard[19]) b. in Bristol, England, probably; m. Mary ——— in England. She d. in Boston, July 12, 1647; m. 2nd, Aug. 10, 1654, Mrs. Rebecca Wheeler. She res. in Dorchester, Mass., and died Dec. 1674. He d. Sept. 17, 1661.

While John resided in Dorchester his uncle, Capt. Wm. Pearse, was sent by Gov. Winthrop to Ireland with his ship "Lyon" for provisions for the colony, as there was a scarcity one year. Oct. 8, 1633, John was selected as one of the first selectmen of Dorchester. He was one of the first grantees of lands in that town prior to 1636.

P. 427, L. 42. *JOHN, Dorchester: Savage has here confounded two persons of the same name, rightly distinguished in the Hist. Dorch. p. 71. His note (p. 659) admits an uncertainty, but does not correct the error of the text.

1. John, Dorchester, cooper, had by his w. Mary, Nehemiah, b. 17 Jan. $163\frac{1}{2}$, and Mary, b. 6 Mar. $163\frac{8}{9}$ (Gen. Reg., Vol. V. p. 244); sold house and land in Dorch., 28 Dec. 1642, to Richard Curtis, his w. not signing (Suff. Deeds, L. 2, F. 151), and prob. rem. to Boston. This is clearly the John who m. Rebecca Wheeler, 10 Aug. 1654, and d. 17 Sept. 1661, and his s. Samuel seems to me to have been b. in Boston 14 Jan. $16\frac{59}{60}$ (Savage, p. 429, l. 6). His will (Suff Prob., no. 276,) mentions estate "at Boston or Dorchester," gives to Nehemiah the testator's "working tools," and provides for the education of Samuel, whom Savage rightly, as I think, judges to be younger than N. Mercy P., who m. Manasses Marston at Charlestown, 22 Aug., 1667 (Charlestown Records), seems to have been the dau. of this John (Suff. Deeds, L. 15, F. 160); but she cannot have been the dau. of Rebecca. Administration on the est. of Rebecca P. was granted to her s., Joseph Wheeler, 21 Dec., 1674. (Suff. Prob. no. 713, L. 5, F. 220.) See also Suff. Deeds, L. 3, F. 190.

I am disposed to identify this John with the John Pears whose name stands seventeenth in the list of inhabitants of

---

* Suffolk Probate Records.

Dorchester in 1641 (Hist. Dorch., p. 424), and who was freem. 18 May, 1631, selectman 1633, 1636, 1639, 1641, and a proprietor of lands in 1656.

John's will is as follows :

In consideration of my unfeigned love unto Rebecca, my wife, and also by way of Restoration of what I married with her and have injoyed of her former husband's estate, I leave the home and land we live in, freely, unto her and also out of that little God hath given mee, my will is she have in such things as may be, to her Content and Comfort, to the value of £13, in necessary as bed, Table, Chaire, pott and other household stuff, as she and my overseers can agree upon, or the value aforesaid payd her in some convenient time after my Decease. For my owne house and land yt I lately purchased in Boston, my will is that my wife during the time of her widowhood after my decease, shall have one halfe of the yearlley rent and profitt of the same and no longer ; yee other halfe of the yearlly profftt of the aforesaid land I dispose of for the education and maintenance of my sonne Samuell and after the Death or Day that my wife shall change her condition by marriage, that all said house and land shall be and Remain, the Inheritance of my sonne Samuel and his heyres forever. For my son Nehemiah Pears I give him all my working tools and implements belonging to my Calling with all the timber and stuffe to work upon, be it at home or elsewhere, Desiring he may by the helpe of God, be a good husband in the use of it, and then I hope he may Live like a man. For my dau. [blank] the wife of Jeremiah Rogers, it is my will that whereas her husband stands indebted unto mee £20 more or less the same I give unto my dau. and her children ; also 20s a peece unto his 3 children after my Decease. For my three daus. Mary, Mercy and Exercise I give unto them the Remainder of my estate be it land, goods, cattle, etc., be it at Boston, Dorchester or else where ; mywill is they have it equally Divided amongst them ; and if any dye before age of 18 or marry these portions to be divided amongst the survivors. For ye equale Administration of the premises I beg ye help of my Loving friends William Killcupp, William Robinson and John Wisewall, to advise and direct upon all occasions, according to law 16:7:61.

John Pears.

Signed in pr'nc of
John Wisewall, Wm. Killcupp
11 Oct., 1671. Power of administration
to the estate granted to Mr. John
Wisewall, Wm Robinson and Wm. Killcupp.

Children :

6.+ i. Nehemiah, b. Jan. 17, 1631 ; m. Phebe Planting and Mrs. Anna Mosley.

ii. Mary, b. Mar. 6, 1638 ; d. bef. 1661.

7.+ iii. Samuel, b, m. Mary ——.

iv. MERCY, b. m. Aug 22, 1667 Manassah Marston, son of John and Sarah of Salem. The father came from Ormsby, Norfolk county, England, in 1637. Mercy was living in 1716. He was b. Sept. 7, 1645 ; d. 1705. Res. Charleston and Salem. He was a blacksmith and later merchant; freeman 1677; Captain and Representative 1691.

v. MEHITABLE, b. m. Jeremiah Rogers. They res. in Dorchester. He was one of the first settlers in Lancaster, Mass. Ch.—Margaret, b. 1653 ; Mehitable, b. Oct. 6, 1658 ; Ichabod, b. May 27, 1660 ; Sarah, d. Sept. 21, 1657.

vi. EXERCISE.

vii. MARY. She was unm. in 1661.

1+. RICHARD[2] PEARCE (Richard[21]), b. Oct. 3, 1643, in Portsmouth R. I., m. Experience ——. They removed to Bristo and died there. He passed away July 19, 1720 ; Richard was freeman of the colony of Portsmouth May, 1663 ; freeman of the town of Portsmouth Apr. 28, 1669 ; was sole executor of his father's will Sept. 10, 1691. Richard Pearce and Experience, his wife, of Bristol, sold 16 acres of land in Portsmouth to William Barrington for £48. He probably settled in Bristol soon after his father's death.

From the Bristol town records we glean the following :

Oct. 11, 1696, Richard Pearse, Deed of 10 acres of land, (bought of Col. Nathaniel Ryfield) to Jeremiah Osborn.

March 10, 1709-10, Richard Pearse, Deed of the above land to Richard Pearse, Jr.

March 15, 1713-14, Richard Pearse. Deed of the 150th part of 600 acres of Commonage to William Munro.

March 24, 1717-18, William Munro, Deed of 16 acres of land to Richard Pearse, Con—£180.

Sept. 3, 1720, Richard Pearse, Deed of 60 acres of land to Richard Pearse, Jr.

Their children born in Bristol were :

6. i. JONATHAN, b. m. Elizabeth ——.

7. ii RICHARD, b. m. { Sarah ——. Susannah Lawton.

iii. ABIGAIL, b. Oct. 3, 1690.

iv. MARY, b. Aug. 17, 1693.

8. v. JEREMIAH, b. Aug. 29, 1695; m. { Submit Carpenter, Sarah ——.

vi. ANNIE, b. Feb. 11, 1698 ; m. May 15, 1728, Thomas Hogins ; res. Bristol.

vii. BENJAMIN, b. Jan. 11, 1703 ; d. at sea Dec. 26, 1778 ; res. Bristol, R. I.

viii. SON, b. —— ; d. at sea June 1737.

2. Ensign John[2] Pearce (Richard[2 1]), b. Sept. 8, 1647, in Portsmouth, R. I.; m. Mary Tallman, who d. in June, 1720. Res. in Portsmouth and Tiverton. John Pearce 27 died at Tiverton Dec. 5, 1707, at 60 years, 2 months and days. He was made a freeman of the town of Portsmouth Apr. 28, 1669, and of the colony from Portsmouth May 2, 1671. In 1681 he made several purchases of lands in Pocassett, afterwards Tiverton (State Records). He probably settled in Pocassett about 1682-3 and was one of the incorporators of Tiverton, 1692. Married Mary, dau. of Peter and Ann Tallman of Portsmouth. Apr. 11, 1689 he sold lands in Pocassett to William Wodell, Jr. Dec. 11, 1706 he sold lands in Portsmouth to Thomas Durfee.

Aug. 3, 1709, an agreement was filed between John Pearce of Tiverton, John Read, Jr., of Freetown and Mary his wife, Samuel Shearman and Sarah his wife of Swanzey, Thomas Cook, Jr., and his wife Elizabeth, John Cook, son of John Cook and Rachel his wife of Tiverton and Alice Pearce, all children of John Pearce, deceased, who died intestate. John was the only son. He was commissioned an Ensign of militia; moderator of town meeting at Tiverton in 1705. He is said to have been a mason by trade. His grave stone still remains with legiable inscription.

Tiverton, R. I., was incorporated as a town Mar. 2, 1692, and among the twenty-seven citizens at that time residing there was John Pearce.

From an inventory of all and singular the goods, chattels and estate of John Pearce of Tiverton, deceased, prized on the Twentyeth day of 10th month December, 1707, William Wilbore, George Pearce and Richard Borden we find the amount to have been 519£ 3s.

Mary Tallman was a daughter of Peter and Ann — Tallman. He was general solicitor of R. I. in 1661.

Mary's will was proved at Taunton, Mass., Jan. 19, 1720. She was from Tiverton, R. I. Witnesses, Benj. Durfee, Thomas Brownell, Jos. Sheffield. John Read, Jr., was executor. The children mentioned in the will were Alice, John, Samuel Sheffield, Sarah Wilcox, Mary Read, Elizabeth Cook, Rachel Cook. The negro woman Rose is given to Alice. The will was signed by mark.

The husband's estate—John—was administered upon Mar. 3, 1708, by his widow Mary.

Their children were:

i. Mary, b. m. John Reed, Jr. They had 12 children b. between Nov. 19, 1690, and Sept. 27, 1715. She d. Aug. 25, 1735. For three years he was a representative to General Court. Res. Fall River.

ii. SUSANNAH, b. 1672; m. Richard Woodall. They both died before 1710. Ch.—Mary, b. Oct. 14, 1691; Susan, b. May 7, 1693; Sarah, b. May 7, 1693 (twins). Richard was a son of Gersham and Mary (Tripp) Woodall. His ancestor William was of Boston and was one of the original purchasers of Shawoneet (Warwick) in 1643.

iii. ANNA, b. Feb. 14, 1674; m. Mar. 5, 1696; Capt. Amos Sheffield, b. June 25, 1673. Ch.—Susanna, b. Oct. 11, 1697; John, b. Jan. 8, 1699; m. Martha Taber; Mary, b. Apr. 2, 1701; Ruth, b. Jan. 10, 1704; m. Benjamin Weaver. She d. Nov. 27, 1706. He was a blacksmith, assessor, selectman, and town treasurer. He was also a deputy to the legislature and a captain. His father-in-law, John Pearce, and wife Mary were the executors to his will. He gives to son John at age his dwelling house and land, mare colt, and a book called "Josephus' Antiquities of the Jews." To his daughters certain land when they are 18. To son John a bed of silk grass, one of deer's hair, and one of flocks and a little gun. The housings and the smith's shop to be re nted till John is of age, and then he to have the shop and tools if he learn the art or mystery of blacksmith, and if not, he to have a third and the other children two-thirds of the proceeds of sale of the shop and tools. Son John to be bound out to what trade he likes best, at 16; the three daughters to be bound out to tailor's trades at 16. Inventory 474£ 4s. 1d.

iv. Sarah, b. m. Samuel Sherman.

v. Elizabeth, b. m. Thomas Cook, Jr.

vi. Rachel, b. m. John Cook.

vii. John, b. 1686.

viii. Alice, b. 1688, m. Blake Perry of Tiverton, R. I., April 19, 1722.

3. HON. GILES[2] PEARCE (Richard [1]), b. July 22, 1651; m. April 13, 1676, Elizabeth Hall, who d. 1698. She was the eldest daughter of William and Mary (———) Hall of Portsmouth. He died November 19, 1698. Res. in East Greenwich and Portsmouth, R. I.

Hon. Giles or Gyles Pearce was born in Portsmouth, R. I., the son of Richard and Susannah (Wright) Pearce; he was admitted a freeman of the colony in 1673, he being of the above town. He was one of the incorporators of the town of East Greenwich, R. I., in 1677, when he was admitted a freeman of that place. The town meeting that year being held at his house. He was moderator of the town meeting in 1685, member of the General Assembly in 1690 and 1696, and town councilman in 1677–1684, 1691 and 1696. His will was admitted to probate in East Greenwich, December 7, 1698.

Giles Pearce was admitted freeman of the town of Portsmouth, April 29, 1693, and of the colony, May 6, 1673. Ear-mark recorded in Portsmouth, July 5, 1673. One of the grantees of East Greenwich, May, 1677. February 20, 1678, bought of John and Susanna Tripp, one-fourth part of a purchase right in Warwick. Moderator of town meeting in East Greenwich, 1690. Town councilman of same town 1691. His will is dated November 15, 1698 and proved December 7, 1698 in East Greenwich. His first two children were born in Portsmouth, and the third in East Greenwich May 20, 1682.

His will was filed Nov. 15, 1698, and proved Dec. 7, 1898. His wife Elizabeth was executor. To her while widow, the occupation and profit of house and land and orchard belonging thereto till son John is of age, he then having ½ of profits and the whole at wife's death. To eldest son Jeremiah, a house, 90 acres, etc., a pair of oxen and 3 cows. To son John, all lands in East Greenwich, undisposed of, a pair of oxen and 3 cows at age. Mentions daughters Susana, eldest, Elizabeth and Mary.

Children :

9. i. Jeremiah b. Jan. 22, 1678; m. Abigail Long.

ii. Susannah, b. May 7, 1679; m. Aug. 6, 1713, Hon. John Warner, b. Jan. 5, 1673 ; d. Nov. 13, 1732. She d. Aug. 4, 1727. Res. Warwick, R. I.; Ch.—Mary, b. Sept. 5, 1714 ; Priscilla, b. June 10, 1716 ; d. March 7, 1716 ; William, b. Mar. 4, 1718. Susanah was his second wife. He during 1702-9-23-25-26-27-29-31 was a deputy to the General Court. His will is dated May 2, 1728, and proved Dec. 23, 1732. Inventory £445. He was a lawyer by profession.

iii. Elizabeth, b. May 27, 1682 ; m. Dec. 30, 1703 ; Hon. Thomas Spencer, M. D., b. July 22, 1679 ; d. Apr. 25, 1752. She d. Sept. 30, 1742. Res. East Greenwich. Ch.—Thomas; Elizabeth, b, Feb. 19, 1714 ; William, b. Sept. 6, 1716 ; Susanah, b. Aug. 18, 1720 ; Dr. Thomas Spencer was the son of John and Susanah Spencer of East Greenwich, R. I. He was born July 22, 1679, and was the first English child born in that town. He was a physician and made freeman in 1703. In 1704-7-10-14-15-19-21-27-29-30-31-33-35-36-37-38-41-48-49-50 and 51 he was a Deputy to the General Court. In 1720-21-27 he was clerk of the assembly. In 1734-5 he was one of the Justices of the Inferior Court of Common Pleas of the county of Providence. In 1738 he was Speaker of the House of Deputies. Dec. 2, 1741, he was appointed a committee to represent and manage the affairs of this colony before the Commons, to hear and determine boundaries between Rhode Island and Massachusetts. In Aug., 1741, he and two others were appointed by the assembly to let off part of Warwick into a township to be called Coventry. May 20, 1752, administration is granted to son-in-law, Thomas Aldrich. Inventory—£2,055, 3s, 10d; viz., wearing apparel, £156; plate, £85, 4s; watch, £25; bonds, £409, 2s, 6d; bonds, supposed to be deposited debts, £33, 1s, 10d; notes, £80, 1s, 10d; books, £24, 10s; three framed maps or plans, £3; two spinning wheels, pewter and table, the whole of his medicines, with the vessels and utensils belonging to his practice, £50; four feather beds, £140; negro man and woman, £400; two horses, three cows, three swine, etc.

Dr. Spencers' father John resided in Newport originally, and while there, Oct. 31, 1677, he, with forty-seven others, were granted 5,000 acres of land to be called East Greenwich.

10. iv. JOHN, b. Jan. 11, 1687; m. Susanah Nicholls.

v. MARY, b. Feb. 7, 1690; m. March 10, 1708, David Vaughn; b. Apr. 29, 1683; m. Dec. 19, 1728. She d. 1728. Res. East Greenwich, R. I. Ch.—Elizabeth, b. Nov. 3, 1710; Margaret, b. Apr. 12, 1713; Mary, b. Dec. !, 1717; Rebecca, b. Apr. 3, 1720; Waity, b. May 13, 1721; m. George Nicholls; Susanah, b. May 13, 1724.

Nott David was born at E. Greenwich Apr. 29, 1683, the son of Geo. Vaughn, b. in Newport, Oct. 20, 1650. Geo. m. Margaret Spink at N., July 26, 1680, and was son of John Vaughn, one of the first of the name who settled R. I. The inventory of David's estate was £2,138-17-4.

4. SAMUEL[2] PEARCE (Richard[1]), b. Dec. 22, 1664; m.——— ———.

Res. Prudence Island, opposite Portsmouth, R. I. Ch.—

11. i. SAMUEL, b. ; m. Esther———.

5. GEORGE[2] PEARCE (Richard[1]), b. July 10, 1662; m. Apr. 7, 1687, Alice Hart, b. Mar. 8, 1664, the dau. of Richard and Hannah Hart, of Portsmouth, d. Mar. 11, 1718; m. 2nd Mar. 22, 1721, Temperance Kirby, b. May 5, 1670, d. Feb. 25, 1761. He d. Aug. 30, 1752. Res. Little Compton, R. I., and in 1696 sold lands to his brother-in-law, Richard Hart. There was a George Pearce and George, Jr., in Little Compton in 1748, who at that time took the oath against bribery and corruption. The following is a copy of the entry of the first marriage of George Pearce from the Portsmouth town records:

On Rhode Island, the seventh day of April, in the year of our Lord one thousand six hundred and eighty-seven, George Pearce, of Portsmouth aforesaid, did take to wife Alice Hart, daughter of Richard Hart, of Portsmouth, and the said George Pearce and Alice Hart here and then, according to law, joined together in marriage before me, John Coggshall, Justice.

Ch.—

i. SUSANNAH, b. Aug. 21, 1688 ; m. Dec. 19, 1706, Edward Thurston, b. Oct. 18, 1679 ; d. May, 1739. She d. Aug. 5, 1711. Ch. : George P., b. Nov. 4, 1709 ; m. Kezia ——— and ——— Grene ; William, b. Apr. 13, 1711 ; d. May 13, 1712. After Susanah's death he m. Oct. 15, 1712, Sarah Carr, by whom he had five children. Res. Little Compton, R. I. Edward Thurston was the eldest son of Jonathan Thurston of Little Compton, R. I., where he was born in 1679. He was a grandson of Edward Thurston, who was the first by that name in the Colony of Rhode Island. According to the Thurston genealogy he must have been there some time previous to 1647, sufficient, at least, to attend to the preliminaries of his marriage, which occurred June, 1647, to Elizabeth Mott, daughter of Adam Mott.* and is the third on the record of the "Society of Friends" at Newport. He is mentioned in the Colonial records as a freeman in 1655, as commissionor, assistant and deputy from Newport for many years from 1663 to 1690. On Aug. 26, 1686 he, with others, signed an address from the Quakers of Rhode Island to the king. He died Mar. 1, 1707, æ 90. She d. Sept. 2, 1694, æ 67. His grandson Edward is mentioned in the will.

12. ii. GEORGE, b. Mar. 2, 1697 ; m. Deborah Searles.

13. iii. JAMES, b. Sept. 4, 1691, ; m. Martha Wilbur.

iv. SAMUEL, b. Feb. 3, 1695 ; d. Jan 29, 1705.

v. MARY, b. May 16, 1700 ; m. Jan. 31, 1755, William Simmons. Res. Little Compton, R. I.

6.+ NEHEMIAH[3] PEARCE (John[2, 1]), b. Jan. 17, 1631 ; m. Phebe Planting, eldest daughter of William Planting ; m. 2nd 1684, Mrs. Ann Mosley, daughter of Isaac Addington, b, Dec. 1, 1646. She d. in Boston, Mass, in Apr. 1691. In 1661 he was a setwork cooper, and and in 1671 was a member of the Ancient and Honorable Artillery Company.

P. 430, l. 19. NEHEMIAH, Boston, 1661, setwork cooper, s. of John, the cooper, of Dorchester and Boston, and his w. Mary, had in 1671, and as late as 1674, a w. Phebe, dau. of William Planting, sen., of Dorchecter, and had by her a dau. Mercy, who was living unmarried in 1696. He had no chn. by his sec. w. Ann, to whom the administration of his estate was granted, 28 Ap., 1691. Manasses Marston was appointed guardian to his dau. Mercy (or Mary). Suff. Deeds, L. 3, F. 519 ; L. 7, F. 224 ; L. 8, F. 282, 480 ; L. 9, F. 5 ; L. 13, F. 421 ; L. 14, F. 297 ; L. 15, F. 160., 161 ; L. 17 F. 68 ; L. 20, F. 201 ; Suff. Prob., No. 1849, L. 8, F. 161 ; L. 13, F. 134-136.)

* Adam Mott and thirty-nine others from Cambridge, England, his second wife Sarah, aged thirty-one years, four children of Adam by a first wife, and M ry Mott, a daughter of Sarah by a former husband, were passengers from London for New England in the "Defence" in July, 1634. One of these children was the wife of Edward Thurston.

Ch.—

i. NANCY, b. Aug. 21, 1673. She was m. in 1696.
ii. PHEBE, b. Aug. 31, 1663 ; d. young.
iii. REBECCA, } children of his second wife.
iv. Mary, }

7.+ SAMUEL[2] PEARCE (John[21]) b. ; m. Mary ——. He d. s. p. in June, 1716. Res. Boston.

P. 431, L. 15. SAMURL, Boston, setwork cooper, s., as I suppose, of John, the cooper, of Dorchester and Boston, mortgaged land in Bofton in 167?, had a w. Mary in 1673. His will, signed 19 May, and proved 11 June, 1716, makes bequests to Zachriah Simons of Bradford, husbandman, testator's niece Phebe Shackley, single woman, his niece Margaret, w. of Samuel Triskett of Brush Hill, husbandman. and her children, and appoints Mercy Pearce of Boston, spinster (daughter of Nehemiah ?), and Sarah Mirick, testator's housekeeper, resid legatees. (See Suff. Deeds, L. 8, F. 74, 198, 215 ; L. 9, F. 119 ; L. 12, F. 63 ; Suff. Prob, No. 3756, L. 19, F. 1314.)

6. JONATHAN[3] PEARCE (Richard[2], Richard[1]), b. —— ; m. —— Elizabeth ——. He d. July 2, 1713. Res. Bristol, R. I., and Rehoboth, Mass.

Ch.—

i. NICHOLAS, b. Nov. 11, 1700.
ii. WILLIAM, b. Mar. 17, 1702.
iii. ISAAC, b. Aug. 13, 1705 ; d. May 21, 1706.
iv. ISAAC, b. May 21, 1706.
v. ELIZABETH, b. Nov. 13, 1707.
vi. MARY, b. Dec. 11, 1709 ; d. June 15, 1710.
vii. THOMAS, b. Aug. 7, 1711.
viii. ABITAH, b. Sept. 23, 1713 ; d. Apr. 15, 1714.

7. RICHARD[3] PEARCE (Richard[2] Richard[1]), b. —— ; m. Sarah —— ; m. 2nd, May 22, 1723, Susanah Lawton of Portsmouth, R. I. Susanah was the daughter of Hon. Isaac and Elizabeth (Tallman) Lawton of Portsmouth, R. I. Isaac was a deputy of the General Court 1696–8–9–1702–4–5–6–8. Susanah was b. Ap. 3, 1689 ; d. July 27, 1768. He d. Oct. 25, 1744. Res. Bristol, R. I. After his death in Sept., 1746, she was united in marriage to John Burden of Portsmouth. His will is at Taunton, Mass., from Bristol, then Mass., Jan. 14, 1745. Edward, Priscilla and Stephen Paine were witnesses. Sons Nathaniel and William executors. The following entries are taken from the Bristol land records :

Feb. 20, 1719. William Gallup, Deed of land to Richard Pearse, Jr. Con. £66.

Feb. 17, 1720-1. Benjamin Cary, Deed of 6¾ acres of land to Richard Pearse, Jr. Con. £66.

Feb. 13, 1726. Richard Pearse, Jr.; Deed of 20 acres of land to Nathaniel Blagrove. Consideration £110.

Feb. 17, 1720-1. Richard Pearse, Jr., Deed 6 acres of land to Benjamin Carey. Con. £66.

Nov. 24, 1742. Richard Pearse, 2 deeds of land to Samuel Oxx; another deed, Dec. 24, 1742, to same.

Dec. 10, 1742. Richard Pearse, Deed of land to Nathaniel Munro. Con. £290.

Nov. 23 and 24. Richard Pearsé, 2 Deeds of land to Nathaniel is worth.

April 6, 1742. Edward Little, Deed of 12 acres of land to Richard Pearse. Con. £300.

July 1, 1743. George Waton, Deed of 41 acres of land to Richard Pearse. Con. £205.

Sept. 10, 1745. Inventory of estate of Richard Pearse, a Negro

Woman	£ 25
Homestead Farm, 110 acres, at £25 per pace	2,750
31 acres of land bought of Capt. Wanton	651
One-half of Still and Stillhouse	650
¾ acre of land, which belonged to Capt. Oxx	80
	£4,155

Chn.—

i. SAMUEL, b. Nov. 2, 1706.

14. ii. NATHANIEL, b. Nov. 23, 1708; m. Mary Lindsay.

iii. SARAH, b. Feb. 8, 1710; d. July 4, 1720.

iv. RICHARD, b. Oct. 6, 1713.

15. v. WILLIAM, b. Sept. 18, 1716; m. Lydia Brown.

vi. EXPERIENCE, b. July 5, 1718; m. Sept., 1737, Ichabod Simmons, of Newport, R. I., and 2nd Aug. 15, 1753, Samuel Whittaker, of Rehoboth.

vii. MARY, b. June 29, 1720; m. Sept., 1745, Joseph Jay, of Bristol.

viii. SUSANNAH, b. Feb. 12, 1724.

ix. ANN, b. Sept. 21, 1725; m. Sept. 16, 1770, Col. Nathaniel Carey, of Bristol.

x. ELIZABETH. b. May 9, 1728; d. Aug. 5, 1746.

8 JEREMIAH[3] PEARCE (Richard[2], Richard[1]), b. Aug. 29, 1695; m. in Swansey, May 16, 1717, Submit Carpenter; m. 2nd Dec. 24, 1744, Sarah Eddy.

He d. Jan. 22, 1761. Res. Bristol, R. I. Ch.—

i. JONATHAN, b. May 13, 1718.

ii. JEREMIAH, b. June 2, 1738.

iii. KEZIAH, b. Apr. 27, 1722; m. Nov. 11, 1742, Ezekiel Smith. Res. Swansey, Mass.

iv. RENEW, b. Sept. 12, 1724.

v. TABITHA, b. Oct. 17, 1726.

vi. GEORGE, b. Mar. 20, 1745; d.———, 1750.

16. vii. THOMAS, b. July 27, 1749; m. Abigail Wardwell.

9 JEREMIAH[3] PEARCE (Giles[2], Richard[1]), b. Jan. 22, 1678; m. ——, Abigail Long, b. June 20, 1682, d. Apr. 22, 1774.

He d. April 25, 1754. Residence South Scituate, R. I. Ch.—

17. i. GILES, b. Aug. 24, 1701; m. Comfort Nichols.
18. ii. PHILLIP, b. Mar. 9, 1703; m. Frances Nichols.
iii. ELIZABETH, b. Feb. 6, 1705; m. Wm. Sweet, of E. Greenwich, R. I., July 20, 1727.
iv. SUSANNAH, b. Apr. 8, 1708; m. —— Olin.
19. v. JEREMIAH, b. Feb. 18, 1711; m. Frances ——.
20. vi. JOHN, b. Mar. 9, 1713; m. Elizabeth Weaver.
vii. WILLIAM, b. Aug. 18, 1716, } prob. d. before 1754,
viii. JAMES, b. Oct. 30, 1719, } as they are not mentioned in their father's will.

The following is a copy of Jeremiah's will in full:

The 11th day of April, in 1752, the 26th year of his Majesties reign, George the Second, By the grace of God and Great Britain, France and Ireland, King Defender of the Faith.

I, Jeremiah Pierce, of East Greenwich, in the county of Kent, in the colony of Rhode Island, *yeoman*, being far advanced in life, but at present in health and of a sound disposing mind and memory, thanks be to Almighty God, thoughts calling to mind the mortality of my body and considering its appointed for all men to die, I make and ordain this to be my last will and testament. That is to say principally and first of all, I give and recommend my soul to God that gave it, and my body I commit to the earth to be decently buried at the discretion of my executor hereinafter named. And as touching such worldly estate as it has pleased God to bless me with, in this world, after all my just debts are paid, I give and dispose of it in the following manner and form.

Item 1st — I bequeath to my beloved wife Abigail Pearce all that my dwelling house and shop and two lots of land whereon the house and shop stands in East Greenwich aforesaid, excepting what I have before disposed of to Isaac Lawton. Said lot and No. 2 and No. 14, the same to be to my said wife during her natural life, and after her disease, said house and shop and lots to be my son John Pearce's during his natural life and at his disease the same and every part thereof to be his son Jeremiah Pearce, his heirs and assigns forever.

Item 2nd.— I bequeath to my said wife during her natural life all that my land and orchard situate in Warwick, bounded southerly on Warwick south line westerly and land of Thomas Aldrich northerly on land of John Greene Esq & others easterly on the country road being about 13 acr. I also give to her during her natural life all my land fronting against the aforesaid land in Warwick to the north of the county road, bounded southerly on land of Thomas Spencer, westerly by land of John Greene Esq & easterly on the salt water & contains about two acres—I also give to my wife during her natural life all that my land in said East Greenwich adjoining to the east side of the country road containing about 15 acres bounded northerly on a highway easterly on the salt water, southerly on land of Thomas Aldrich, westerly on the country road.

Item 3rd.—I give to my son Giles Pearce all my land situated in Warwick to the eastward of the county road bounded southerly on land of Thomas Spencer, westerly on the salt water and northerly on land of John Green Esq. containing about three acres, the same after my said wifes decease, to be my said son Giles Pearce his heirs aud assigns forever. I also bequeath to my son Giles my two lots of thatch bed and upland in Warwick in that part called Chipponoxit being Nos. 8 and 15, upon condition that he or his heirs, executors or administrators pay or causeth to be paid to my daughters Elizabeth Sweet and Susannah Olin each of them forty pounds in bills of credit (old tenor) in one year after my decease, then said lots be to him, his heirs and assigns forever. But in failure of paying said legacies to my said daughters as aforesaid, then my will is that my said daughters Elizabeth and Susannah shall have the said lots of thatch bed to be equally divided between them and to be their heirs and assigns forever.

Item 4th—I bequeath to my son Giles one and a half acres out of the corner of my land in East Greenwich aforesaid laying near to where Rufus Green now dwells, to be layed in the corner of my said land adjoining to the county road and to be laid as square as may be and the same after my wife's decease to be to him, my said son, Giles his heirs and assigns forever.

Item 5th.—I give to my granddaughter, Mary Estis, all that my land in East Greenwich, with my orchard therein containing about 13 acres, bounded west, northerly by the county road, southerly on land of Thomas Aldrich, easterly on the salt water, northeasterly partily on a high way near Rufus Green Esq dwelling house and partly on land of my son Giles Pearce which I have herein given him out of said tract of land after my aforesaid wifes disease upon conditions that my said grand daughter Mary Estis her heirs executors or administrator pay to her two brothers namely Benjamine Pearce and Phillip Pearce in consideration thereof each of them one hundred pounds bills of public credit (old tenor) Provided they live to return from sea where they have been for many years missing unhurd of. Then the said land and orchard all to be to my said grand daughter Mary Estis her heirs and assigns forever.

Item 6th.—I give to my grand son Caleb Pearce that part of my lot of land in Warwick to the westward of the country roads bounded northerly on land of John Green Esq and partly on land of Thomas Comstock easterly on the county roads southerly on the stone wall on the north side of my orchard and so to extend westward until it comes to the west end of said wall on a square across to the north side thereof the same after my said wifes decease to be to him his heirs and assigns forever—I also give to my grandson Caleb Pearce my quarter of a lot No. 12 on Chipponoxit island being chiefly thatch bed upon condition that he pays to his sister Mercy Pearce five pounds in bills of credit in one year after my desease, then the same to be him, his heirs and assigns forever.

Item 7th.—I give to my grand son James Pearce all the residue of my land and orchard and *barn* thereon being to the westward of the county road in Warwick bounded southerly on Warwick south line westerly on land of Thomas Aldrich northerly on land of Ebenezer Cook and John Green Esq Easterly partly on land herein given to Caleb Pearce and partly on the county road and a house lot of said Caleb Pearce all after my said wifes decease to be to him my said grandson James Pearce his *heirs* and assigns forever, always, provided he or his heirs or *executors* or administrator pay or cause to be paid to his sister Barbary Pearce the sum of 5 pounds in bills of credit in one year after my death.

Item 8th.—I give all my Coopers tools to be equally divided betwixt my two grand sons *namely* Caleb and James Pearce. *Item* I give to my wife one *cow* to be delivered to her, by my executors. I also give to my wife the use of all my household goods of every kind whatever for her comfort during her natural life and after her decease the same and every part thereby to be equally divided between my two daughters namely Elizabeth Sweet and Susannah Olin and all the residue and remainder of my estate both real and personal. I give and bequeath to my said son Giles Pearce, his heirs and assigns forever, And I do hereby ordain, constitute, and appoint my said son Giles Pearce to be my executor, to execute this my last will and testament according to the true intent and meaning thereof. The inventory of his estate which was taken May 10, 1754, amounted to £820–3–3.

10 JOHN[3] PEARCE (Giles,[2] Richard[1]), b. Jan. 11, 1687; m. June 9, 1709, Susanah Nicholls. He d. 1739. Res. East Greenwich, R. I. His will was admitted to probate Apr. 28, 1739.

Ch.—

i. GILES, b. Sept. 21, 1710; d. Feb. 27, 1711.
ii. GILES, b. Apr. 22, 1712; d. Mar. 17, 1713.
iii. SUSANNAH, b. Jan. 10, 1714; m. Apr. 3. 1733, Thomas Spencer. She d. 1748. Res. No. Kingston, R. I.
21 iv. JOHN, b. Aug. 4, 1722; m. Alice Tibbetts.
22 v. THOMAS, b. ; m. Rebecca Scranton.
vi. ELIZABETH, b. ; m. Caleb Carr, Nov. 9, 1740. Res. No. Kingston.
23 vii. GILES, b. m. Desire Case.
viii. MARY, b.

11 SAMUEL[3] PEARCE (Samuel,[2] Richard[1]) b. ; m. Esther He d. aged 104. Res. Prudence Isle, R.I.

Ch.—

i. JOHN, b. April 11, 1745; killed on board ship.
ii. MARTHA, b. June 5, 1747; m. James Allen. Res. Prudence Island, and removed to Amsterdam, N. Y., dur-

ing the revolutionary war. Ch.—Daniel, m. Hannah Wall; Samuel, both these sons followed the seas until after the war of 1812. They died of yellow fever in the West Indies. Daniel's dau. Elizabeth, b. Mar. 6, 1802; m. David Pierce (see Pierce Genealogy p. 250) John, Thomas,* Cyrus, Matthew, Harry, Martha, Cynthia, m. ——— Davis; Susan, m. ——— Davis; Juliana,

iii. SARAH. b. Jan. 14, 1749.

iv. DORCAS, b. Oct. 16, 1750; m. John Walford. Ch.—John and James. She removed with her brother Michael to New York State and was the first white person to die in Augusta, Ontario county, now the town of Yates, Middlesex Co.

12. v. SAMUEL, b. April 13, 1752; m. Hannah Jerrauld.

vi. ESTHER, b. June 20, 1754; d. unm. in 1854. She always claimed that she was decended from one of two brothers who settled in Woburn, Mass.

25. vii. THOMAS, b. Oct. 8, 1756; m. Martha Jerrauld.

viii. MICHAEL, b. Oct. 9, 1757; m. Sarah Allen.

12 GEORGE[3] PEARCE (George[2], Richard[1]), b. Mar. 2, 1697; m. Feb. 20, 1717, Deborah Searles, b. Nov. 17, 1695; d. May 16, 1776. He d. Feb. 22, 1764. Res. Little Compton, R. I. Ch.—

i. ALICE, b. Nov. 4, 1718; d. Mar. 28, 1719.

26. ii. JEPTHA, b. Feb. 20, 1722; m. Elizabeth Rouse.

iii. TEMPERANCE, b. Jan. 26, 1723; m. Oct. 9, 1745, Thomas Gibbs, b. June 15, 1721. She d. 1750. Ch.—Alice, b. July 26, 1747. Res. Little Compton.

iv. JEREMIAH, b. Dec. 22, 1725; d. London, England, Oct. 17, 1750.

27. v. NATHANIEL, b. Oct. 13, 1727; m. Sarah Rouse.

vi. SARAH, b. Jan. 12, 1729; m. 1745, Josiah Sawyer, Jr. b. 1719; d. 1792. She d. Aug. 28, 1780, in Little Comp, ton. Ch.—Samuel, b. 1747, d. 1804; Thomas- b. 1749; Anstras, b. Oct. 1751, d. Oct. 12th, 1835; Pris-, silla, b. 1753; Josiah, Jr., b. 1755; Martha, b. 1757; John, b. 1759; Sarah, b. 1761; name unknown, b. 1763; name unknown, 1765; Jeremiah and George, twins, b. 1768; name unknown, b. 1770; Isaac, b. 1772.

---

* Died in Amsterdam on the 20th inst., Mr. Thomas Allen, in the 88th year of his age. Mr. Allen was a member of the Presbyterian church in this place and held the office of Ruling Elder for 47 years—first in the church at Manny's Corners, and then in the church at Amsterdam village, from the time of its organization to the time of his death. He conscientiously discharged his, duties as a Christian and an officer in the church, resting alone on Christ for the hope of his personal justification in the sight of God. He was a Christian of the old school, and loved the doctrines of grace and rested on them as a sure foundation. His last sickness was protracted and painful, during which he was sustained by the consolation of the gospel, and he died in the hope of a glorious and blessed immortality.

vii. SARAH, b. Nov. 11, 1720 ; d. Feb. 20, 1721.

viii. RUTH, b. Sept. 20, 1731 ; m. Oct. 24, 1750, John Horswell. She d. Little C., 1801. Ch.—Mary, b. Mar. 4, 1751 ; Betsey, b, Aug. 26, 1753 ; Pearce, b. Sept. 3, 1755 ; d. 1756 ; Pearce, b. Feb. 2, 1757 ; Deborah, b. Apr. 10, 1759 ; Ruth, b. Apr. 21, 1761.

ix. ANSTRAS, b. Nov. 12, 1733 ; m. June 24, 1753, Thomas Faber. Res. Tiverton, R. I.

x. DEBORAH, b. Feb. 23, 1735 ; m. Christopher Manchester. She d. Apr. 25, 1795.

xi. RICHARD, b. Apr. 19, 1738 : d. Mar. 15, 1817, Tiverton, R. I.

13 JAMES[3] PEARCE (George[2] Richard[1]), b. Sept. 4, 1691; m. 1712 ; Martha Wilbur, b. Oct. 22, 1690 ; d. 1760. She was the daughter of Samuel and Mary (Potter) Wilbur of Little Compton, R. I. His will was proved June 17, 1740. He gave to his daughter Martha Pierce, £40. The inventory of his estate amounted to £5,344–13–3. He d. Sept. 24, 1755. Res. Little Compton and Tiverton, R. I. Ch.—

28. i. JAMES, b. Sept. 1719 ; m. Sarah Simmons.

29. ii. WILLIAM b. Jan. 19, 1713 ; m. Elzabeth Woodman and Anna ———.

iii. SUSANNA, b. May 24, 1715 ; m. John Dennis.

iv. MARTHA, b. Aug. 4, 1717 ; m. Joseph Tompkins.

30. v. GILES, b. Mar. 23, 1722 ; m. Mercy Rouse.

vi. MARY, b. Oct. 17, 1724 ; m. William Woodman.

31. vii. GEORGE, b. Sept. 12, 1727 ; m. Deborah Woodman and Priscilla Woodman.

viii. ALICE, b. Jan. 1, 1729.

ix. PHEBE, b. Sept. 21, 1731 ; d. unm. Sept. 20, 1755.

32. x. SAMUEL, b. Jan. 29, 1733 ; m. Betty Simmons.

14 NATHANIEL[4] PEARCE (Richard,[3] Richard,[2] Richard,[1]) b. Nov. 23, 1708 ; m. Apr. 6, 1732, Mary Lindsay. Sept. 22, 1746, Nathaniel and his brother William deeded land to John Lindsay for £78–15s. They Res. Bristol, R. I. Ch.—

33. i. SAMUEL, b. Oct. 25, 1733 ; m. Mary ———.

ii. JOHN, b. Mar. 28, 1735 ; d. 1736.

34. iii. RICHARD, b. Jan. 15, 1737 ; m. Phebe Monroe.

iv. NATHANIEL, b. Aug. 5, 1739 ; m. Nov. 15, 1767, Mrs. Lydia Peckham, Res. Bristol and Rehoboth.

v. CHRISTOPHER, b. July 5, 1741 ; d. Nov. 27, 1743.

vi. ELIZABETH, b. Feb. 17, 1742 ; d. Aug. 6, 1746.

vii. THOMAS, b. Mar. 6, 1744 ; d.

viii. MARY, b. Apr. 3, 1747 ; d. Dec. 23, 1748.

ix. THOMAS, b. Mar. 24, 1749.

x. WILLIAM, b. Apr. 2, 1753.

xi. SARAH, b. Aug. 26, 1754 ; d. Jan. 16, 1755.

15 WILLIAM[4] PEARCE (Richard,[3] Richard,[2] Richard,[1]) b. Sept. 18, 1716; m. Apr. 22, 1742, Lydia Brown. Res. Bristol, R. I. William Pearce purchased the property known as Bristol Ferry in 1753, of Job Lawton. There was an old fort not far from the house at Bristol Ferry. It was this fort which prevented the British from passing on its way to burn Fall River and other places during the Revolutionary war. The Yankees made it so hot for them they were obliged to anchor their fleet, and manned their barges, thinking to pass hugging the south shore, but they were nearly all sunk, and the attempt was abandoned. At this time—the Revolution—the house stood a short distance to the N. E. of the present location, and in that house two of the sentries were killed by a cannon ball fired from the British fort upon the other side of the River, or Bay, about one mile distant. They were repeatedly warned of the danger, but did not heed it. The ball first struck the water, then a sharp rock, at the foot of the road, then glanced and passed through the side of the house, a partition, and through one man and lodged in the other, killing both. His son George Pearce has related that one day the cannon balls were flying so fast that the family were sent to Bristol for safety, and while going over the top of the Ferry Hill, on horseback behind his mother, a cannon ball passed between the horse's legs. Persons there have frequently ploughed out grape shot, and 8 and 12 pounders, once the half of a 24lb ball. The embankment of the fort is plainly to be seen, also the powder magazine. The British had possession of the entire Island of R. I., at one time, with a fort at the N. end opposite the Ferry. Members of this family have been wardens of St. Michael's church, Bristol, for sixty years. William Pearce's name appears in the old Colony records as assisting about the fort and victualling the soldiers. A man was dragged from the Ferry House, during the war of 1812, cropped and branded for some misdemeanor. Ch.—

i. SARAH, b. Dec. 21, 1742; m. ——— Monroe.

35. ii. GEORGE, b. Sept. 15, 1744; m. Hannah ———.

iii. SUSANAH, b. Aug. 31, 1746.

iv. ELIZABETH, b. June 20, 1748; m. ——— Darling.

v. WILLIAM, b. ———; m. ———. Res. in Swansey and was instrumental in organizing the First church there.

vi. LYDIA, b. ———; m. ——— Clark,

16 THOMAS[4] PEARCE (Jeremiah[3], Richard[2], Richard[1]), b. July 27, 1749; m. Dec. 5, 1771, Abigail Wardwell, b. 1751; d. Mar. 10, 1810. He d. Dec. 20, 1823. Res. Bristol, R. I. Ch.—

36. i. William, b. Nov. 3, 1772; m. Mary Gladding and Sally Smith.
ii. Stephen, b. Dec. 29, 1775.
iii. Jeremiah b. June 21, 1777.
iv. Mary, b. , 1783; m. June 10, 1805, David Fisk. She d. in Bristol, R. I., Oct. 29, 1861.
37. v. Josiah, b. ——; m. Sarah Wilson.

17 Hon. Giles[4] Pearce (Jeremiah[3], Giles[2], Richard[1]), b. Aug. 24, 1701; m. Feb. 14, 1724, Comfort Nichols, b. Mar. 7, 1701; d. June 9, 1777. He d. Dec. 22, 1763. Res. East Greenwich, R. I. Giles was for many years town clerk of East Greenwich and several times deputy to the General Assembly. His will was approved in 1764. His son William was executor. His wife was a daughter of Thomas and Mary (Reynolds) Nichols. Ch.—

38. i. Jeremiah, b. June 2, 1726; m. Margaret ——.
ii. Joseph, b. Apr. 24, 1728.
39. iii. George, b. Apr. 24, 1730; m. Mary Green.
iv. Ruth, b. Dec. 18, 1732.
40. v. William, b. Jan. 22, 1735; m. Catherine Green.
vi. Sarah, b. May 10, 1739.

18 Phillip[4] Pearce (Jeremiah[3], Giles[2], Richard[1]), b. May 9, 1703; m. Oct. 17, 1733, Frances Nichols, born Nov. 29, 1697. She was a sister of Hon. Giles' wife. They res. in East Greenwich, R. I.

i. Mary, b. ——; m. —— Estie.
ii. Benjamin, b. } did they come back from sea?
iii. Phillip, b. }

19 Jeremiah[4] Pearce (Jeremiah[3], Giles[2], Richard[1]), b. Feb. 18, 1711; m. Frances ——. Ch—.

41. i. Caleb, b. July 15, 1734; m. Margaret Pearce.
ii. Mary, b. Feb. 21, 1736.
iii. James, b. July 7, 1737.
iv. Barbara, b. July 24, 1738.

20 John[4] Pearce (Jeremiah[3], Giles[2], Richard[1]), b. Mar. 9, 1713; m. Aug. 22, 1736, Elizabeth Weaver. He d. Oct. 19, 1798. Res. East Greenwich, R. I. Ch.—

i. Susannah, b. Apr. 2, 1737.
ii. William, b. June 16, 1739.
42. iii. Job, b. Nov. 15, 1741; m. Temperance Green,
iv. Jeremiah, b. Apr. 14, 1744.
v. Edward, b. June 25, 1747.
vi. Elizabeth, b. Mar. 9, 1751.
43. vii. Phillip, b. Jan. 14, 1754; m. Mary Mumford.
viii. Charles, b. Feb. 22, 1758.

21 John[4] Pearce (John[3], Giles[2], Richard[1]), b. Aug. 4, 1722; m. Apr. 13, 1739, Alice Tibbets. Res. N. Kingston, R. I. Ch.—

i. SARAH, b. Nov. 17, 1740.

44. JOHN, b. June 14, 1746 ; m. Mary Spencer.

22 THOMAS[4] PEARCE (John,[3] Giles,[2] Richard[1]), b. m. Oct. 14, 1743, Rebecca Scranton, dau. of Stephen of Warwich, R. I. He was admitted freeman in 1457. Res. East Greenwich and Warwick, R. I. Ch.—

i. SUSANNAH, b. Oct. 27, 1744 ; m. July 2, 1763, in E. G., Robert Brattle.

45. ii. GILES, b. Feb. 6, 1746, m. Elizabeth Pearce.

46. iii. STEPHEN, b. July 20, 1749 ; m. Lydia Rice.

47. iv. DANIEL, b. Mar. 3, 1752 ; m. Mary Bentley, or Sweet.

v. M RY, b. Dec. 8, 1754 ; m. ——— Lewis and Capt. John Warner.

48. vi. MOSES, b. Feb. 19, 1757 ; m. Sarah Bentley.

vii. THOMAS, b. May 25, 1761 ; d. s. p.

49. viii ISAAC, b. Apr. 12, 1764 ; m. Sarah Vaughn.

ix. REBECCA, b. Apr. 12, 1764 ; m. Henry Miles.

23 GILES,[4] PEARCE (John,[3] Giles,[2] Richard[1]), b. ; m. Desire Case, b. Sept. 15, 1733 ; d. Sept. 15, 1803. He d. Apr. 10, 1793. Res. East Greenwich, R. I., Block Island and North Kingston.

Giles Pearce was admitted a Freeman of Rhode Island in 1745. He married Desire, daughter of Joseph Case, Esq., of North Kingston. He was the youngest son of John Pearce and Susannah his wife. A few years of his married life was spent in East Greenwich, and after the large landed estate of his father John had been spent in law suits by the executors of his estate, and finding that nothing of any value would be left for him, he removed soon after 1758 to Block Island, where he improved the Sands, Hull and Rathburn farms and became the largest stock raiser, especially of sheep, upon the Island and second to but few in the Colony. In 1775, James Rhodes and Gideon Hoxie were a committee appointed by the general assembly of the Colony to oversee all the stock on the Island, exhibited unto said assembly an account of the stock taken from said Island belonging to sundry persons, together with the valuation thereof. The largest number by far were taken for Giles Pearce, being:

241 fat sheep and lambs valued at..	78£ 6s. 6d.
441 sheep valued at......	110£ 5s. 0d.
Total 682 sheep and lambs. Total value..	188£ 11s.6 d,

In the proceedings of the General Assembly, held for the colony of Providence, the 31st day of Oct., 1775, the following appears as per the R. I. Colony Records :

And the said account being duly examined It was voted and resolved that the same be and is hereby allowed and that the account thereof being 534£ 9s. 6d.

lawful money be paid out of the general treasury to the person to whom the same is rightfully due as mentioned in said account.

A correspondent, writing to me, says: Between 1760 and 1770 he removed from East Greenwieh to New Shoreham, or Block Island, where he lived during the war of the Revolution, when, during those times, the authorities took from the island most of the stock belonging to the inhabitants of the island, and Giles Pearce at that time was one of the largest owners of sheep on the island, and a large number of fat sheep and lambs were taken from him. Whether he was ever paid for them or not I do not know.

In 1782 he purchased quite a large tract of land in North Kingston, Narragansett, and in 1783, as soon after the war as permission could be procured, he and his large family of sons and daughters moved here. He died in 1797, aud his will was admitted to probate in North Kingston July, 1797. Ch.—

50. i. John, b. Feb. 19, 1766; m. Polly Davis and Sarah Brown,
ii. Sarah, b. Jan. 2, 1751; m. Nehemiah Wilson and rem. to New York.
iii. Lucy, b. Sept. 2, 1753.
iv. Elisha, b, Oct. 30, 1755; d. 1764.
v. Anna, b. May 14, 1758; m. Robert Reynolds and rev. to Vermont.
51. vi. Joseph, b. Sept. 14, 1760; m. Sarah Havens.
52. vii. Giles, b. 1763; m. Elizabeth Dodge and Susanah Gardiner.
viii. Susanah, b. , 1769; d. Oct. 17, 1831, in N. K.
ix. Desire, b. ; m. Oliver Rose.
x. Thomas, b. , 1770; m. Mary Cole. He d. in 1810 in No. Kingston and she afterwards m. her nephew Giles Pearce, Jr.

24 Samuel[4] Pearce (Samuel[3], Samuel[2], Richard[1]), b. Apr. 13, 1752; m. Dec. 22, 1776, Hannah Jerrauld. They were married in Warwick, R. I. She was the daughter of Dr. Dutee Jerrauld, *the* physician in that place. Res. Isle of Providence and Portsmouth, R. I. Ch.—

53. i. Dutee, J. b Apr., 1780; m. Abby C. Perry and Harriet Boss.
ii. Wm. T., b. ; d. s. p.
iii. Nancy, b. ; m. Solomon Townsend.

25 Thomas[4] Pearce (Samuel[3], Samuel[2], Richard[1]), b. Oct. 8, 1756; m. Oct. 10, 1773, Martha Jerrauld, daughter, of Dr. Dutee of Warwick, R. I. He was killed on board ship. Res. Tolland, Ct.

25½. Michael[4] Pearce (Samuel[3], Samuel[2], Richard[1]), b. Oct. 9, 1757; m. , 1775, in Portsmouth, R. I., Sarah Allen,

b. Apr. 17, 1760 ; d. Feb 11, 1839. He d. 1844. Res. Middlesex, Yates Co., N. Y. Ch.—

53-1. i SAMUEL, b. July 27, 1792 ; m. Eliza Larned.

53-2. ii. ASA, b. , 1776 ; m. Martha Eggleston Richards.

53-3. iii. JOB, b. Sept. 30, 1786 ; m. Lucretia Wykoff and Terrence Shaw.

53-4. iv. THOMAS, b. Sept. 4, 1789 ; m. Elida Garrison.

54-5. v. JOHN, b. , 1794 ; m. Candace Case.

vi SARAH, b. Sept. 19, 1796 ; m. Dec. 21, 1817, Dr. James H. Harris, b. Mar. 3, 1795 ; d. Oct. 24, 1836. She d. at Middlesex, July 28, 1847. Ch—Michael P., b. June 8, 1819, d. June 12, 1819 ; Susanah P., b. Mar. 8, 1821, d. May 1821; Sarah A., b. June 16, 1822, d. June 24, 1822: Ozella E., b. 19, 1835, m. O. E. Shorey. Res. Minneapolis, Minn., P. O. box 679; James D., b. Sept. 26, 1823; Irving L. b., Sept. 1, 1826, d. Oct. 27, 1830 ; John M. b. Aug. 24, 1829 ; Wm. B., b. July 13, 1832. Res. Rushville, N. Y.

vii. SUSANAH, b. Dec. 19, 1799 ; m. Thomas Patten. She d. Apr. 4, 1883, s. p., at Middlesex.

26 JEPTHA[4] PEARCE (George[3], George[2], Richard[1]), b. Feb. 20, 1722 : m. Nov., 1749, Eliza Rouse, b. Feb. 23, 1724 ; d. . He d. Oct. 22, 1770. Res. Little Compton, R. I. Ch.—

54. i. ISAAC, b. Nov. 1759 ; m. Susanna Stoddard.

ii. RUTH, b. Apr. 7, 1753.

iii. ELIZABETH, b. Oct. 17, 1756 ; d. July 15, 1849.

iv. JEREMIAH, b. Jan. 15, 1758.

v. DEBORAH, b. , 1760 ; d. Jan. 22. 1778.

vi. HANNAH, b. Oct 22, 1761.

vii. ELIZABETH, b. Apr. 22, 1751 ; d. June 22, 1753.

27 NATHANIEL[4] PEARCE (George[3], George[2], Richard[1]), b. Oct. 13, 1727 ; m. Dec. 1, 1750, Sarah Rouse, b. Jan. 14, 1728 ; d. Nov. 23, 1812. He d. Feb. 19, 1801. Res. Tiverton, R. I. Ch.—

i. PHEBE, b. Mar. 21, 1752.

ii. MARY, b. Apr. 30, 1754.

iii. ELIZABETH, b. Nov. 14, 1756.

55. iv. JOHN, b. Apr. 26, 1758 ; m. Deborah Hicks.

v. GEORGE, b. ; d at sea in 1792.

vi. VALENTINE, b. Feb. 14, 1759 ; d. , 1775.

vii. NATHANIEL, b. Dec. 17, 1761 ; d. at sea, 1779.

viii. SARAH, b. , 1762.

56. xi. JOSEPH, b. Jan. 26, 1764 ; m. Anna Hillard and Priscilla Palmer.

28 JAMES[4] PEARCE (James[3], George[2], Richard[1]), b. Sept. 24, 1719 ; m. Sept. 14, 1749, Sarah Simmons, b. Jan. 27, 1730 ; d. Dec. 24, 1785. He d. Sept. 14, 1767. Res. Little Compton, R. I.

Ch.—

57. i. WRIGHT, b. July 27, 1750 ; m. Antrace Sawyer.
58. ii. STEPHEN, b. Dec. 20, 1753 ; m. Abigail Taylor.
59. iii. JOHN, b. Aug 24, 1755 ; m. Lydia Palmer.
60. iv. EZEKIEL, b Mar. 24, 1760 ; m. Sarah Pearce.
v. ICHABOD, b. Sept. 30, 1758 ; d. Oct 27, 1762.
61. vi. ICHABOD, b. Nov. 24, 1762 ; m. Lucy Simmons.
vii. SIMEON, b. Jan. 26, 1766. Res. Paris, N. Y.
viii. EZRAH, b. Mar. 21, 1761 ; d. young.

29 WILLIAM[4] PEARCE (James[3], George[2], Richard[1]), b. June 14, 1713 ; m. Nov. 2, 1735, Elizabeth Woodman. She d. and he m. Jul. Anna ———. Res. Little Compton, R. I. Ch.—

62. i. JAMES, b. Oct. 9, 1740 ; m. Deborah Hunt.
63. ii. RICHARD, b. May 26, 1734 ; m Mary Ellis.
iii. JOHN, b. June 30, 1749 ; d. young.
iv. ELIZABETH, b. Sept. 1749 ; d. young.
v. PETER, b. Nov. 10, 1754.
vi. ELIZABETH, b. Aug. 23, 1756.
vii. WM., b. Apr. 5, 1758.
viii. JOHN, b. Aug. 3, 1760.
ix. SUSANAH, b. ———.

30 GILES[4] PEARCE (James[3], George[2], Richard[1]), b Mar. 21, 1722 ; m. Aug. 28. 1755, Mercy Rouse, b. Jan. 13, 1723. He d. May , 1792. Res. Tiverton and Little Compton, R. I. Ch.—

i. HANNAH, b. Oct 18, 1745 ; m. ——— Taylor.
ii. MARTHA, b. June , 1747 ; m. Caleb Church.
iii. SARAH, b Apr. 22, 1748 ; m. Philip Seabury.
iv. RACHEL, b. Apr. 14, 1750 ; m. Josiah Seabury.
v. ELIZABETH, b. Oct. 19, 1751 ; m. Wm. Brownell.
64. vi. ROUSE, b. July 4, 1753 ; m. Mary Brownell.
65. vii. JAMES, b. Aug. 15, 1755 ; m Phebe Wood.
viii. MERCY, b. Dec. 11, 1759 ; m. Job. Taber.
ix. LYDIA, b. July 29, 1760 ; m. Wm. Brownell.
x. ABIGAIL, b. Mar. 3, 1763.
xi. REBECCA, b. May 13, 1766 ; m. Peleg Seabury.

31 GEORGE[4] PEARCE (James[3], George[2], Richard[1]), b. Sept. 12, 1727 ; m Oct. 25, 1750, Deborah Woodman, b. Oct. 21, 1726 ; d. Mar. 20, 1760 ; m. 2d, Feb. 4, 1762, Priscilla Woodman, b. July 1, 1721 ; d. May 7, 1791, s. p. He d. Nov. , 1780. Res. Little Compton, R. I. Ch.—

i. JEREMIAH, b. Oct. 26, 1749 ; d. Dec. 25, 1751.
ii. ISAAC, b. Aug. 28, 1756 ; d. Nov. 3, 1756.
iii. DEBORAH, b. June 26, 1758 ; d. Feb. 26, 1759.

32 SAMUEL[4] PEARCE (James[3], George[2], Richard[1]), b. Jan. 29, 1733 ; m. Nov. 12, 1755, Betty Simmons, b. Mar. 8, 1733.

He was born in Massachusetts and while his children were all residing at home moved to Little Compton,

Rhode Island. After living there at that time he moved to Warren, Bristol County, where he ever afterwards resided. His sons were Jeremiah, John, Samuel and James. He was a master mechanic—contractor and builder. Several of the larger buildings in Warren, which he built, are standing to this day. Among the number is the Baptist Church. Res. Little Compton and Warren, R. I. Ch.—

66. i. SAMUEL b. Mar. 19, 1764; m. Ruth Martin.
67. ii. JEREMIAH, b. Mar. 7, 1760; m. Nancy Brown.
68. iii. JOHN, b. Feb. 16, 1768; m. Patience Arnold, Mary Luther and Annie———.
iv. JAMES, b. Dec. 10, 1765; rem. to North Carolina.
v. MARY, b. Mar. 2, 1775; d. Nov. 13, 1798.
vi. ABIGAIL, b. June 10, 1776.
vii. JOSEPH, b. Dec. 18, 1761.
viii. PHEBE, b. Sept. 8, 1756.
ix. PRISCILLA, b. Feb. 1, 1758.

33 SAMUEL[5] PEARCE, (Nathaniel[4], Richard[3], Richard[2], Richard[1]), b. Oct. 25, 1733; m. Mary———, b. , 1735; d. Dec. 30, 1760. Res. Bristol, R. I. Ch.—

i. MARY, b. June 27, 1755; d. Aug. 6, 1812.
ii. JOHN, b. Feb. 4, 1760; d. Dec. 26, 1760.

34 CAPT. RICHARD[5] PEARCE, (Nathaniel[4], Richard[3], Richard[2], Richard[1]), b. June 15, 1737; m. Phebe Monroe, b. June 16, 1743. He d. 1809. Res. Bristol, R. I., and Rehoboth, Mass. His will is proved in Taunton, Mass., June 6, 1809. Wm. Blarding, James Wheaton and Stephen Bourne were witnesses. Phebe, the widow, was executor. Ch.—

i. PHEBE, b. Oct. 5, 1760; m. Mar. 19, 1785. Samuel Smith; he res. in Bristol and d. April 22, 1847. Ch— Sarah, b. Feb. 17, 1786; Ruth, b. Aug. 15, 1787; Benjamin, b Jan. 11, 1793.
69. ii. RICHARD, b. Oct. 27, 1762; m. Cardace ———.
70. iii. NATHANIEL, b Oct 4, 1764; m. Lucy Rogerson.
iv. LYDIA, b. Feb 13, 1767 d. Nov. ; m. in 1825.
v. MARY, b. July 2, 1771; m. Mar. 27, 1794, Robert Rogerson. Res. Rehoboth. Ch. John and Robert.
vi. TIMOTHY, b. Feb. 14, 1775; a physician; rem. to New York State.
71. vii. ROBERT, b. July 18, 1777; m. Lydia Blanding.

35 GEORGE[5] PEARCE (William[4], Richard[3], Richard[2], Richard[1]), b. Sept. 15, 1744; m. Hannah ———. Res. Bristol, R. I. Ch.—

72. i. WILLIAM, b. Mar. 2, 1766; m. Elizabeth Gifford,
73. ii. GEORGE, b. Apr. 24, 1768; m. ——— ———.
iii. MARY, b. June 4, 1770; m. ——— Steere, and res. Harwick, N. Y.

iv. HANNAH, b. Dec. 22, 1772; m. —— Field, and res. in Hartwick, N. Y.

36 CAPT. WILLIAM^5 PEARCE, (Thomas^4, Jeremiah^3, Richard^2, Richard^1), b. Nov. 3, 1772; m. 1794, Mary Gladding; m. 2d, 1805. Sally Smith, b. June 27, 1780; d. Aug. 27, 1843. He d. Feb. 3, 1868. Res. Bristol, R. I.

"The memory of the just is blessed." Seldom has this sentiment been more beautifully illustrated in any community, than in ours, in the case of the venerated patriarch of our church, our oldest and highly esteemed fellow-citizen, Capt. William Pearce, Of the pure stock of the Pilgrims, the sixth in direct descent from John Howland, of the Mayflower. Capt. Pearce, was in early life convinced of his need of a new nature. In his eighteenth year, he heard Jesse Lee preach the first Methodist sermon in Bristol, R. I., from the words, "Therefore, if any man be in Christ, he is a new creature; old things are passed away; behold, all things are become new." So clearly cut were the impressions of that discourse, that the wear of seventy-seven years failed to efface them from his memory. Within a short time previous to his death, I have heard him repeat the text, and characterize the subject and the manner of the preacher as something "entirely new" in those times. In May, 1792, Rev. Lemuel Smith organized the first class in Bristol. William Pearce was one of the original sixteen members. In Sept. mber following, Rev. Ezekiel Cooper, Presiding Elder of Boston District, visited the infant church and administered the ordinances. Bro. Pearce was baptized, and received the Holy Sacrament for the first time. From this "day of small things," through her varied experience of nearly three quarters of a century, this church has ever found in him a fast friend, unwavering in his love and devotion. In her feebleness, in her shame, in her fiery trials, as in her strength, her honor and her triumphs he stood unflinchingly by her; whoever else proved faithless, William Pearce remained faithful to the end. In the discharge of his religious duties, our brother was exemplary. In the closet and at the family altar he sought the divine blessing, in the strength of which he maintained an eminently consistent and useful Christian life. He delighted in the services of the sanctuary, and highly appreciated the peculiar institutions of his beloved Methodism. Enjoying the love and confidence of his brethren, he was charged with official responsibiity for many years, and always proved himself a wise counselor, and an earnest, devoted and faithful servant.

His fellow-citizens indicated their appreciation of his ability and integrity by electing him for many years a member of the Town Council and Court of Probate; several times a member of the State Legislature, and for several years a Justice of the Court of Common Pleas. An original corporator of the Freeman's Bank of Bristol, he served as a Director for fifty years. Much of his active life was spent in mercantile pursuits. He was always distinguished for temperance, prudence and strict integrity. Born in this town, Nov. 3d., 1772, when the war-clouds were gathering for the storm of the Revolution, he attained his majority in time to cast his maiden vote for the re-election of George Washington to the Presidency; and, near the end of his pilgrimage of almost a hundred years, when the war-clouds of a fiercer storm were still hanging over the land, he participated in another Presidential contest, and cast his vote for the re-election of our second Washington, the immortal Abraham Lincoln. Other rare distinctions were enjoyed by our brother. In his family were entertained as honored guests Francis Asbury and Thomas Coke, the pioneer bishops of our church, the fathers respectively of Sabbath Schools and modern missions. Here, too, sat and talked and prayed such apostolic men as Jesse Lee, Joshua Soule and Ayrshire Cooper.

The closing scene of this long and well-spent life was calm and sincere. On the 2d. of February, 1867, about midnight, just as common was passing into holy time, the saintly spirit of this veteran of the cross, disrobed of its mortal vestments, took its upward flight to mingle with "the spirits of just men made perfect."

His funeral was celebrated the following Wednesday, in the church, where a large concourse gathered to do honor to the memory of this good man. Rev. Dr. Shepard, of the Congregational Church, Revs. John Livesey and David H. Ela, of the Providence Conference, assisted the pastor, Rev. T. Snowden Thomas, in the solemn services. A profound impression was made upon the entire community by the death and funeral of Father Pearce, and contributed not a little to the growing religious interest, which has resulted so gloriously in reviving our churches and converting many scores of sinners. Bristol Phœnix, R. I., April 27, 1867.

T.

Ch.—

i. Susan T., b. Sept. 8, 1816; d. unmarried, May 26, 1840.

ii. Mary A., b. Aug. 22, 1798; m. Apr. 1818, Allen Wardwell, b. July 29, 1791; d. July 28, 1821. She d. Dec. 11, 1851. Ch.: Wm. A., b. Feb. 19, 1819. Res. Bristol, R. I.

74. iii. RICHARD S., b. June 12, 1808; m. Hope C. Reed.
iv. ABBY W., b. May , 1801. d. Sept. 21,1878.
75. v. JOHN W. b. Dec. 18, 1818. m. Mary S. Monroe.
76. vi. THOMAS, b. May 27,1821. m. Mary E. Coit.
vii. HARRIET, b. July 5, 1810; d. May 22, 1821.
viii. JEREMIAH, b. Sept. 1, 1812; d. June 5, 1835.
77. ix. GEORGE P., b. July 12, 1814; m. Phebe Leonard.

37 JOSIAH[5] PEARCE (Thomas[4], Jeremiah[3], Richard[2], Richard[1]), b. ——; m. June 1, 1804, Sarah Wilson. He d. Aug. 14, 1814. Res. Bristol, R. I. Ch.—

i. SARAH M., b. , 1808; m. —— Bowers. Res. Bristol, and d. June 9, 1872.
ii. JOSIAH, b. ——; d. Oct. 11, 1814.
iii. THOMAS, b. , 1804.

38 JEREMIAH[5] PEARCE (Giles[4], Jeremiah[3], Giles[2], Richard[1]), b. June 2, 1726; m. ——, Margaret ——, b. 1730; d. Aug. 13, 1803. She m. 2nd Sept. 16, 1792, Hopkins Cook of East Greenwich and d. there. Jeremiah died before 1792. Res. East Greenwich, R. I. Ch.—

78. i. JEREMIAH, b. June 20, 1751; m. Mary Gorton.
ii. MOSES, b. ——.
iii. ELIZABTH, b. Dec. , 1755; d. June 9, 1774.
iv. OLIVER, b. Nov. 10, 1759.

39 GEORGE[5] PEARCE (Giles[4], Jeremiah[3], Giles[2], Richard[1]), b. Apr. 24, 1730; m. Dec. 2, 1753, Mary Green, b. Jan. 6, 1732; d. Nov. 11, 1789. George, b. 1730, was at the time of the Revolutionary war, living at W. Greenwich. R. I. He one night, with two companions, left E. Greenwich in a row-boat with muffled oars for an island which is in Narraganset bay, where several British ships were lying. There was a noted colonel with soldiers in camp on that island. The colonel was a little way from the body of soldiers and they succeeded in capturing him and put him into their boat and got safely away to E. Greenwich where he was taken by other Americans and imprisoned. Res. East Greenwich and Exeter, R. I. Ch.—

i. AMEY, b. Sept. 19, 1754; m. Dec. 16, 1774 Oliver Spink. Res. North Kingston, R. I.
ii. CHRISTOPHER, b. Oct. 3, 1759.
79. iii. GILES, b. Apr. 22, 1765; m. Hannah Arnold.

40 WILLIAM[5] PEARCE (Giles[4], Jeremiah[3], Giles[2], Richard[1]), b. Jan. 22, 1735; m. June 1, 1760, Catherine Green. Res. East Greenwich, R. I. Ch.—

i. AUSTUS, b. May 13, 1761.
ii. PHEBE, b. Dec. 7, 1762.
iii. SARAH, b. Dec. 5, 1764.
iv. CATHERINE, b. Apr. 21, 1766.

v. HANNAH, b. June 27, 1768.
vi. DEBORAH, b. Apr. 17, 1769.
vii. MARY, b. Oct. 23, 1771.
viii. GILES, b. Sept. 19, 1775.
ix. COMFORT.
x. DESIRE, b. Oct. 20, 1777.

41 CALEB[5] PEARCE (Jeremiah[4], Jeremiah[3], Giles[2], Richard[1]), b. July 15, 1734; m. June 3, 1753 Mrs. Margaret Pearce. He died Aug. 1775. Res. East Greenwich and Warwick, R. I. Ch.—

i. ELIZABETH, b. ———; m. Giles Pearce, s. of Thomas, b. Feb. 6, 1746.

42 JOB[5] PEARCE (John[4], Jeremiah[3], Giles[2], Richard[1]), b. Nov. 15, 1741; m. July 1, 1770, Temperance Green. They res. East Greenwich, R. I. Ch.—

79½. i. JOB, b. Oct. 29, 1781; m. Elizabeth Dean.
ii. CHARLES, b. Mar. 24, 1783.

43 PHILLIP[5] PEARCE (John[4], Jeremiah[3], Giles[2], Richard[1]), b. Jan. 14, 1754; m. Feb. 20, 1777, Mercy Mumford. He d. Sept. 26. 1820. Res. East Greenwich, R. I. Ch.—

i. POLLY, b. April 22, 1778; d. Aug. 9, 1819.
ii. JOHN M., b. Mar. 13, 1780.
iii. MERCY M., b. Oct 23, 1784; d. Jan. 21, 1787.
80. iv. STEPHEN M., b. Mar. 15, 1782: m. Sukey Fry.
v. CHARLES, b. June. 15, 1786.
vi. HANNAH F, b. Feb. 28, 1788.
81. vii. PHILLIP, b. Apr. 1, 1790; m. Hannah Wall.
82. viii. ROBINSON, b. , 179–; m. Abby Boyd.
83. ix. GRANGE M., b. Apr. 29, 1801; m. Celia Gorton.

44. JOHN[5] PEARCE (John[4], John[3]. Giles[2], Richard[1]), b. June 14, 1746; m. Feb. 28, 1771, Mary Spencer. Res. East Greenwich, R. I. Ch.—

i. REBECCA, b. Feb. 13, 1769.
ii. GEORGE, b. June 14, 1775; m. Sept. 1, 1816 Catherine Wander. Res. East Greenwich, R. I.
iii. ALICE, b. Oct. 4, 1781; m. July 11, 1805, Benjamin Bateman. Res. East. Greenwich, R. I.
iv. WELTHY, b. Sept. 13, 1785; m. Thomas Pearce.

45. GILES[5] PEARCE (Thomas[4], John[3], Giles[2], Richard[1]), b. Feb. 6, 1746; m. Warwick, R. I., Oct. 13, 1775, Elizabeth Pearce. She was a dau. of Caleb Pearce. They res. in East Greenwich, R. I., and Warwick, R. I. Ch.—

i. BETSEY, b. Apr. 14, 1776; m. Jan. 7, 1798, Wm. Casey. Res. Easton, N. Y.
ii. LUCY, b. May 10, 1778; m. ——— Wickes.
iii. MARGARET, b. Nov. 19, 1785; m ——— Budlong.

iv. HANNAH, b. Dec. 13, 1786 ; m. ———.
v. CALEB G. b. May 18, 1789 ; drowned at sea.
vi. MARY, b. Apr. 14, 1794 ; m. ——— Parrish.

46. STEPHEN[5] PEARCE (Thomas[4], John[3], Giles[2], Richard[1]), b. July 20, 1749; m. Apr. 25, 1773, Lydia Rice. They res. E. Greenwich, R. I. Ch.—

i. DANIEL, b. June 15, 1774.
ii. STEPHEN, b. Feb. 14, 1777.
iii. ANNA, b. Jan. 18, 1779.
iv. SAMUEL R., or James R., b. ——— 26, 1781 ; m. ——— Sprague. Ch.—Hattie, Lydy and Delia.
v. THOMAS, b. ———; m. Wealthy Pearce.
84. vi. EARL, b. ——— . m. Eliza R. Taylor.
vii. HATTIE, b. ——— ; d. ———.
viii. LYDIA, b. ——— ; m. Cromwell Salisbury.
ix. REBECCA, b ———.

47. DANIEL[5] PEARCE (Thomas[4], John[3], Giles[2], Richard[1]), b. Mar. 3, 1752 ; m. Mary Bentley or Mary Sweet, b. ———, 1760 ; d. Feb. 12, 1839. He d. Feb. 12, 1834. They res. in East Greenwich, R, I. Ch.—

i. PELEG, b. Apr. 27, 1798 ; d. unm.
ii. ELIZA, b. July, 17, 1796.
iii. SUSANAH, b. Apr. 2, 1798 ; d. unm.
iv. GILES B., b. Aug. 13, 1799.
85. v. JAMES B., b. Mar. 24, 1801 ; m. Mary Pinnegar.
86. vi. CHRISTOPHER B., b. Apr. 13, 1799; m. Martha W. Glanding.
vii. HOPE, b. ——— ; m. ——— Spencer.
viii. MARY, b. ——— ; m. Welcome Arnold.

48. MOSES[5] PEARCE (Thomas[4], John[3], Giles[2], Richard[1]), b. Feb. 19, 1757 ; m. Dec. 25, 1785, Sarah Bently, b. Aug. 31, 1764 ; d. Jan. 18, 1805. Res. East, Greenwich, R. I. He d. of yellow fever and was buried at sea in 1796. Res. at Surinam, S. A.

87. i. BENJAMIN B., b. Sept. 1, 1786 ; m. Susan Walker.
ii. FANNY, b. Nov. 14, 1788 ; m. William Roberts, b. June 28, 1789 ; d. Aug. 13, 1867. Ch.—James E., b. June 2, 1816, m. Maria S. Bently; William A., b. July 20, 1813 ; m. Mercy Vaughn ; Moses P. b. Oct. 30, 1826, m. Caroline Capron and Elizabeth Russell; Melissa E., b. May, 13, 1821. Res. S. Scituate, R. I.
iii. HARRIETT, b. Jan. 19, 1791 ; m. ——— Andros.

49. ISAAC[5] PEARCE (Thomas[4], John[3], Giles[2], Richard[1]), b. Apr. 12, 1764 ; m. ———, Sarah Vaughn.

81. i. AMY, b. ——— ; m. ———Thompson.
82. ii. AARON, b. ——— ; m. Sally Angell.
83. iii. MYRAH, b. ——— ; d. unm.

84. iv. SALLY, b. ——; d. unm.
85. v. REBECCA, b. ——.
86. vi. THOMAS A., b. —— ; d. unm. in Smithfield, R. I.

50. JOHN[5] PEARCE (Giles[4], John[3], Giles[2], Richard[1]), b. Feb. 19, 1776 ; m. Polly Davis ——; d. ——, 1820; m. 2nd, Nov. 6, 1825, Sarah Brown, b. May 21, 1788 ; d. Dec. 30, 1859. He d. July 11, 1848, in Prov. Res. North Kingston, R. I. Ch.—

88. i. JOHN B., b. July 19, 1827 ; m. Izitt C. Gardner, Mary G. Brown, Abby C. B. Gardner.
89. ii. THOMAS C. b. Sept. 27, 1829 ; m. Amy A. Brown.

51. JOSEPH[5] PEARCE (Giles[4], John[3], Giles[2], Richard[1]), b. Sept. 14 1760 ; m. Sarah Havens, b. Feb. 11, 1760 ; d. ——, 1845. He d. ——, 1814. Res. No. Kingston, R. I. Ch.—

i. SYBIL, b. Nov. 15, 1780 ; d. young.
ii. MERCY, b. Nov. 3, 1782 ; m. Wm. D. Cole, b. Sept. 27, 1780 ; d. Oct. 31, 1842. She d. Mar. 15, 1847. Res. No. Kingston, R. I. Ch.—Wm. A., b. Aug. 21, 1815 ; m. Elizabeth C. Mawney. Res. Eagle Creek. Scott Co., Minn.
iii. MARGARET, b. Oct. 3, 1784 ; m. June 3, 1815, Edward Cole, b. Apr. 18,1786 ; d. Feb. 5, 1852. She d. Apr. 10, 1862. Res. No. Kington, R. I. Ch.—Sarah A., b. Mar. 10, 1816, d. Jan. 3, 1868; Edward, b. Dec. 4, 1818, d. Dec. 5, 1818 ; Maria, b. July 31, 1820, m. Ezra N. Gardiner ; Sybil P., b. June 28, 1822, m. Wm. G. Congdon ; Jos. E., b. Mar. 18, 1824, m. Màry K. Peckham.
iv. SYBIL, b. Dec. 14, 1786.
90. v. ELISHA, b. Feb. 19, 1789 ; m. Amey Gardner and Rebecca Pearce.
91. vi. JOSEPH, b. July 19, 1791 ; m. Molly Champlin.
vii. SARAH, b. Oct. 19, 1773 ; d. young.
viii. RHODES, b. May 29, 1796 ; d. ——, 1842.
92. ix. SAMUEL, b. Aug. 27, 1798 ; m. Mary Hazard.
x. BENJAMIN, b. —— ; d. young.
xi. SARAH, b. Apr. 14, 1807 ; m. June 1, 1835, Hazard Burlingame. She d. No. K. Dec. 11, 1848.

52. GILES[5] PEARCE (Giles[4], John[3], Giles[2], Richard[1]), b. —— 1763 ; m Elizabeth Dodge ——. She d. ——, 1810, and he m. 2nd Sarah Gardiner. He d. Jan. 25, 1844. Res. North Kingston, R. I. His second wife was a daughter of Ezekiel Gardner of No. K. His portion of his father's estate was s. w. of Roon's farm, where he built a new house in 1866-7 and where he died. Ch.—

93. i. WILLIAM, b. Apr. 2, 1789; m. Waity Northup and Abigail Sanford.
ii. REBECCA, b. ——, 1793 ; m. Elisha Pearce.

94 iii. GILES, b. ——, 1795 ; m. Mrs. Mary (Cole) Pearce.
iv. EDWARD, b. ——, 1800 ; d. ——, 1817,
v. DESIRE, b. Jan. 9, 1805 ; m. Joseph Brown.

53 HON. DUTEE J.[5] PEARCE, (Samuel[4], Samuel[3], Samuel[2], Richard[1]), b. Apr. ——, 1780, on Prudence Island ; m. Apr. 18. 1811, Abby C. Perry, b. Feb. 9. 1793 ; d. July 4, 1827 ; m. 2d Dec. 12, 1829, Harriet Boss, b. July 12, 1797, Res. Newport, R. I. He d. May 9, 1849.

He died at his residence in Newport, R. I., May 9. 1849, æ 69, of erysipelas. He was born April, 1780, on the Island of Prudence and was therefore sixty-nine years of age at the time of his death. He graduated with much honor at Brown University, and after completing his study of law, he began his practice of the legal profession in Newport, where he remained until the time of his death. Mr. Pearce became early interested in political affairs and in 1819 he was elected Attorney General of the State, which office he filled until 1825. He was then appointed United States District Attorney for the Rhode Island district, and in November, 1835, he was elected representative to Congress, in which capacity he continued to serve the people of Rhode Island until 1837, when he was succeeded by the Hon. Robert B. Cranston.—[*Newport News*.

Pearce, Dutee, was born on the Island of Prudence, Rhode Island, in 1780 ; received a classical education, graduating at Brown Univesity in 1808 ; studied law, was admitted to the bar, and commenced practice at Newport ; was United States Attorney for the District of Rhode Island ; was Adjutant General of Rhode Island 1819–1825 ; was a presidential elector on the Monroe ticket in 1821 ; was for several years a member of the State House of Representatives ; was elected a representative from Rhode Island in the Nineteenth Congress as a Democrat; was re-elected to the Twentieth Congress ; was re-elected to the Twenty-first Congress, receiving 1,871 majority ; was re-elected to the Twenty-second Congress, receiving 619 majority ; was re-elected to the Twenty-third Congress ; was re-elected to the Twenty-fourth Congress, receiving 238 majority over R. B. Cranston, Whig, Serving from December 5, 1825, to March 3, 1837 ; died in Newport, Rhode Island, May 9, 1849.—[*From Poore's Political Register and Congressional Directory* 1776–1876. *Copied for Fred. C. Pierce, Esq. by Ben. Perley Poore.*

Ch.— .

i. HARRIET B., b. Jan 5, 1836 ; m. —— Bailey Res. Newport.
95. ii. DUTEE J., b. July 27, 1833 ; m. Martha Palmer.
iii. HANNAH J., b. Jan. 3, 1812 ; d. unm. Mar. —, 1865.
iv. ABIGAIL C., b. July 12, 1813 ; m. July 12, 1830, —— Casey. She d. in 1862. Ch.—Silas and Thomas L.

Thomas Lincoln Casey, the engineer has finished probably the highest structure ever reared, the Washington monument, the capstone of which is 555 feet above the ground. When it was placed in position a few years ago the national flag was unfurled from its summit, and the booming of artillery announced the completion of a wonderful piece of masonry, finished, that is, as regards its exterior structure. Within two years its base and interior will have been completed, also, and the visitor will find comfortable means of ascent to the summit from within the monument. An an elevator and iron stairway will be provided for the purpose.

The corner-stone of the building was laid July 4, 1848. Robert C. Winthrop, Speaker of the House of Representatives, made the principal address on that occasion. In six years' time the height of 175 feet was reached, upon which $230,000 had been spent. Nothing was done toward furthering the work during the next twenty-five years. In 1876 interest in the neglected building revived, and after Congress had voted the necessary appropriation work was resumed in earnest, about six years ago, with Col. Thomas Lincoln Casey as engineer in charge of it.

The following details as to the dimensions and materials of the monument will be read with interest: Measuring from the zero mark, or brass bolt set in the masonry of the foundation at the southwest corner, it is 555 feet and four inches high. As the foundations are thirty-six feet eight inches deep; total height from the foundation bed is 592 feet. At its base the obelisk measures fifty-five one and a half inches square, and the walls fifteen feet and a quarter of an inch thick. The pyramidal top begins at the 500-foot mark, where the dimensions are thirty-four feet five and half inches square and eighteen inches thick. The batter of the structure is one and a quarter inches to one foot. Marble used in the construction was quarried in Maryland. The top of the capstone has a shining point of aluminium, a metal which oxidizes slowly and is superior as a conductor of lightning. This metalic point is connected with a copper rod, which leads down through the center of the capstone to each of the four columns which form the elevator frame in the main shaft. At the base of the monument these leaders are conducted to the wall beneath the center of the foundation, the whole arrangement forming what is believed to be a perfect electrical conductor. Congress has appropriated $900,000 to the erection of the monument. As $230,000 had been spent previously, its entire cost thus far has been more than $1,100,000.

Great honor attaches to Colonel Casey on account of his eminent skill and success in completing the erection of the obelisk known as the Washington monument. He is a member of the Corps of Engineers, United States Army, and was born in Madison Barracks, Sacketts Harbor, New York, May 10, 1841. The late General Silas Casey, of the United States army, was a brother of the distinguished engineer. His family on both sides has been prominent in the annals of Rhode Island for more than two hundred years.

President Polk appointed him a cadet "at large" in the West Point Military Academy, where he graduated in 1852. He was then commissioned a brevet second lieutenant in thecorps of engineers. Subsequently he was employed upon the military and civil works in the ordnance bureau as an instructor in engineering at the Military Academy, West Point, and in connection with engineer troops on the Pacific coast. His most important duty during the civil war was the construction of defences on the coast of Maine and New Hampshire. After the war Col. Casey was engaged in the Engineer's Bureau, Washington. In 1877 he was assigned to the charge of public buildings and grounds in the Dist. Columbia; the construction of the State, war and navy buildings, and the Washington aqueduct. His selection as chief engineer to complete the Washington National Monument was made in 1878. At the present time his duties relate to the construction of the buildings for the State, War and Navy departments ; improvements at the grave of of Thomas Jefferson, at Monticello, Va., and the erection of monuments to commemorate and mark the birthplace and headquarters of George Washington.

Outside of eminence in his chosen pursuit of engineering, Colonel Casey is a genealogist of reputation, and a writer marked by taste and refinement. He is a member of the Society of Cincinnati of Massachusetts, of the Loyal Legion of the United States, of the American Society of Civil Engineers, of the New England Historical and Genealogical Society, and of other learned bodies. —1886.

v. Ann T., b. May 15, 1815 : d. unm.

vi. Catherine P., b. May 3, 1816. Res. Narraganset Pier, R. I.

vii. Samuel, b. Aug. 7, 1818 ; d. unm. Mar. ——, 1874.

viii. Dutee, J., b. June —, 1820 ; d. ——, 1823.

53-1 Samuel[5] Pearce (Michael[4], Samuel[3], Samuel[2], Richard[1]), b. July 27, 1792. m. Feb. 14, 1815, Eliza Larned, b. Mar. 26, 1799, d. Feb. 26. 1876. He d. Dec. 13, 1875. Res. Clifton Springs, N. Y. and Chicago, Ill. Ch.—

96. i. J. IRVING, b. July 27, 1827 ; m. Margaret E. Wilkins,
97 ii. WM. L. b. Jan. 28, 1816 ; m. Margaret Hasbrook.
98. iii. MYRON, L., b. Dec. 16, 1821 ; m. Hattie A. Pestana.
iv. SAMUEL D., b. Sept. 18, 1829 ; d. Dec. 22, 1862.
v. FRANCES M., b. June 29, 1835 ; m. Horatio O. Stone. She d. Mar. 12, 1854, at Clifton Springs, N. Y.

53-2 ASA[5] PEARCE (Michael[4], Samuel[3], Samuel[2], Richard[1]).. b. 1776, m. Jan. 1811, Martha Eggleston Richards, b. 1771, d. 1846. He d. Feb. 23, 1813. Res. Middlesex, N. Y. Ch.—

i. ASA W., b. Apr. 4. 1813. Res. M. D. Rushville, N. Y.

53-3 JOB[5] PEARCE (Michael[4], Samuel[3], Samuel[2] Richard[1]), b. Sept. 30, 1786, m. Lucretia Wykoff, b. 1802, d. Oct. 19, 1838 ; m. Terrence Shaw. Res. Middlesex, N. Y. Ch.—

99. i. WM. W. b. Sept. 14, 1838, m. Louise Carey.
ii. MARY A. b. May 7, 1833, m. Oct. 5, 1854, Geo. Beckett b., Mar. 27, 1826. Res. Rushville, N. Y. Ch.—Fred'k I. b. Oct. 11, 1855 ; m. Clara Romand and Emma Van Epps. Res. Rushville, N. Y.; Sarah F., b. July 14, 1858 ; m. John Adamson.
iii. SARAH E. b. ———, 1842 ; d. ———, 1857.

53-4 THOMAS[5] PEARCE (Michael[4], Samuel[3], Samuel[2], Richard[1]), b. Sept. 4, 1789 ; m. Oct. 15, 1808, Elida Garrison, b. Aug. 29, 1790, d. Sept. 25, 1847. He d. Dec. 26, 1875. Res. Middlesex, N. Y. Ch.—

100. i. WILEY K., b. Sept. 18, 1812 ; m. Sarah J. Foster and Sarah R. Lindsley.
ii. MICHAEL A., b. Oct. 1, 1820 ; m. Mary Dimmick and Mrs. Sarah C. Wyman. Res. Penn Yan, Yates Co., N. Y.
iii. ALMIRA, b. Aug. 29, 1809 ; m. ——— Brown. She d. Apr. 24, 1882.
iv. ELCIE, b. May 21, 1811 ; m. Holland Williams. She d. Nov. 25, 1882. Res. Mason, Mich.
v. JULIAN P., b. Oct. 9, 1814 ; m. Oct. 1, 1835, Lorenzo D. Brooks, b. Apr. 1, 1807, d. Dec. 22, 1880. Res. 303 No. Main st., Madison, Wis. Ch.—Henrietta E., b. June 12, 1837 ; m. Albert W. Curtis ; res. 708 Grand av., Milwaukee, Wis.; Cornelia C. b. Apr. 30, 1842 ; m. Russell Thorpe ; res. Rawhide Butts, Wyo. Ter.; Estell L. b. June 28, 1844 ; m. R. H. Vosburgh ; res. Douglas, Wyo. T.

53-5 JOHN[5] PEARCE (Michael[4], Samuel[3], Samuel[2], Richard[1]), b. ———, 1794 ; m. 1817, Candace Case, b. Oct. —, 1795, d. June —, 1881. He d. June —, 1824. He was dragged by a horse, with the halter around his waist, which caused his death. Res. Middlesex, N. Y. Ch.—

101. i. DANIEL C., b. Sept. 3, 1818 ; m. Sarah A. Fisher.
ii. LAURA, b. Oct. 9, 1824 ; m. Apr. 20, 1843, Guy Shaw, b. Dec. 4, 1820. Res. Penn Yan, N. Y. Ch.—Wealthy, b. Mar. 14, 1844 ; unm.; Elizabeth, June 17, 1848 ; m. E. B. Porter ; res. Penn Yan; Marvin B., b. June 10, 1855 ; unm.; res. Penn Yan.
iii. JOB, b. ———, 1821 ; m. 1846 and died, s. p., on an overland trip to California in 1849.

54 ISAAC[5] PEARCE (Jeptha[4], George[3], George[2], Richard[1]), b. Nov. —, 1759 ; m. Aug. 1, 1784, Susanna Stoddard, b. ———, 1764, d. Apr. 1, 1825. He d. May 21, 1825. Res. Little Compton, R. I. Ch.—

102. i. NATHANIEL, b. June 30, 1787 ; m. Susanna Simmons.
ii. DEBORAH, b. Apr. 1, 1785 ; m. June 17, 1804, Thomas Sanford, b. May 15, 1782, d. May 3, 1823 She d. Aug. 8, 1868. Res. L. C. Ch.—Eliza W., b. July —, 1812 ; m. Gardiner Anthony, res. Westport Point, Mass.; Priscilla C., Thomas L., Susan S., Joseph, Ruth B., Mary, b. May —, 1807, Clarissa.
iii. ELIZABETH, b. Nov. 27, 1789 ; m. Aug. 23, 1818, John Crosby. He d. Apr. 28, 1852. She d. ———, 1867. Res. Martha's Vineyard, Mass. Ch.— Sarah P., b. Feb. —, 1819 ; Susan E., b. July 1822 ; Rebecca P., b. ——, 1820 ; John L. b. Dec. 25. 1824 ; res. Little Compton ; Hannah P., b. June —, 1826 ; Thomas, b. Sept. 20, 1829 ; Mary M., b. Aug. —, 1832.
iv. WALTER W., b. May 11, 1792 ; d. unm. Nov. 7, 1811.
v. LYDIA, b. Dec. 22, 1794; m. Dec. 5. 1819, Abiel Simmons, b. Feb. 27, 1793, d. July 1, 1856. She d. Mar. 15, 1862. Res. Little Compton, R. I. Ch.—Walter W., b. Jan. 29, 1813, d. Nov. 3, 1845; Orin W., b. July 3, 1815 ; res. Little Compton, R. I ; Alexander C., b. May 5, 1817 ; res. Little Compton; Jane M., b. Sept. 4, 1819 ; B. Wilson, b. Feb. 15, 1822, d. Dec. 17, 1842 ; Andrew E.. b. Dec. 24, 1824, d. Oct. 26, 1845 ; Albert H., b. May 13, 1827 ; Fred. H., b. Dec. 22, 1830 ; Susan B., b. Dec. 28, 1832, d. Feb. 17, 1883.
vi. HANNAH, b. Dec, 19, 1794 ; m. Dec. 5, 1819, George Wilbur ; d. Dec. —, 1824. She d. Nov. 18, 1824. Res. L. C. Ch.—Geo. E. ; Caroline, b. July 31, 1822, m. Fred. C. Woodcock ; res. 4 Ferry st., Fall River, Mass.
103. vii. JONATHAN D., b. Apr. 15, 1801 ; m. Hannah P. Head.

55 JOHN[5] PEARCE (Nathaniel[4], George[3], George[2], Richard[1]), b. Apr. 26, 1758; m. Jan. —, 1783, Deborah Hicks, b. Sept. 8, 1761 ; d. Oct. 14, 1834. He d. Nov. 13, 1827. Res. Tiverton, R. I. Ch.—

104. i. JOHN, b. Oct. 19, 1793 ; m. Lucinda C. Trout.
ii. MARY, b. Dec. 24, 1784 ; m. ——— Records and, 2d,

Elery Gray. By first husband, s. p.; by second, six children, one Sylvester H. Res. New Berne, N. C.

iii. GEORGE, b. Jan. 31, 1787. Went west and d. 1849.

iv. NATHANIEL, b. May 11, 1789. Went west.

v. JEREMIAH, b. June 21, 1791; m. and res. Cumberland, R. I., and d. there Nov. 10, 1841, leaving a son and daughter.

vi. PHILLIP, b. Apr. 17, 1796; m. Fanny Gray and had five children.

vii. SARAH, b. Oct. 13, 1799; d. s. p.

viii. BETSEY, b. Dec. 15, 1802. She married twice. Her second husband was a Borden, by whom she had four children. One son res. in Texas, two daughters in Fall River and one in California.

105. ix. PELEG, b. June 31, 1804; m. Sarah Gray.

56 COL. JOSEPH[5] PEARCE (Nathaniel[4], George[3], George[2], Richard[1]), b. Jan. 26, 1764; m. ———, 1790, Ann Hillard, b. Aug. 18, 1769, d. June 27, 1816; m. 2nd, Nov. 16, 1817, Priscilla Palmer, b. Nov. 6, 1781, d. Feb. 27, 1823. He d. Aug. 6, 1836. Res. Tiverton, R. I. Ch.—

i. JONATHAN H., b. ———, 1791; d. 1791.

ii. PHEBE, b. June 14. 1792; d. May —, 1812.

iii. BENJAMIN, b. Dec. 3, 1896; d. Oct. 2, 1822.

106. iv. VAL., b. Oct. 14, 1799; m. Eliza Woodman.

v. NANCY, b. May 16, 1802; m. Oct. 12, 1822, James Pearce, b. July 6, 1802. She d. July 28, 1856. Ch.— b. in Little Compton, R. I.: Sarah A. b. May 28, 1831. d. Nov. 14, 1845; Harriet N. b. Dec. 13, 1832, m. Horatio W. Richmond.

107. vi. JOSEPH, b. Nov. 4, 1804; m. Phebe Pearce.

108. vii. NATHANIEL, b. Dec. 19, 1809; m. Bethany Brightman.

viii. ANN, b. Apr. 23, 1807; m. Thomas Records, b. 1797, d Mar. 21, 1881. She d. in Little Compton Apr. 5, 1860. Ch.—David B., b. Oct. 17, 1832, d. Dec. 21, 1841; Philander, b. Dec. 21, 1835, m. Mary Sisson; res. Westport, Mass.

ix. PHEBE, b. June 6, 1820; m. Feb. 10, 1841, Josiah S. Pearce, b. Apr. 22, 1818, d. Nov. 16, 1869. She d. in Little Compton, R. I., Apr. 30, 1880. Ch.—

i. *Sarah A.*, b. Nov. 3, 1846; m. June 1, 1886, William S. Liscomb, b, Mar. —, 1847. Res. Providence, R. I., s. p.

ii. *Mary J.*, b. Feb. 13, 1849; m. June 11, 1872, Asa R. Howland, b. Aug. 19, 1845. Res. Adamsville, R. I. Ch.—Geo. W., b. Oct 20, 1874; Stephen R., b. Jan. 12, 1876.

iii. *John T.*, b. Oct. 17, 1851.

iv. *Isabel M.*, b. May 20, 1854; m. Clarence O. Gray; m. 2nd, Feb. 28,1886, George E. Cobb. Res. L. C. Ch.—Deborah B. b. Oct. 15, 1876.

x. PRISCILLA, b. Feb. 13, 1823; m. Geo. Hubard. She d. Feb. 5, 1887. Ch.—Geo. D. Res. Concord, Mass.

57 WRIGHT[5] PEARCE (James[4], James[3], George[2], Richard[1]), b. July 27, 1750; m. ———, 1771, Antrace Sawyer, b. Oct. 30, 1751, d. Oct. 12, 1835. He d. Apr. 8, 1829. Res. Little Compton, R. I. Ch.—

109. i. GODFREY, b. Oct. 3, 1772; m. Sarah Simmons.
110. ii. TIMOTHY, b. July 17, 1779; m. Hannah Dennis and ——— Webber.
iii. ABRAHAM, b. Apr. 12, 1792; m. Ruth Bailey. He d. s. p. Sept. —, 1862.
111. iv. THOMAS, b. Sept. 6, 1784; m. Elizabeth Tompkins.
v. SARAH, b. Apr. 29, 1778; m. Benjamin Pearce, son of Rouse.
vi. PRISCILLA, b. Sept. 28, 1776; d. Sept. 25, 1778.
vii. PRISCILLA, b. July 23, 1790; d, Sept. 17, 1790.

58 STEPHEN[5] PEARCE (James[4], James[3], George[2], Richard[1]), b. Dec. 20, 1753; m. Feb. 18, 1776, Abigail Taylor, b. Nov. 12, 1758, d. Oct. 28, 1826. He d. May 14, 1843. Res. Little Compton, R. I., and Paris, Oneida Co., New York.

Stephen Pearce (second son of James Pearce and Sarah Simmons), born at Little Compton, R. I, Dec. 20, 1753.

In 1776 he entered the Revolutionary army as ensign in the second company of infantry, from Little Compton; was soon after promoted to first lieutenant; served during the war, and at its close he retired from the service as captain of the second company in the second battalion of the Newport county troops.

In 1791, with his wife and four children, he removed from Little Compton to Paris Hill, Oneida Co., New York, where he became a pioneer settler in a wild region which he lived to see populous and prosperous. He was for many years a deacon and a prominent member of the Congregational church at Paris Hill. In the war of 1812, notwithstanding his advanced age, he again entered the American army, to fill the place of his son George, who had been drafted, but who was by his duty to his family compelled to remain at home; and the veteran of the Revolution served as a private soldier on the Canadian frontier. He died at Waterville, Oneida Cor, N. Y., May 14th, 1843, and was buried at Paris Hill.

Abigail Taylor, the wife of Stephen Pearce, was a daughter of Andrew Taylor of Providence, R. I. Her father, Andrew Taylor, was a merchant and traded in West India goods and slaves. He had been at one time very wealthy, and he provided for his daughter Abigail and her family the little farm on which she lived and died, in Paris, Oneida Co. N. Y. In his last years he was poor, but still an active man, of strong will and purposes. Ch.—

i. JAMES, b. Nov. 7, 1776. He sailed from New York city in a merchant vessel, as second mate, in 1796, and was lost on the Barbary coast, not far from 1800.

112. ii. GEORGE T., b. Aug. 3, 1779; m. Mercy S. Simmons.

iii. LUCY S., b. Aug. 29, 1782; m. Nov. 8, 1800, Simeon Walker, b. Jan. 2, 1776, d. Nov. 24, 1847. She d. Aug. 15, 1867. Res. Waterville, N. Y. He was a soldier of the war of 1812, and after his death his widow received a land warrant from the United States government for his services. Ch.—Lyman, b. Feb. 8, 1802, m. Martha Tracey; Orrin, b. Aug. 11, 1806 m. Diadamia Moore and Hulda M. Hubbard; Eliza, b. Aug. 6, 1803, m. Samuel Farnham; Caroline, b. Dec. 10, 1808, m. Shubal Hubbard; Lucy, b. Dec. 23, 1810, m. Leman Stilson; Simeon, b. Nov. —, 1815; Julia A. b. June 5, 1818, m. Alonzo Ingersoll; Martha A., b. Nov. 11, 1820, d. April 25, 1874; Herman T., b. June 8, 1823, d. Dec. 1, 1840; Morris D., b. Mar. 4, 1825; d. Feb. 7, 1859.

iv. DEBORAH T., b. July 6, 1785; m. Feb. 15,1808, Reuben Tower, b. Feb. 15, 1787, d. Mar. 14, 1832. She d. Dec. 30, 1864. Res. Paris, N. Y. He was born in Rutland, Worcester Co., Mass., and died in St. Augustine, Florida. His body is interred in the Waterville, N. Y., cemetery. Ch.—Charlemange, b. Apr. 18, 1809, m. June 14, 1847, Amelia M. Bartle. Res. 228 So. 7th st., Philadelphia, Pa. In sending data to the writer, he adds: Here I give you a copy of what I wrote respecting her and her father, Stephen Pearce, in February, 1833: "She was only five years old when her "father moved into that town from Little Compton, R. "I. She was born there July 6, 1785. The name of "her grandfather and greatgrandfather, who both lived "in Little Compton, was James Pearce. (My grand-"father Pearce, who now sits in the room with me alone "reading the Bible, has just told me this. He had one "brother older than himself, whose name was Wright. "He succeeded. under the English law of primogeni-"ture which then prevailed, to the large farm of his "father, and the other boys all scattered. His brothers "Ezekiel and Simon came with my grandfather into "Paris.") I remember now, besides, that my grandfather, Stephen Pearce, time and again told me stories of his whaling voyages and catching of whales, in the South Pacific ocean. Whaling was the great industry of his day and the region where he lived, and he made many voyages on board of whaling ships as a common hand. Julius, b. Apr. 17, 1811, m. Sept. 12, 1832, Delia Hersey; res. Carthage, Mo.; Henrietta, b. Augt 30, 1814, m. Putnam Page; res. Waterville, N. Y.: Fayette B., b. Jan. 29, 1817, m. three times; res.

Fort Wayne, Ind. Fayette Bartholomew Tower (son of Reuben and Deborah (Pearce) Tower), born at Waterville, N. Y.; died there Feb. 16th 1857. Commenced life as civil engineer on the Chenango canal; afterwards served with distinction as engineer on the Croton aqueduct, and was author of an eminent work entitled "Illustration of the Croton Aqueduct," the only one devoted to that subject. Removed in 1848 to Cumberland, Maryland, where he engaged largely in manufacturing. Was mayor of Cumberland when the cholera raged there in 1850, and became conspicuous for the zeal and devotion with which he remained at his post, visiting and caring for the aflicted, and refusing all entreaties to leave until the epidemic was over. Was member of the House of Delegates of Maryland in the winter of 1855–6, where he contracted consumption, from which he died the following winter. DeWitt, b. Jan. 20. 1821, m. Anna Williams. He died in Brooklyn, N. Y., Oct. 22, 1873; James M., b. Mar. 21, 1823, m. Catherine Osborne, res. Jersey City, N. J.; Francis M., b. July 31, 1825, m. Sarah Rawson, res. 170 So. Oxford st., Brooklyn, N. Y.; Reuben, b. June 17, 1829, res. Waterville, N. Y.

v. Mary T., b. Dec. 16, 1790; m. June 22, 1808, Eleazer Tompkins, b. June 5, 1786, d. May 19, 1872. She d. Jan. 2, 1849. Res. Paris, Tompkins Co. N. Y.; buried at Sangerfield. Ch.—Lucius H., b. Sept, 13, 1809, m. Cornelia Claus; Deborah T., b. Jnne 23, 1812, m. W. C. Burritt; Mary, b. Oct. 19, 1813, m. Jos. N. Winchell, res. West Winfield, N. Y.; Stephen P., b. July 4, 1815.

113. vi. James, b. Nov. 30, 1803; m. Lucy Barnes and Joanna Polleys.

vii. Emma, b. Apr. 8, 1796; m. June 26, 1815, Zeriah F. Rowell, b. Apr. 12, 1789, d. Oct. 10, 1877. He was a soldier in the war of 1812. She d. Feb 22, 1878. Res. Waterville, N. Y. Ch.—Emeline R., b. June 6, 1816, m. Alpheus C. Babcock; Jane E., b. Apr. 21, 1818, David B. Fancher; Albert, b. Dec. 13, 1819, m. Elizabeth McGraw; James P., b. Nov. 4, 1821, m. Lucy C. Wilmot; Harriet, b. Sept. 6, 1824, d. June 2, 1835; Stephen P., b. Aug. 11, 1826, m. Hannah Fuller. He served in the war for several months, but was discharged for disability. In 1862 he re-enlisted in the 50th Mass. Vols. as First Sergt. of Co. D. for nine months and was discharged with the regiment. Abigail P., b. Aug. 11, 1826, m. Solomon Wolworth; Henry, b. July 9, 1830, d. Sept. 1, 1832; Laura L., b. Oct. 6, 1832, m. Willis A. Wilbur; Charles, b. Apr. 18, 1835, m. Harriett F. Baldwin; Henry S., b. Nov. 20, 1837. His address is Waterville, N. Y. He enlisted in July, 1862, in the

117th regiment New York Vols., Co. D., and served in the army until the close of the war. Andrew T., b. Apr. 16, 1843, d. Oct. 27, 1864. He enlisted in July, 1862; promoted to corporal Oct. 15th 1862; to sergeant May 18th, 1863; killed in action before Richmond, Va., Oct. 27th, 1864. His remains are buried at Waterville, N. Y. The Grand Army Post of Waterville bears his name.

viii. NANCY, b. Sept. 30, 1798; m. Joseph Greenhill, b. 1797, d. Nov. —. 1863. She d. May 25, 1854. Res. Paris, N. Y. Ch.—Edwin D., b. Apr. —, 1857; Francis H., d. May —, 1885: Geo. D., m. Ellen Stiles; res. Utica, N. Y.; Wm. M., m. Adaline Burlingame; res. Waterville; Joseph E., m. Maria Reese, res. Utica.

114 ANDREW T., b. June 16, 1793; m. Harriett S. Hale.

59. JOHN[5] PEARCE (James[4], James[3], George[2], Richard[1]), b. Aug. 24, 1755; m. Lydia Palmer. He d.———1793. Res. Little Compton R. I. Ch.—

i. NATHAN, b. ———; d. unm.

115. ii. BENJAMIN, b. ——— 1780; m. Esther Hazard.

iii. JOHN, b. ———; d. unm.

iv. SARAH, b. ———; m. ——— Tompkins.

v. ELIZABETH, b. ———. unm.

60 EZEKIEL[5] PEARCE (James[4], James[3], George[2], Richard[1]), b. Mar. 24, 1760; m. Sarah Pearce [———], b. Feb. 4, 1766, d. July 24, 1848. He d. May 10, 1838. Res. Little Compton, R. I. Ch.—

116. i. NATHANIEL, b. Apr. 12, 1800; m. Clarissa Simmons.

ii. EZEKIEL, b. Nov. 1, 1805; m. Oct. 14, 1829, Phebe Simmons, b. July 4, 1807, d. Dec. 21, 1884, s. p. Res. Clayville, N. Y.

iii. SALOME, b. May 11, 1787; m. Jan. 17, 1804, James Saxton, b. May 30, 1782, d. Aug. 13, 1848. She d. Feb. 7, 1867. Ch.—Benjamin, b. Jan. 17, 1810, res. Berlin, Wis.; Sarah, b. Dec. 4, 1804, d. Oct. 26, 1820; Fred'k, b. Sept. 1. 1806, d. Dec. —, 1881; Antris, b. Feb. 26, 1808, d. Apr. 15, 1840; Salome, b. Jan. 25, 1812, d. May 6, 1866; Arnold, b Apr. 9, 1814, d. Mar. 8, 1853, Adelia, b. July 23, 1816, d. Aug. 11, 1838; Joshua, b. Mar. 12, 1820, d. ———, 1881; Ray. b, Mar. 10, 1822, res. Dodge, Minn.; Rhoda, b. Apr. 25, 1824, d. Dec. 15, 1853; George. b. Sept. 22, 1827, d. Sept. 26, 1853.

117. iv. VAL., b. Jan. 28, 1791; m. Mercy Simmons, Catharine Boss and Antrice Pearce.

v. JOSHUA, b. Oct. 20, 1792; d. April 7, 1816.

vi. MARY, b. Oct. 11, 1796, m. June 9, 1825, George Brownell, b. Mar. 11, 1784, d. June 25, 1864. She d. Jan. 15, 1866. Res. Newport, R. I. Ch.— Joseph W. b. July 12, 1830, m. Adaline J. Hill, res. Galva, Ill.; Sarah M.

b. Mar. 22, 1826, d. Aug. 23, 1842; Nancy N. b. Nov. 28, 1827, m. John Lohmas; Harriet B. b. Aug. 2, 1832, d. Sept. 25, 1832; Ezekiel P. b. Apr. 20, 1834, m. Sarah P. Lohmas, res. Cassville, N. Y.; Geo. B. b. Feb. 27, 1836, m. Harriet J. Oatley; Andulusia, b. July 12, 1830, m. Geo. Monroe, res. New Castle, Pa.

vii. Geo. B. Apr. 12, 1800, m. Nov. 1, 1821, Sally Simmons, b. Apr. 22, 1803, d. Jan. 9, 1877, s. p. Res. Clayville, N. Y.

61 Ichabod^5 Pearce (James^4, James^3, George^2, Richard^1), b. Mar. 24, 1762 ; m. Lucy Simmons, b. ——— 1771, d. Nov. 26, 1859. He d Dec. 11, 1844. Res. Little Compton, R. I. Ch.—

118. i. Pardon S. b. Dec. 3, 1792 ; m. Eliful Allen.
ii. Jonathan, b. ———.
iii. Clarinda, b. ———.
iv. Cinderella, b. ———; m. ——— Brownell. Res. 328 4th st. So. Boston, Mass.
v. Cynthia, b. ———.

62 Capt. James^5 Pearce (James^4, James^3, George^2, Richard), b. Oct. 9, 1740 ; m. July 14, 1762, Deborah Hunt, b. May 6, 1739. He d. Mar. 2, 1821. Res. Little Compton, R. I. He was captain of one of the Little Compton companies during the Revolutionary war and took a very active part in the successful struggle for independence. Ch.—

i. Samuel, b. Feb. 13, 1763 ; d. Mar. 21, 1827, New Bedford, Mass.
ii. Elizabeth, b. July 1, 1764 ; m. Samuel Hillard. Res. L. C.
119. iii. Wm., b. June 7, 1766 ; m. Eleanor Pearce [ ].
iv. Sarah, b. Mar. 12, 1767 ; m. Owen Wilbur. Res. Madison, N. Y.
v. Loring, b. Mar. 19. 1774.
vi. Abigail, b. May 3, 1778.

63 Richard^5 Pearce (William^4, James^3, George^2, Richard^1), b. May 26, 1744 ; m. Mary Ellis, b. ———, 1745, d. ——, 1818. He d. Mar. 15, 1817. Res. Little Compton, R. I. Ch.—

i. Jonathan, b. Apr. 22, 1764.

64 Rouse^5 Pearce (Giles^4, James^3, George^2, Richard^1), b. July 4, 1753, m. Dec. 19, 1776, Mary Brownell, b. July 5, 1754, d. Apr. —, 1854. He d. Dec. 24, 1831. Res. Little Compton, R. I. Ch.—

i. Bradford, b. Dec. 25, 1791 ; m. Fannie Tompkins. He d. June 28, 1869, in Little Compton, R. I.
120. ii. Benjamin, b. May 19, 1784 ; m. Sarah Pearce [ ].
121. iii. Giles, b. Feb. 2, 1778 ; m. Sarah Champlin.
iv. Stephen, b. July 5, 1780.

v. Geo. R., b. Mar. 21, 1782.
vi. Cornelius, b. Apr. 27, 1787.
vii. Ellery, b. July 25, 1789.
viii. Sarah, b. Oct. 27, 1793.
ix. Mary, b. May 25, 1796.

65 James[5] Pearce (Giles[4]. James[3], George[2], Richard[1]), b. Aug. 15, 1755; m. Phebe Wood, b. Mar. 9, 1763; d. June 25, 1842. He d. July 22, 1820. Res. Tiverton, R. I. Ch.—

122. i. Giles, b. Apr. 1, 1794; m. Content Hall.
ii. John. b. Feb. 8, 1790. Has a dau. Phebe res. in Albany, N. Y,
iii. George W.. b. July 11, 1797.
iv. Phebe, b. Oct. 13, 1807; m. Sept. 14, 1833, Amos A. Hale, b. May 20, 1806, d. Feb. 6, 1870. Ch.—Eliza E., b. Aug. 10, 1834, unm.; Ruth, b. Apr. 26, 1839, d. Aug. 21, 1846; Benj., b. Apr. 26, 1843, d. Aug. 29, 1846; res. Republic, O.
v. Sally, b. Dec. 28, 1787; m. ——— Jaynes.
vi. Deborah, b. Jan. 26, 1786; m. ——— Dennison.
vii. Desire, b. Apr. 1, 1800; m. ——— Gilbert.
viii. Susanna, b. Mar. 17, 1792; m. ——— Tripp.
ix. Lydia W., b. ———; m. ——— Dodge. Res. Kingston, Mo.
123. x. Abel S., b. Feb. 7, 1805: m. Sarah Hering.

66 Samuel[5] Pearce (Samuel[4], James[3], George[2], Richard[1]), b. Mar. 19, 1764; m. Feb. 26, 1788, Ruth Martin, b. ———. 1754, d. ———, 1834. He d. Dec. 2, 1793. He was born in Little Compton, R. I., and while quite young removed with his parents to Warren where, with other brothers, he learned the the carpenter's trade with his father. Later he was married to Ruth Martin of Barrington. His union was blessed with two sons and three daughters. Thus surrounded by a young family he removed to Providence, where he resided several years, and then purchased a small farm in Plainfield, Windham Co., Conn, where he died, leaving his children quite young; but his widow survived him many years. The only public position that he ever held was that of deacon of a Baptist church. He was well sustained by a devoted wife. Ch.—

i. George, b. July 1, 1788; d. Aug. 29, 1788.
124. ii. Sanford, b. Apr. 23, 1789; m. Lydia Sherman.
iii. Polly, b. ———; m. Benjamin Fisk. Res. Coldwater, Mich.
iv. Betsy, b. ———; m. E. B. Tyler. Res. Oneida County, N. Y.
v. Abigail, b. Dec. 25, 1791; m. James Hale. Abigail d. Mar. 4, 1851. They had three sons, one Alfred E., b.

July 23, 1813. Hon. Alfred E. Hale was born at West Killingly, Windham Co., Conn., July 23rd, 1813.

When he was four years old his father died and he went to live with his uncle, Stephen Hale of Plainfield. While living with his uncle his advantages for school were very limited, the nearest school being (Horse Hill) four miles distant.

At the age of sixteen years he, in company with his mother, moved to New Post, Herkimer Co. N. Y. While living here he learned the shoemakers' trade with another uncle and worked at it most of the time until he was married, June 13th, 1837. His wife was Miss Julia Ann Post of Newport.

About this time stories began to reach the east about the great Rock River Valley. The excitement continued until the fall of 1839, when Mr. Hale decided to visit the far west Late in October of that year he reached Newburg, on the Kishwaukee river. He was much pleased with the country and, after looking around for some time, he decided on a location a short distance west of what is now the village of Cherry Valley.

After selecting his home in the west, Mr. Hale returned to the east and made preparation to move the following spring. In June, 1840, he reached his new home again in company with his family, which consisted of his wife, one child and his mother.

Mr. Hale, like many of the early settlers, often saw hard times, and often had to resort to his trade of shoemaking, it being about the only thing that would bring in any money.

March 4th, 1851, Mr. Hale's mother died, and July 29th, 1852, his wife died, leaving four children, the youngest being but nine months old. Mr. Hale married again April 12th, 1854, to Miss Harriet Ball, who had a short time before moved with her parents from near Prescott, Canada, and settled near Garden Prairie, Boone Co. Ill. Mr. Hale always lived on the farm he purchased from the goverment, with the exception of about one year, during which time he kept hotel at Cherry Valley. Mr. Hale often expressed a desire to visit the land of his nativity, and in the fall of 1870, with his wife he paid a visit the scenes of his childhood, as he stated to many of his friends, for the last time, which proved to be too true. On the morning of November 3d he went to the barn to assist his son-in-law to move away a load of fodder. After doing this he again returned to the house, opened his desk and began writing a letter. One of the family stepping into the room and noticing his head fall back, immediately called to the son-in-law, who reached the house in a moment, only to find that life was extinct. Heart disease had done its work, and the body that but a few moments before was so busy was now cold in death.

Mr. Hale being an early settler and having a large acquaintance, his funeral was attended by a large concourse of people, who came to pay a last tribute to a departed friend.

Mr. Hale filled many places of public trust. He was Justice of the Peace for many years, and at the breaking out of the war he was appointed Assistant U. S. Marshal. In November, 1860, he was elected to the Legislature. He took his seat in January and served his term with distinction.

Mr. Hale was a whole-souled generous man; was always ready to do a kiud aet and to help a neighbor. During the war he distinguished himself by looking after the wants of the families of those who had gone to the front, and many a family can attest to his generosity during those trying times.

67 JEREMIAH[5] PEARCE (Samuel[4], James[3], George[2], Richard[1]), b. Mar. 7, 1760; m. Nancy Bowen. Jeremiah was a blacksmith by occupation, and carried on the business for several years after his marriage in Warren. He subsequently removed to Fairfieid, Herkimer Co., N. Y. On the same highway, two miles north of him, grew up the village of Fairfield. There was located a noted college and popular medical school, which was transferred to Geneva and later to Buffalo. After his removal west he was a farmer, held several different town offices and was an intelligent man, an upright citizen and a good neighbor. He d. ———, 1834. Res. Warren, R. I., and Fairfield and Herkimer, N. Y. Ch.—

125. i. JOSEPH, b. July 31, 1785 ; m. ——— ——— and Mary Carey.

126. ii. GEORGE, b. May 14, 1803 ; m. Sophronia Haskins.

iii. BETSEY, b. June 1, 1787.

68. JOHN[5] PEARCE (Samuel[4], James[3], George[2], Richard[1]). b. Feb. 15, 1768 ; m. Nov. 27, 1785, Patience Arnold ; m. 2nd, Dec. 17, 1794, Mary Luther, b. 1769, d. June 7, 1809 ; m. 3rd, 1809, Annie ———. John Pearce resided in Warren, R. I., with the exception of two years he was with his brother James in North Carolina, while a young man. Like his father he was a master builder. He erected not only fine residences but elegant churches in his home town and across the line in the old Bay State. He served his townspeople in offices of usefulness and trust and was by all regarded as an upright man and citizen. He d. Mar. 2, 1848. Ch.—

127. i. JOHN, b. May 28, 1802 ; m. Mary T. Hale and Mary H. Jones.

ii. Polly, b. ——, 1797 ; m. Oct. 21, 1816, Job Luther. She d. July 22, 1871. Res. Warren, R. I.
128. iii. Samuel, b. Dec. 30, 1810 ; m. Elizabeth H. Chase.

69 Richard[6] Pearce (Richard[5], Nathaniel[4], Richard[3], Richard[2], Richard[1]), b. Oct. 27, 1762 ; m. Candace ——. Res. Dighton and rem. to Vermont. Ch.—

i. Mary, b. Feb. 4, 1782.
ii. Jonathan, b. Apr. 7, 1784.
iii. James, b. June, 16, 1786.
iv. Richard, May 29, 1788.
v. Phebe, b. June 27, 1790.
vi. Robt. M., b, Dec. 24, 1791.
vii. Rufus, b. June 8, 1794.
viii. Emily, b, Mar. 11, 1796.

70 Nathaniel[6] Pearce (Richard[5], Nathaniel[4], Richard[3], Richard[2], Richard[1]), b. Oct. 4, 1764, m. Dec. 25, 1787 Lucy Rogerson, b. 1764, d. Jan. 22, 1805. He d. Nov. 28, 1810. Res. Rehoboth, Mass. Ch.—

129. i Geo. A. b. Oct. 19, 1788, m. Lucretia Carpenter.
ii. Lucy b. July 12, 1790, m. Jan. 21, 1808, Martin Horton, s. p. Res. Rehoboth.
iii. Nathaniel b. Nov. 7, 1793, unm. Went West, Ohio and Kentucky.
iv. William H. b. Sept. 5, 1797, d. June 5. 1810.
v. Betsy R. b. Aug. 28. 1799, m. Jonathan Reynolds, one son J. Augustine. Res. Bristol, R. I.
130. vi. Albert S. b. Apr. 1, 1804, m. Mary S. Bradford.

71 Robert[6] Pearce (Richard[5], Nathaniel[4], Richard[3], Richard,[2] Richard[1]), b. July 18, 1777, m. May 3, 1798, Lydia Blanding, b. Feb. 22, 1778, d. Dec. 17, 1833, He d. Jan. 3. 1832. Res. Rehoboth, Mass. Ch.—

131. i. Gilbert D. b. Dec. 16, 1809, m. Eliza Wheaton,
ii. Elizabeth M. b. May 23, 1811, m. Noah Pierce, Nov. 4, 1832. He was b. Dec. 6, 1805, d. Jan. 4, 1869. Res. Rehoboth. Ch.— Edward B. b. Sept. 3, 1833, d. Dec. 14, 1837 ; Aurelia M. b. Jan. 2, 1838 ; Eliza B. b. Aug. 15, 1839 ; Edward B. b. May 14, 1844, m. Mary E. Williams ; Ann P. b. Aug. 26, 1847, m. Charles Perry ; William L. b. May 23, 1851 ; d. Mar. 9, 1852. Res. Rehoboth, Mass.
132. iii. James Henry, b. May 29. 1818, m. Mary A. Brown.
iv. Aurelia P. b. Dec. 14, 1798, m. Jas. Murray.
v. Wm. A. b. May 25, 1801, d. Aug. 1822.
133. vi. Robert M. b Oct. 27, 1803, m. Lucy Blanding.
vii. Abraham B. b. 1805, d. May 1822.
viii. Susan B. b. Sept. 1815, d. 1816.

72 WILLIAM[6] PEARCE (George[5], William[4], Richard[3], Richard[2], Richard[1]), b. Mar. 2, 1766, m. Elizabeth Gifford, b. Feb. 27, 1769, d. Jan. 25, 1826. He d. June 19, 1844. Res. Bristol, R. I. Ch.—

134. i. GEORGE b. Nov. 14, 1787, m. Elizabeth T. Childs.

ii. HANNAH, b. Aug. 8, 1800, m. Rev. Erastus De Wolff. She d. Dec. 4, 1851. A friend in writing of Rev. De Wolff says : Of the birth and early life of the Rev. Erastus De Wolff—I know absolutely nothing. My impression is that he was born in Penn. about the year 1808. In early manhood he removed to Rhode Island, studied for the ministry in the Episcopal Church, and was ordained by Bishop Henshaw. It was while in Bristol, R. I., that he became acquainted with and subsequently married Hannah Pearce.

Erastus De Wolff had charge of the Tower Hill Church, South Rhode Island, as a missionary for eight months in 1835. In 1834 he held the same position for seven months in Westerly, not far from Tower Hill. He was then called to the rectorship of Tower Hill Church, which position he held for four years. This church is one of the oldest in Rhode Island and was built by an English endowment, as were several others. In the pulpit or reading desk may still be seen the old bible inserted by the venerable English society for the propogation of the gospel in foreign parts. Mrs. De Wolff took with her to Tower Hill the first piano in the town, given her by her father and took it to the church and played it during service. She was a very fine singer and much beloved by every one.

In 1839 he removed with his family to the then far West, viz— near Dixon, Lee County, Illinois. The family resided on a large farm near Dixon from 1839 until the time of the mother's death in 1851. The father being engaged in missionary work all over that sparsely settled country, extending the services of the Church as far Aurora and other points on Fox River Tiskilwa, Princeton, Providence and other points south. After the mother's death he removed to Philadelphia, established a mission called St. Barnabas. I think in Nineteenth street which finally secured a little brick church and became quite flourishing doing an excellent work among the poor. While in Philadelphia he married an estimable widow lady by the name of Jones.

During the late civil war, in perfect health, he was sent from Philadelphia as a member of the Sanitary Commission, to look after our poor wounded soldiers, who by the hundred were being brought to Harrison Landing. Working night and day over the poor sufferers he soon became, prostrated himself, and only lived a few days after reaching his home in Philadelphia. Their child was Rev. Erastus Jr. b. in Bristol, R. I. Res. at Racine Junction, Wis. He m. Caroline A. Wasson. Ch.— Erastus jr. b. Nov. 15, 1865, now in Denver, Colorado; Robert Warren, b. Oct. 18, 1866; Hannah Lucy, b. Sept. 7, 1869, d. Nov. 16, 1885; Grace Caroline b. Oct. 5, 1871 ; Esther E. b. June 11, 1876. Mrs. Caroline De Wolff died of consumption Jan 14, 1886.

Rev. Erastus De Wolff the second son of Erastus and Hannah (Pearce) De Wolff was born in Bristol, R. I. Nov. 11, 1834. In 1839 his parents removed to Lee County, Ill., where his youth was passed upon a large farm. This was prior to the district school even, and his parents employed a teacher, and established a school in his own house, where his only brother Willliam Willis, his two sisters Elizabeth Pearce and Mary Ann, he and the children of two or three other families received the best of instruction in the common English branches. In 1851, his brother and himself were sent to Jubilee College in Peoria Co., Ill., where they remained until the period of their graduation. His brother (two years older than himself), receiving his diploma in 1855, and Erastus in 1856.

After recovering his health, like his father he studied for the ministry of the Episcopal Church partly at dear old Jubilee his Alma Mater, and partly at the General Theological Seminary in New York City. He was ordained by Bishop Whitehouse in the Cathedral, Chicago in 1861 and immediately entered upon missionary work at Onaga, Ill. Dec. 9th, 1863. While rector of the Church of the Redeemer, Wilmington, Ill., he married Miss. Caroline A. Wasson, of Amboy, Lee Co., Ill. In 1872, he removed with his family to Wis., and became rector of St. John's Church, Sparta. He later engaged in missionary work in Milwaukee and vicinity.

During the past three years he has been engaged in missionary work at Western Union, Racine Co., Wis. He is still engaged in this work at St. Paul's Mission and School where they feel that they are doing a good and noble work for the Master.

iii. Polly, b. July 29, 1794, d. s. p. Jan. 11, 1825.
135. iv. Wm. b. Mar. 8, 1798, m. Mary Coit.
v. Hannah, b. Oct. 4, 1790, d. young.

73 George[6], Pearce (George[5], William[4], Richard[3], Richard[2], Richard[1]), b. Apr. 24, 1768, m. ——, Res. Hartwick, N. Y. Ch.—

i. REUBEN b. ———, m. ——— in Hartwick, N. Y. had sons Marshall, Robert and Reuben.

74 CAPT. RICHARD S[6] PEARCE (William[5], Thomas[4], Jeremiah[3], Richard[2], Richard[1]). b. June 12, 1808, m. June 20, 1830, Hope C. Reed, b. Oct. 2, 1809, d. Dec. 26, 1878. Res. Bristol, R. I. Ch.—

i. HARRIET T. b. Sept. 20, 1832, m. Dec. 19, 1860, Evan A. Fisk, b. June 12, 1826. Res. Milford Mass. Ch.— Walter A. b. Nov. 13, 1864, d. June 25, 1868; Cora L. b. May 29, 1869, d. Apr. 21, 1872.
ii. ELIZABETH B. b. July 6, 1834, m. Nov. 24, 1862, Andrew J. Gale, b. July 20, 1836. Res. 42 Central street, Providence, R. I. Ch.— Lillian P., b. Feb. 21. 1864; Chas. A. b. Apr. 11, 1867.
136. iii. GEORGE T. b. Feb. 7, 1837, m. Martha Moore and Sarah J. Pearce.
137. iv. RICHARD S. Apr. 2, 1839, m. Addie F. Sweet.
v. WILLIAM F. b. Apr. 20, 1841, unm. Res. Bristol, R. I.
vi. THOMAS E., b. } May 13, 1844, d. Nov. ——, 1848.
vii. MARY A., b. } May 13, 1844, m. Dec. 29, 1870, Thomas Moore, b. May 8, 1845, d. Jan. 8. 1871. Ch— Thomas b. Oct. 1871, d. 1872. She m. 2nd. May 10, 1876, Charles F. Nixon. Res. Woonsockett, R. I. Ch.— Hattie S. b. Oct. 31, 1877; Chas. A. b. Aug. 23, 1879; Gracie V. b. Nov. 6, 1883.
138. viii. OLIVER C., b. Apr. 10, 1848, m. Mary T. Fowler.

75 JOHN W.[6] PEARCE (William[5], James[4], Jeremiah[3], Richard[2], Richard[1]), b. Dec. 18, 1818; m. May 21, 1843, Mary S. Monroe, b. Mar. 20, 1821. He d. s. p. Aug. 1, 1881. Res. Bristol. R. I.

76 THOMAS[6] PEARCE (William[5], Thomas[4], Jeremiah[3], Richard[2], Richard[1]), b. May 27, 1821; m. Jan. 8, 1844, Mary E. Coit, b. June 3, 1824, d. June 26, 1879. He d. Apr. 12, 1850. Res. Bristol, R. I. Ch.—

139. i. WILLIAM T., b. Apr. 20, 1846; m. Hannah B. Briggs.

77 GEORGE P.[6] PEARCE (William[5], Thomas[4]. Jeremiah[3], Richard[2], Richard[1]), b. July 12, 1814; m. July 19, 1840, Phebe Leonard, b. Mar. 12, 1820. He d. Nov. 19, 1843. Res. Bristol, R. I. Ch.—

i. SUSAN T., b. Feb. 8, 1842; m. May 21, 1863 James E. Blackmer of Providence, R. I. She d. Mar. 21, 1875, leaving one son, Charles A., b. Nov. 23, 1863. Res. East Prov.

78 JEREMIAH[6] PEARCE (Jeremiah[5], Giles[4], Jeremiah[3], Giles[2], Richard[1]), b. June 20, 1751; m. May 2, 1773, Mary Gorton. Res. East Greenwich, R. I. Ch.—

i. JEREMIAH, b. June 2, 1791.

ii. MARY, b. Oct. 23, 1786 ; m. March 8, 1807, John Mowrey. Res. East Greenwich. One son, Rev. Gideon B., is rector of Trinity Episcopal Chuch, in Chicago, at 26th st.

140. iii. NATHAN, b. Apr. 12, 1784, m. Freelove Boyde.

iv. PEGGY A., b. Oct. 20, 1795 ; m. Oct. 19, 1815, Oliver C. W. Arnold, b. June 17. 1792, d. Apr. 14, 1845. She d. Jan. 29, 1883. Ch. b. East Greenwich and Compton, R. I.: Ann E., b. Sept. 11, 1838, m. Albert C. Greene ; John G., b. Feb. 27, 1833, drowned June 28, 1841 ; Henry M. b. Aug. 25, 1835; went to sea N. & K. ; Wm. E., b. Aug. 15, 1816, m. Lucy Cottrell ; Mary A., b. Oct. 21, 1820, m. Sabin Ballou; Freelove A. b. May 5, 1825 ; Oliver C., b. July 12, 1827, d. Aug. 18, 1827 ; Olive, b. Sept. 10 1828, d. s. day ; Susan P., b. July 19, 1830, m. Caleb Williams.

v. JOHN G., b. Aug. 13, 1776 ; d. May 10, 1777.

79 GILES[6] PEARCE (George[5], Giles[4], Jeremiah[3], Giles[2], Richard[1]), b. Apr. 22, 1765 ; m. Mar. 24, 1785, Hannah Arnold ; d May 15, 1821. Giles removed to Rutland, Vermont, in 1800, and then moved to Hamburg, N. Y., ten miles south of Buffalo, in 1814. where he spent the remainder of his life, Res. N. Kingston, R. I., Rutland, Vt., and Hamburg, N. Y. He d. Nov. 8, 1835. Ch.—

i. GILES, JR., b. Mar. 25, 1807 ; m. Harriett ———, and had dau. Harriett, who died.

ii. ANNIE, b. May 13, 1809 ; d. June 24, 1828.

141. iii. GEORGE, b. Mar. 5, 1786 ; m. Lydia Littlefield.

iv. AMEY, b. Dec. 12, 1787 ; m. 1808, Meacham, b. ———, 1780, d. ———, 1823. She d. Oct. 11, 1864. Res. Abbott's Corner, N Y. Ch.—Lucia, m. ——— Turner ; Mary, b. May 16, 1812, m. Wm. Randlett, Nov. 8, 1870. He was b. 1790, d. Oct. 22, 1882 ; res. South Dayton, N. Y.; Laura; Louisa, m. ——— Richards, res. Wichita, Ks.; Hannah, m. ——— Andrews, res. Springville, N. Y.; Jesse; George.

v. SARAH, b. May 23, 1789 ; m: Aaron Parker. Ch.—Francis B., Perry G., res. Buffalo, N. Y., lawyer; Horace, res. Detroit, Mich.

142. v–2. JOSEPH A., b. Jan. 15, 1805 ; m. Rachel C. Morse.

143. vi. OLIVER S., b. Feb. 11, 1791 ; m. Susan Hammond.

vii. RUTH. b. Aug. 29, 1792 . d. Jan. 3, 1804.

viii. DORCAS, b. Feb. 25, 1796 ; m. Moses Baker. Ch.—Nathalita, Darius O., Wm. Lafayette, Edward, Everett S., Res. Buffalo, N. Y., Geo. M., res. Buffalo, Elizabeth, Mary A.

ix. HANNAH, b. Dec. 18, 1797 ; m. Sanford Williams. Ch.—Robert E., Mary A. m. ——— Northrop, res. Brodhead, Wis., Amy G. and Lucina.

x. PATIENCE, b. May 10, 1800 . d. unm. ———, 1821.

xi. MARY, b. Sept. 9, 1802 ; d. June 2, 1804.

79½ JOB[6] PEARCE (Job[5], John[4], Jeremiah[3], Giles[2], Richard[1]), b. Oct. 29, 1781 ; m. Sept. 1, 1805, Elizabeth Dean, b. 1782, d. Dec. 17, 1857. Res. East Greenwich, R. I. Ch.—

144. i. CHARLES, b. June 7, 1806 ; m. Ruby W. Gorton.

ii. DANIEL R., b. Aug. 19, 1807 ; d. Oct. 15, 1868.

iii. SARAH P., b. Dec. 14, 1808 ; m. Mar. 15, 1835, Chas. C. Eldridge, b. March 12, 1812, d. Aug. —, 1845, res. East Greenwich, R. I. Ch.—Eleanor E., b. Jan, 12, 1836 ; James, b. Oct. 12, 1837, res. Holden, Johnson Co., Mo.; Chas. C., b, Sept. 29, 1839 ; Lucy, b. June, 20, 1842 ; Henry P., b. Mar. 20, 1844.

145. iv. JOB, b. Mar. 30, 1811 ; m. Maria A. Briggs.

v. MARY M. Sept. 22, 1813 . d. unm. July 10, 1877.

80 STEPHEN M.[6] PEARCE (Phillip[5], John[4], Jeremiah[3], Giles[2], Richard[1]), b. Mar. 15, 1782 ; m. Nov. 9, 1806, Sukey Fry, d. Aug. 12, 1873. He d. Aug. 5, 1830. Res. Coventry, R. I. Ch.—

146. i. CHARLES, b. Sept. 29, 1811 ; m. Mariah Atwood.

81 PHILLIP[6] PEARCE (Phillip[5], John[4], Jeremiah[3], Giles[2], Richard[1]), b. Apr. 1, 1790 ; m. Nov. 1, 1816, Hannah Wall, b, Apr. 16, 1798, d. Apr. 16, 1861. He d. July 27, 1835. Res. East Greenwich, R. I. Ch.—

147. i. SAMUEL W. b. May 11, 1818 ; m. Cornelia Sherman.

ii. PHILLIP H., b. Dec. 11, 1821 ; unm. Res. East Greenwich.

82 ROBINSON[6] PEARCE (Phillip[5], John[4], Jeremiah[3], Giles[2], Richard[1]), b. ———, 179– ; m. Abby Boyd. d. Aug. 1, 1872. He d. ——, 1856. Res. East Greenwich, R. I. Ch.—

148. i. WM. R., b Aug. 11, 1827; m. Hannah Sheridan and Sarah I. Rand.

ii. HANNAH H., b. Aug. 5, 1832 ; d. unm. July 12, 1883.

iii. ALBERT A., b. Mar. 4, 1836 ; m. Elizabeth Coon. Res. 20 Aborn st., Prov. R. I.

149. iv. ROBINSON, b. Aug. 10, 1822 ; m. Raby B. Brown and Sarah Dening.

83 GEORGE[6] PEARCE (Phillip[5], John[4], Jeremiah[3], Giles[2], Richard[1]), b. Apr. 29, 1801 ; m. Apr. 25, 1824, Celia Gorton. He d. Apr. 29, 1883. Res. East Greenwich, R. I. Ch.—

i. MARY A., b. May 9, 1825 ; m. July 19, 1865, Robert T. Sands.

ii. BENJAMIN, b. Mar. 11, 1827 ; d. Aug. 4, 1827.

iii. GEORGE, b. May 17, 1829 ; d. Sept. 30, 1830.

iv. EDWARD, b. July 12, 1833 ; d. Sept. 7, 1836.

v. LYDIA, b. Apr. 26, 1835 ; d. Oct. 30, 1839.

vi. ALBERT M., b. Mar. 14, 1838.
vii. CELIA A., b. July 16, 1844 ; m. Mar. 17, 1864, Stukly W. Spencer.
viii. HARRIETT, b. Mar. 23, 1847 ; d. Aug. 3; 1847.

84 EARL[6] PEARCE (Stephen[5], Thomas[4], John[3], Giles[2], Richard[1]), b. ——— ; m. Eliza R. Taylor, b. Jan. 18, 1799, d. Dec. 14, 1881. He d. at sea in Sept., 1830. Res. East Greenwich, R. I. Ch.—

i. DANIEL, b. Feb. 25, 1828. Res. 34 Friendship st., Providence, R. I.
ii. DAUGHTER ; m. G. B. Mowrey. Res. 3141 Dearborn st., Chicago, Ill.
iii. ANNA E., b. Mar. 18, 1821 ; m. May 28, 1845, Nahum Tainter, b. June 14, 1821. Res. Birds Island, Minn. Ch.—Henry A., b. June 26, 1846, d. May 17, 1856 ; Laurilla A., b. Nov. 3, 1850, m. Norman Hickok, June 26, 1874, d. Mar. 18, 1882 ; Clifton M., b. April 8, 1868, d. Mar. 19, 1863.
iv. DAUGHTER, m. ——— Aldrich. Res. 159 Friendship st., Providence, R. I.
v. CARRIE F. Res. Pascoag, R. I.

85 JAMES B.[6] PEARCE (Daniel[5], Thomas[4], John[3], Giles[3], Richard[1]), b. Mar, 24, 1801 ; m. Apr. 3, 1823, Mary Pinnegar, b. May 11, 1808, d. Mar. 30, 1862. He d. Jan. 29, 1885. Res. East Greenwich, R. I. Ch.—

150. i. JAS. C., b. Mar. 25, 1830 ; m. Lucretia Foster.
ii. MARY E., b. June 28, 1828.
iii. SUSAN R., b. Mar. 27, 1831. Res. E. Greenwich.
iv. SARAH A., b. Aug. 19, 1833, m. June 21, 1859, Samuel M; Knowles. Res. East Greenwich, R. I.
151. v. DANIEL A., b. May 9, 1838 ; m. Emily G. Vaughn.

86 CHRISTOPHER B.[6] PEARCE (Daniel[5], Thomas[4], John[3], Giles[2], Richard[1]), b. Apr. 13, 1779 ; m. May 1, 1826, Martha W. Gladding, b. Sept. 3, 1809, d. Oct. 25, 1859. He d. July 12, 1875. Res. Prov. R. I. Ch.—

i. FREELOVE G., b. Jan. 11, 1827 ; m. Apr. 29, 1851, Chas. H. Sheldon. She d. Jan. 6, 1856.
ii. ALBERT H., b. June 5, 1828 ; d. Aug. 2, 1829.
iii. MARY E., b. Jan. 30, 1831.
iv. WM. A. b. Mar. 9, 1833 ; d. Apr. 2, 1833.
152. v. CHRISTOPHER A., b. Feb. 10, 1835 ; m. Clara Fisher.
vi. MARTHA W., b. Apr. 13, 1837 ; d. May 11, 1838.
153. vii. EDWARD H., b. Aug. 4, 1838 ; m. Kate L. Anthony.
viii. MARTHA W., b. Apr. 11, 1841 ; m. Oct. 12, 1864, Chas. H. Sheldon.
ix. AUGUSTUS F., b. June 22, 1843 ; d. Mar. 9, 1844.
x. LOUISE F., b. July 14, 1846 ; d. June 8, 1868.

87 BENJAMIN B.[6] PEARCE (Moses[5], Thomas[4], John[3], Giles[2], Richard[1]), b. Sept. 1, 1786; m. ———, 1806, Susan Walker, b. Mar. 21, 1784, d. July 30, 1869. He was born in East Greenwich; was a tanner and currier in Pawtucket, where he was a deacon of the First Baptist church. She was a daughter of Nathaniel and Sarah (Whitford) Walker of Rehoboth. He was an excellent mechanic and resided in Pawtucket; was an ensign and lieutenant in R. I. militia during the Revolutionory war; was taken prisoner and confined in Old Jersey Prison Ship and subjected to the severest hardships. Ch.—

154 i. HENRY N., b. Oct. 19, 1820; m. Nancy H. Sheppard.
155. ii. MOSES, b. July 3, 1808; m. Harriett G. Hathaway.
156. iii. GEORGE, b. Apr. 27. 1810; m. Harriett N. Brown.
157. iv. WM. B., b. Aug. 12, 1818; m. Amanda Peet, Catherine Roath, Martha Freeman.
v. MARY G., b. Mar. 9, 1826; m. Wm. H. Pierce.
vi. SUSAN E, b. Dec. 15, 1823. Res. unm. in Elmwood, R. I.
vii. LYNDON W., b. July 25, 1812; d. unm. 1840.
viii. SARAH N., b. July 25, 1815; d. ———. 1835.

88 JOHN B.[6] PEARCE (John[4], Giles[4], John[3], Giles[3], Richard[1]), b. July 19, 1827; m. Nov. 17, 1846, Izitt C. Gardner, b. June 7, 1827, d. July 17, 1848; m. 2nd, Oct. 17, 1853, Mary G. Brown, b. Apr. 21, 1830, d. Nov. 10, 1858; m. 3rd, Aug. 8, 1859, Abby C. B. Gardner. He d. Mar. 26, 1885. Res. Wickford, R. I. John B. Pearce began business in Providence in 1817, and was unsuccessful. After the death of his father, wife and child in Providence, which occurred between Aug. 11 and 21, 1848, he went to California, arriving there in Aug. 1849; he returned home in Dec. 1851, living at Panama, in South America from Dec., 1850 to Dec. 1851. He was then employed, on his return to America, first as a clerk in the print works of Wm. Lanham, in Johnston, and afterwards at the Manchester print works in Littlefield until 1856, when he returned and settled in Providence, where he was elected Alderman of the Seventh ward, May, 1861, re-elected in 1862 and 1863. He resigned in April, 1864, and entered the United States volunteer army as First Lieut. Co. A, 14th Regt. R. I. Heavy Artillery, and served until the end of the rebellion, arriving home in Nov., 1865. He found his family living in Wickford, to which place he had removed them prior to his enlistment. In 1867 he was elected president of the town council of his native town, which place he held for five successive years, and in 1868 he was elected Senator to represent North Kingston in the State Senate and was re-elected in 1869; was elected town clerk in June, 1873, which place he held until his death in 1885. Ch.—

i. IZITTE G., b. Feb. 12, 1855; d. Mar. 31, 1880.
158. ii. THOS. J., b. June 20, 1857; m. Sarah M. Wightman.

89 THOMAS E.[6] PEARCE (John[5], Giles[5], John[3], Giles[2], Richard[1]), b. Sept. 27, 1829 ; m. Oct. 20, 1851, Amy A. Brown, b. July 15, 1836. They res. in Wickford, R. I. He is proprietor of the celebrated Cold Spring House, which is pleasantly situated on the western shore of Narraganset bay, at a few rods from the beach, and commands a broad view of Narraganset bay, one of the most beautiful sheets of water on the R. I. coast, affording unequalled opportunities for boating, fishing and bathing, sports which may be enjoyed at any time with perfect safety, and for which every convenience is provided. Cold Spring Beach, which extends in front of the house. has long been noted as the finest on the bay and is entirely free from the dangerous undertow so prevalent in surf bathing. At a short distance from the house lies the old village of Wickford, which quietly nestles at the head of Wickford bay, and affords many pleasant nooks, Ch.—

159. i. JOHN F., b. Aug. 17, 1852 ; m. Emma F. Sprink.
ii. CHRISTOPHER P., b. Sept. 28, 1854 ; m. Jan. 25, 1882, Hattie L. Waldron, b. Aug. 20, 1858. Res. s. p. Wickford, R. I.
160. iii. THOMAS W., b. Mar. 21, 1859 ; m. Hattie A. Sunderland.
iv. AMY A. B., b. Mar. 6, 1869.

90 ELISHA[6] PEARCE (Joseph[5], Giles[4], John[3], Giles[2], Richard[1]), b. Feb. 19, 1789 ; m. Amey Gardiner ; m. 2nd, Rebecca Pearce, daughter of Giles, b. ———, 1793, d. May 13, 1871. He d. Sept. 7, 1864. Res. No. Kingston, R. I. Ch.—

i. JOSEPH, b. Aug. 23, 1815 ; d. Nov. 20, 1836.
ii. SUSAN, b. Dec. 23, 1816 ; m. Benjamin Smith.
iii. EZEKIEL, b. Mar. 25, 1818.
iv. ELISHA, b. Mar. 25, 1818.
v. AMEY A. b. Dec. 24, 1820 ; m. Sept. 28, 1837, Benjamin Champlin, b. ———, 1817, d. June 20, 1872. Ch.— Charles G., m. Mary Knowles.

91 JOSEPH[6] PEARCE, (Joseph[5], Giles[4], John[3], Giles[2], Richard[1]), b. July 19, 1791 ; m. Molly Champlin. He d. Aug. 23, 1836. Ch.—

i. BENJAMIN.
ii. THOMAS.
iii. ALBERT.
iv. ABBY.

92 SAMUEL[6] PEARCE (Joseph[5], Giles[4], John[3], Giles[2], Richard[1]), b. Aug. 27, 1798 ; m. Feb. 21, 1830, Mary Hazard. He d. Oct. 11, 1874. Res. North Kingston, R. I. Ch.—

i. MARY E., b. Dec. 8, 1836 ; d. Oct. 3, 1854.
ii. JOSEPH, b. Mar. 31, 1838 ; d. young.
iii. JOSEPHINE, b, Oct. 6, 1840 ; d. Mar. 7, 1873.
iv. F. HENRY, b. Feb. 18, 1842 ; d. ———, 1848.

v. SAMUEL, b. Sept. 8, 1843 ; d. young.
vi ANNA L., b. Dec. 11, 1844 ; d. young.
vii. SAMUEL B., b. Nov. 12, 1851 ; d. young.

93 WILLIAM[6] PEARCE (Giles[5], Giles[4], John[3], Giles[2], Richard[1]), b. Apr. 2, 1789 ; m. Nov. 13, 1812 Waity Northrup, d. Nov. 27, 1812; m. 2nd, Oct. 15, 1815, Abigail Sanford, b. June 3, 1796, d. Mar. 11, 1876. He d. June 11, 1856. Res. North Kingston, R. I. Wm. Pierce married for his second wife Abigail, dau. of Hon. Esbon Sanford. After this marriage they went to live in the upper house at Bissell's mills, which stood on the corner of the main road and Trench avenue. Here he remained until the spring of 1819, when he removed to the Wm. Northrup's farm, west of the old North Ferry in North Kingston. He remained there until the spring of 1840, when he went to live upon the farm of his father. Ch.—

i. ELIZABETH D., b. Jan 13, 1817 ; m. Apr. 21, 1836, Daniel Tefft. Res. North Kingston, R. I. Ch.—Elizabeth, b. Aug. 21, 1837, m. Nathan Van Alstyne; Wm. A., b. June 5, 1840, d. June 10, 1865. Wm. Tefft enlisted Oct. 25, 1861, in the late war of the rebellion as a private in the 7th R. I. Battery, and for bravery and firmness shown at the capture of Fort Macon received a commission as Second Lieutenant in 1863, and enlisted in the 3d R. I. Cavalry ; was taken prisoner at Red River campaign, in Nov. 1864, and consigned to Andersonville prison, where he remained until May, 1865. From the privations and brutal treatment received in that hell-hole he died at his home June 10, 1865. Caroline A., b. June 24, 1844, d, June 16, 1865 ; Eldora, b. July 10, 1852, m. John A. Hawkins, Prov.; Daniel A.. b. Aug. 18, 1857, m. Anna M. Carroll, Prov.; Lydia A., b. Mar. 28, 1855 ; Emma P., b. June 20, 1861, d. Apr. 15, 1883.

161. ii. WM. E., b. Aug. 15, 1819 ; m. Phebe A. Rodman.

iii. ABBY C., b. Aug. 5, 1821 ; m. Jan. 2, 1842, Varnum W. Gardiner. She d. June 22, 1850. Res. Peacedale, R. I. Ch.—Wm. V., b. Jan. 19 1843, m. Susanna Brown, res. Peacedale, R. I.; Esbon S., b. June 10, 1847 ; Abby C., b. June 10, 1849, m. Byron Arnold.

iv. LYDIA S., b. June 8, 1824 ; m. Dec. 25, 1843, Wilbour Hazard. Res. Hamilton, R. I. Ch.—Sarah R., b. Nov. 16, 1844; Wilbour, b. Apr. 19, 1846, m. Isabel Carr.

162. v. ESBON S., b. Feb. 1, 1827 ; m. Elizabeth Hall.

163. vi. ALBERT C., b. Oct. 8, 1829 ; m. Caroline F. Gardiner.

vii. MARY A., b. Mar. 17, 1832 ; m. Dec. 9, 1867, Wm. A. Holloway. She d. Dec. 24, 1881.

164. viii. PELEG F., b. Mar. 15, 1835 ; m. Harriett N. Rodman.

ix. JOS. S., b. Mar. 2, 1838 ; d. Aug. 15, 1852.

94 Giles^{6} Pearce (Giles^{5}, Giles^{4}, John^{3}, Giles^{2}, Richard^{1}), b. ———, 1795 ; m. ———, 1813, Mrs. Mary (Cole) Pearce. Res. North Kingston. R. I. He d. Oct. 14, 1841. Ch.—

i. Wm., b. Mar. 12, 1814 ; d. ———, 1841.
ii. Elizabeth, b. May 3, 1816 ; m. Mar. 13, 1848, Jonathan N. Hazard. Ch.—Charles, b. Aug 27, 1849 ; Mary, b. Mar. 18, 1852, b. Oct. 18, 1853 ; Darius, b. June 7, 1855 ; George, b. June 10, 1858.
165. iii. Edward, b. Apr. 29, 1819 ; m. Frances M. Clark.
iv. Darius, b. Aug. 23, 1824. Went to California in 1848.

95 Dutee J.^{6} Pearce (Dutee J.^{5}, Samuel^{4}, Samuel^{3}, Samuel^{2}, Richard^{1}), b. July 27, 1833; m. June 11, 1862, Martha Palmer, b. Nov. 15, 1842. Res. Foxboro, Mass. Ch.—

i. Dutee J., b. Aug. 11, 1864.
ii. Catherine, b. May 19, 1870.
iii. Harriet, b. Mar. 31, 1875.
iv. Candace E., b. Apr. 28, 1877.

96 J. Irving^{6} Pearce (Samuel^{5}, Michael^{4}, Samuel^{3}, Samuel^{2}, Richard^{1}), b. July 27, 1827 ; m. Jan, 28, 1849, Margaret E. Wilkins, b. Apr. 30, 1826. Res. Sherman House, Chicago, Ill. Ch.—

i. Grace E., b. Nov. 28, 1852 ; m. Feb. 19, 1878, Henry A. Blair, b. July 6, 1852. Res. 225 Michigan av., Chicago, Ill. Ch.—Natalie, b. July 28, 1883.
ii. Myron, b. Sept. 22, 1856.
iii. John I., b. Feb. 3, 1860.
iv. Perley P.; dead.
v. Fannie ; dead.

97 William L.^{6} Pearce (Samuel^{5}, Michael^{4}, Samuel^{3}, Samuel^{2}, Richard^{1}), b. Jan. 28, 1816 ; m. Sept. 19, 1839, Margaret Hasbrook, b. Oct. 4, 1815. He died Aug. 11, 1874. Res. Joliet, Ill. Ch.—

i. Margaret, b. July 24, 1840 ; m. Apr. 2, 1868, James G. Elwood. Res. Joliet, Ill. Ch.— Ward P., b. Jan. 17, 1869 ; Wm. N., b. Mar. 17, 1871 ; Louise M., b. Apr. 8, 1873 ; Margaret P., b. July 20, 1875, d. Jan. 14, 1878 ; Elsie P., b. Sept. 7, 1878.
ii. Wm. C., b. May 5, 1844 ; d. June 6, 1845.
166. iii. Samuel, b. Feb. 9, 1848 ; m. Mary E. Clark.
iv. Lewis H., b. Jan. 4, 1850 ; d. May 13, 1852.
v. Charles G., b. Mar. 16, 1860 ; d. Sept. 15, 1861.

98 Myron L.^{6} Pearce (Samuel^{5}, Michael^{4}, Samuel^{3}, Samuel^{2}, Richard^{1}), b. Dec. 16, 1821 ; m. Hattie A. Pestana, b. Dec. 3, 1835. Res. 2548 Prairie av. Chicago, Ill. Ch.—

i. Francis M., b. Sept. 14, 1860.
ii. Myron A., b. July 14, 1864.

iii. MARY E., b. May 21, 1866 ; d. Jan. 16, 1871.
iv. HARRIETT, b. Sept. 25, 1876.

99 WILLIAM W.[6] PEARCE (Job[5], Michael[4], Samuel[3], Samuel[2], Richard[1]), b. Sept. 14, 1838 ; m. Oct. 10, 1860, Louise Carey, b. July 4, 1842. Res. Rushville, N. Y. Ch.—

i. FRANK J„ b. Sept. 27, 1870 ; d. Mar. 27, 1874.

100 WILEY K.[6] PEARCE (Thomas[5], Michael[4] Samuel[3], Samuel[2], Richard[1]), b. Sept. 18, 1812; m. Mar. 20, 1834, Sarah J. Foster, b. Mar. 15, 1813, d. May 13, 1862 ; m. 2nd, Nov. 15, 1863, Sarah R. Lindsley, b. May 4, 1842, d. June 28, 1882. Res. Stoney Creek, Washtenaw Co. Mich. Ch.—

i. EDWARD, b. Jan. 31, 1836 ; m. Aug. 1, 1872. Res. Ludington, Mich.
ii. NANCY J., Feb. 19, 1838 ; m. Mar. 31, 1864, Levi Rogers. Res. Stoney Creek, Mich.
iii. CULYER G., b. Dec. 15, 1839 ; d. Jan. 28, 1849.
iv. CHAS. S., b. Aug. 17, 1843 ; m. June 5, 1867. Res. Grass Lake, Mich.
v. LAURENS S., b. July 6, 1847 ; d. June 6, 1882.
vi. CANDACE A., b. Feb. 19, 1849.
vii. MARY A., b. Apr. 10, 1853 ; m. Aug. 7, 1877, Chas. Tedder. Res. Whitacre, Mich.
viii. FLORA J., b. July 29, 1865 ; m. Dec. 5, 1863, John M. Sweet. Res. Stony Creek, Mich.

101 DANIEL C.[6] PEARCE (John[5], Michael[4], Samuel[3], Samuel[2]. Richard[1]), b. Sept. 3, 1818 ; m. Jan. 21, 1841, Sarah A. Fisher, b. Nov. 3, 1818, d. June 8, 1884. Res. Rushville, N. Y. Ch.—

167. i. JOHN F., b. Nov. 12, 1841 ; m. Lucy B. Green.
ii. JAS M., b. Oct. 27, 1844. Res. Syracuse, N. Y.
iii. MARY B., b. Mar. 4, 1848 ; m. Nov. 10, 1870, Samuel L. Powers, b. Feb. 8, 1848. Res. Potter, N. Y. Ch.—Isabel S. b. May 23, 1873.
iv. GUY S., b. b. Oct. 12, 1851; m. Della Hunt. Ch.—Ada S. b. Oct. 4, 1877. Res. Gorham, N. Y.
v. FRANK, b. Feb. 15, 1855 ; unm. Res. Rushville, N. Y.

102 NATHANIEL[6] PEARCE (Isaac[5], Jeptha[4], George[3], George[2], Richard[6]), b. June 30, 1787 ; m. Nov. 2, 1809, Susanna Simmons, b. Nov. 2, 1789, d. Oct. 12, 1845. He d. Mar. 28, 1868. Res. Little Compton, R. I. Ch.—

168. i. EDWIN, b. Jan. 17, 1815 ; m. Eliza Winchester.
ii. FALLY S., b. Mar. 26, 1810 ; d. Mar. 9, 1856.
iii. MARY, b. Feb. 16, 1813 ; d. Dec. 28, 1828,
iv. BENJ. C. b. Oct. 5. 1819 ; d. May 10, 1830.
v. ANN M., b. June 19, 1821 ; m. May 14, 1879, Rev. Jas. Burlinghame, b. May 13, 1794, d. Aug. 30, 1881, s. p., res. Greene, R. I.

169. vi. WM. S., b. June 25, 1824 ; m. Amelia McDonald.
vii. NAT'H S., b. May 30, 1828 ; d. June 2, 1830

103 JONATHAN D.[6] PEARCE (Isaac[5], Jeptha[4], George[3], George[2], Richard[1]), b. Apr. 15, 1801 ; m. Feb. 16, 1823, Hannah P. Head, b. Apr. 4, 1803, d. Dec. 3, 1879. From early life she maintained a consistent Christian character and in her death the poor felt that they had truly lost a friend. He d. Aug. 3, 1866. Mr. P. was a respected citizen, a blacksmith and a farmer. Res. Little Compton, R. I. Ch.—

i. MIRANDA, b. Feb. 22, 1824 ; unm. Res. Little Compton.
ii. GEO. W., b. Feb. 12, 1826 ; m. Nov. —, 1849, and d. Oct. 27, 1851. Res. Little Compton.
iii. HANNAH, b. Mar. 8, 1828 ; m. Jan. 15, 1849, L. Chester Gifford, b. July 20. 1820, d. June 9, 1878. Ch.—Chas. L., b. Dec. 23, 1849 ; Geo. C., b. Jan. 23, 1851 ; Julia M., b. Mar. 23, 1856.
iv. FRED. H., b. Nov. 29, 1880 ; unm.
v. MARY D., b. Oct. 2, 1832 ; m. Oct. 17, 1857, Asaph P. Tabor, d. Oct. 21, 1859 ; m. 2nd, Mar. 25, 1865, Benjamin C. Borden. Res. Fall River, P. O. Box 533. Ch.—Lizzie D., b. Jan. 9, 1859 ; Abel P., b. May 11, 1866 ; Frank E., b. May 5, 1869.

170. vi. ABEL H. b. June 29, 1834, m. Fanny Lacy and Harriet James.
vii. JULIA A. b. Aug. 2, 1837, m. Sept. 28, 1856, Aaron Bradford, d. July, 1879, m. 2nd. Nov. 8, 1880, Joshua Cole. Ch.— Geo. P. b. July 26, 1857 ; Lizzie b. Jan. 1, 1860 ; Frank I. b. Mar. 21, 1862.
171. viii. JONATHAN E. b. Dec. 6, 1839, m. Nannie Lacy.
ix. SUSAN E. b. Nov. 20, 1841, m. Apr. 20, 1869, m. Wiley M. Huykendall, res. Texas. Ch.— Robert G. b. May 15, 1870 ; Isaac b. Oct. 15, 1874, d. June 23, 1875 ; Isaac G. b. June 19, 1876 ; Eugene B. b. Sept. 13, 1878, d. June 23, 1879 ; Electa M. b. Apr. 15, 1883.
x. ISAAC B. Nov. 21, 1841, d. Aug. 3, 1845.

104 JOHN[6] PEARCE (John[5], Nathaniel[4], George[3], George[2], Richard[1]), b. Oct. 19, 1793, m. Aug. 13, 1818, Lucinda C. Trout, b. Feb. 8, 1797, d. June 29, 1880. He d. Mar. 1, 1885. Res. Philadelphia, Pa. Ch.—

172. i. JOHN S., b. Dec. 18, 1828 ; m. Margaret E. Campbell and Rose A. Cragle.
ii. ELIZABETH, A., b. July 10, 1819 ; m. Sept. 10, 1851, Richard Adams. Res. 1730 Ridge av., Phila., Pa. Ch.—Richard A., b. Aug. 4, 1852 ; John P., b. Aug. 29, 1855 ; Kate D., b. Aug. 8, 1857, d. June 15, 1859 ; Chas. W. b. Apr. 19, 1860 ; Samuel C., b. Mar. 20, 1862.
iii. MARY S., b. Apr. 27, 1821 ; m. Sept. 21, 1864, John T. Brown, b. Jan. 1. 1817, d. May 29, 1883, s. p. Res.

1823 South st., Phil., Pa.

iv. KATHARINE T., b. Apr. 15, 1823 ; m. Jan. 29, 1849, Alex. J. Dougherty, June 15, 1826, d. Apr. 8, 1858. Res. West Chester, Pa. Ch.—Lucretia P., b. Nov. 1, 1849, m. Samuel Lewis. Res. West Chester.

173. v. WM. K., b. Sept. 19, 1832 ; m. Lizzie G. Miller.

105 PELEG[6] PEARCE (John[5], Nathaniel[4], George[3], George[2], Richard[1]), b. Jan. 31, 1804 ; m. Sarah Gray, b. Sept. 21, 1804, d. May 7, 1873. He d. Nov. 24, 1880. Res. Tiverton Four Corners, R. I. Ch.—

i. SAMUEL G., b. Dec. 27, 1723 ; m. 1854 Abby F. Homer. He d. Oct. 1, 1876, s. p.

ii. JOHN C., b. Oct. 4, 1829 ; m. 1852, Sarah Caswell ; m. 2d, 1860, Susan Lacy. He d. Dec. 9, 1884. Res. Tiverton Four Corners, R. I.

iii. BETSEY S., b. Nov. 9, 1827 ; d. May 4, 1832.

174. iv. ALEX. S., b. July 17, 1826 ; m. Ann W. Hambly.

v. ELERY G., b. Mar. 10, 1839 ; m. 1870 Louisa Clark. Res. San Francisco, Cal.

vi. ANN E., b. Mar. 30, 1841; m. Wm. Glazier.

vii. SARAH M., b. Sept. 6, 1844 , m. David Burges in 1862, and d. July 11, 1863. Res. New Bedford, Mass.

106 VAL.[6] PEARCE (Joseph[5], Nathaniel[4], George[3], George[2], Richard[1]), b. Oct. 14, 1799 ; m. Eliza Woodman, b. Sept. 13, 1800, d. Mar. , 1870. He d. Dec. 23, 1852. Res. Little Compton, R. I. Ch.—

175. i. BENJAMIN S., b. Aug. 30, 1827 ; m. Phebe A. Brayton.

ii. NATHANIEL W., b. Aug.28, 1831 ; d. May , 1832.

iii. GEORGE W., b. July 7, 1834 ; d. Jan. , 1853.

iv. OLIVER V., b. May 15, 1839.

107 JOSEPH[6] PEARCE (Joseph[5], Nathaniel[4], George[3], George[2], Richard[1]), b. Nov. 4, 1804 ; m. Feb. 29, 1832, Phebe Pearce [ ], b. May 23, 1813. He d. July 4, 1874. Res. Little Compton, R. I. Ch.—

176. i. HENRY C., b. Jan. 11, 1834 ; m. Catharine C. Chester.

ii. EMERSON P., b. Apr. 24, 1836 ; m. May 3, 1863, Kate McLeod, b Dec. 29, 1840. Res. 27 Hammond street, Providence, R. I., s. p

iii. DAVID H., b. May 6, 1838 ; m. Nov. 20, 1873, Lillian E. Rice, b. June 26, 1850 Res. 25 Division st., Provi- R. I., s. p.

iv. ALFRED G., b. Dec. 20, 1840 ; m. Oct. 3, 1870, Julia A. White. b. May 11, 1849. Res 104 Eddy street, Providence, R. I.

v. JOSEPH B., b. Aug. 28, 1843 ; m. Dec. 15, 1864, Cynthia R. Wilbur, b. Feb. 2, 1840. Res. Adamsville, R. I., s. p.

177. vi. Elery A., b. July 18, 1846 ; m. Leah M. Freeborn.
vii. James N., b. June 18, 1848 ; unm.
viii. Frank N., b. Nov. 5, 1851 ; unm.
ix. Geo. W., b. Nov. 19, 1853 ; m. Dec. 3, 1885, Ida D. Williams, b. Sept. 4, 1856. Res. Hills Grove, R. I., s. p.
x. Nannie A., b. May 6, 1856 ; unm. Res Adamsville, R. I.

108 Nathaniel[6] Pearce (Joseph[5], Nathaniel[4], George[3], George[2], Richard[1]), b. Dec. 19, 1809 ; Feb. 27, 1831, Bethany Brightman. He d. Apr. 12, 1878. Res. Little Compton, R. I. Ch —

i. Anna, H., b June 13, 1832 ; unm.
ii. Rachel A., b. Apr. 9, 1837 ; m. Apr. , 1874, Gardner T. Dean. Ch.—Robert A., b. Oct. 19, 1881. Res. L. C.
178. iii. Nathaniel A., b. Aug. 24, 1839 ; m. Mary T. Davis.
iv. Bethana B., b. Jan. 5, 1842 ; m. June 26, 1866, Robert A. Brown ; d. s. p., Jan. 25, 1877 ; m. 2nd, June 12, 1883, Philip H. Borden. Res. Fall River.
v. Catharine B., b. Nov. 30, 1844 ; d. Apr. 27, 1850.
179. vi. Orin F, b. June 26, 1847 ; m. Mary E. Blair.
vii. Chas H., b. Feb 18, 1854 ; m. July 5, 1884, Mary E. Tyler, s. p. Res. Fall River, Mass.

109 Godfrey[6] Pearce (Wright[5], James[4], James[3]. George[2], Richard[1]), b. Oct. 3, 1772 ; m. Sarah Simmons, b. Dec. 25, 1775, d. Apr. 2, 1856. He d. July 13, 1849. Res. Little Compton, R I. Ch.—

i. George S., b. Mar. 14, 1809 ; m. May 1, 1830, Harriett Barney; 2nd, July 12, 1846, Susannah F. Gore; and 3rd, Mary L. Gordridge. Res. s. p., Rantoul, Ill.
180. ii. James, b. July 6, 1802 ; m. Nancy Pearce [56-v.].
iii. Antrace, b. May 3, 1804; m. Val. Pearce.

110 Timothy[6] Pearce (Wright[5], James[4], James[3], George[2], Richard[1]), b. July 17, 1779 ; m. Sept. 14, 1805, Hannah Dennis ; and 2nd, ——— Wilbur. Res. Tiverton, R. I., and Madison, N. Y. They had nine children.

111 Thomas[6] Pearce (Wright[5], James[4], James[3], George[2], Richard[1]), b. Sept. 6, 1784 ; m. Feb. 26, 1810, Eliphal Tompkins, b. Mar. 15, 1790, d. Feb. 1, 1868. They res. in Little Compton, R. I., and town records say : "Thomas, the son of Wright Pearce and Austus, his wife, and Eliphal, the daughter of John Tompkins and Comfort, his wife, was joined in marriage Feb. 26, 1810." Ch.—

181. i. Abner T., b. Oct. 4, 1811 ; m. Sarah R. Briggs.
ii. Fred'k S., b. Mar. 30, 1813 ; m. Nov. 11, 1839, Lois M. Lee, b. June 25, 1815. Res., s. p., Fairhaven, Mass.
182. iii. Franklin, b. June 20, 1820 ; m. Elizabeth Najac.
iv. Geo. T., b. July 28, 1826. Res. San Francisco, Cal.

v. LOUISA, b. Oct. 22, 1815; m. ——— Barber. Res. Norwich, Ct.

vi. MARIA, b. Aug. 14, 1828; m. Sept, 24, 1848, David B. Grinnell, b. July 1826. Res. Fall River. Mass. Ch.—Harriett M., b. Sept. 15, 1849, d. May 12, 1865; Fred. A., b. May 18, 1853; Richard L., b. Aug. 21, 1858, m. Alzadah Cummings; Cora L., b. Sept. 1, 1862; m. Samuel R. Cory.

vii JOSEPH S. b. Apr. 22, 1818; m. Phebe Pearce [ ].

viii. JOHN T., b. Aug. 25, 1824; d. July 24, 1843.

112 GEORGE T.[6] PEARCE (Stephen[5], James[4], James[3], George[2], Richard[1]), b. Aug. 3, 1779; m. Mercy S. Simmons, b. July 17, 1784, d. Aug 5, 1845, at Richfield, N. Y. He d. Aug. 25, 1848, at Leonidas, Mich. Res. Paris, N. Y. Ch.—

183. i. ADDISON L., b. Apr. 3, 1807; m Sarah Stillwell.

184. ii. GAMALIEL, b. Aug. 27, 1808; m. Polly Brown.

iii. ABIGAIL T. b. June 6, 1810; m. Dec. 10, 1833, John J. Foote. Res. Harford, N. Y. Ch.—George, James, Charles, Algernon and Henry.

iv. MERCY, b. Feb. 20, 1812; m. Feb. 10, 1830, Nathaniel Tompkins, b. Aug. 23, 1810. Res. Paris, N. Y. She d. Feb. 19. 1837. Ch.—Julia S. b. Dec. 4. 1836, m. Wm. R. Damon and Geo. H. Knapp. Res. Centerville, Mich.

v. MARY, b. Apr. 12, 1813; m. May 26, 1836, John J. Foote [iii.].

vi. JULIETTE, b. May 26, 1815; m. Feb. 28, 1838, Nathaniel Tompkins [iv.]. Res. Harford, N. Y., and Centerville, Mich. Ch.—Rosetta, b. Dec. 1, 1839, d. July 5, 1866; Mary H., b. May 1, 1841, m. Peter Carr, res. Cimmarron, Kansas; Julius H., b. July 31, 1843, m. Ella Hopkins, res. Colon, Mich.; Mertie L., b. July 28, 1855, m. William H. White, res. Fulton, N. Y.; Laura J., b July 8, 1855, m. Peter Stout, res. Centerville; Elizabeth B., b. Aug. 24, 1853, m. Charles Wardsworth. Res. Leonidas, Mich.

vii. NANCY, b. Feb. 26, 1817; m. Oct. 16. 1839, Amasa Bemis. She d. Feb. 29 1849. Both are buried at Richford, Tioga Co., N. Y. Ch.—Clark, b. , 1841; d. Sept. 30, 1843. There were other children, but I cannot learn their names nor place of residence, if living. It is thought Mr. Bemis was born at Marathon, Cortland Co., N. Y. It is thought also that he is dead.

113 JAMES[6] PEARCE (Stephen[5], James[4], James[3], George[2], Richard[1]), b. Nov. 30, 1803; m. Mar. 4, 1824, Lucy Barnes, b. May 31, 1803, d. Sept. 3, 1856; m. 2nd, Nov. 5, 1857, Joanna Polleys, Res. Oriskany Falls, N. Y.

James Pearce (youngest son of Stephen Pearce and Abigail Taylor Pearce) was born at Paris Hill, Oneida Co., N.

Y., Nov. 30, 1803. In Sept., 1827, he was commissioned by Governor De Witt Clinton as lieutenant in the 20th regiment of New York infantay, which position he filled for several years. When the State canals were constructed, he engaged in the work as contractor, first on the Chenango and afterwards on the Erie canal, and these engagements took him to Syracuse, where he resided from 1840 to 1856, devoting much of his time to constructing various public works, as contractor and builder. He removed in 1856 to Horicon, Wisconson, where he resided until 1874, and where for several years he held the office of justice. He died August 5th, 1874, at Hastings, Nebraska, while on his way to visit his daughter in Colorado, and he was buried in the last named State, at Colorado Springs. Ch.—

i. Charles N., b. May 1, 1825 ; d. , 1826.
ii. Maria E., b. Feb. 8, 1828 ; m. Feb. 25, 1846, Garrett S. Barnes, b. Nov. 28, 1818 ; d. May 6, 1863. Res. Colorado Springs, Col. Ch.—James Pearce, b. Oct 31, 1847, m. J. Emily Hart, Horicon, Wis., June 18, 1868 ; Lucy Coburn, b. Feb. 6, 1852, m.. Reuben Spencer Barnes, Aug. 8, 1871 ; Etta Decker, b. Jan. 25, 1857 ; Perrit Smith, b. Dec. 6, 1860 ; Marion Oscar Barnes, b. Feb. 27, 1865 ; Irene Stillman, b. July 14, 1868, P. O., Colorado Springs, Colorado.
iii. Francis M., b. July 26, 1833 ; d. , 1837,
185. iv. James O., b. Feb. 3, 1836 ; m. Ada Butterfield.

114 Andrew T.[6] Pearce (Stephen[5], James[4], James[3], George[2], Richard[1]), b. June 16, 1793 ; m. July 5, 1818, Harriett Hale, d. Mar. 27, 1881. He d. June 22, 1840. Res. Sangerfield, N. Y. Ch.—

i. Randolph H., b. Mar. 9, 1821 ; m. Sept. 15, 1845, Mary A. Sweet. He d. New York, N. Y., s. p., Sept. 8, 1856.
ii. Harriett C., b. May 31, 1823 ; m July 27, 1847, Emery G. Bissell, b. Sept. 8, 1818, d. Oct. 12, 1857. Res. Waterville, N. Y.
186. iii. Wellington C., b. Aug. 12, 1825 ; m. Sarah Crandall.
iv. Helen J., b. Nov. 11, 1827 ; m. June 20, 1849, Charles B. Sperry. Res. Allen's Grove, Wis., and Beatrice, Neb. Ch.—Andrew P., b. May 16, 1853, m. Elsie M. Bescker ; Helen A., b. June 23, 1859, d. Sept. 8, 1860 ; Mary C. b. July 9, 1861 ; Harriett A., b. Aug. 21, 1866.
187 v. Albert A., b. Apr. 1, 1833 ; m. Lucinda R. Mott.

115 Benjamin[6] Pearce (John[5], James[4], James[3], George[2], Richard[1]), b. , 1780 ; m. Esther Hazard, b. 1780, d. Aug. , 1836. He d. Sept. 19, 1819. Res. Newport, R. I. Ch.—

188. i. Benjamin, b. Feb. 17, 1813 ; m. Susan P. Nickerson.
ii. Walter, b. , 1809 ; m. Sarah Slack. Res. Mobile, Ala., s. p.

189. iii. Geo. H., b. , 1809 ; m. Abby S. Pearce.
iv. Catherine H., b. , 1811 ; m. July 24, 1854, Aleck Q. Liscomb. Res. Cumberland, Ohio.
v. John, b. , 1815 ; d. , 1835.
vi. James A. H., b. 1817 ; m. Elizabeth B. Broughton. They res, in Norfolk, Va. He d. , 1837, leaving a son James.

116 Nathaniel[6] Pearce (Ezekiel[5], James[4], James[3], George[2] Richard[1],) b. April 12, 1800 ; m. Jan. 26, 1825, Clarissa Simmons, b. March 7, 1804, d. May 22, 1879. Res. Paris, N. Y. ; Dartford, Green, Lake Co., Wis. Ch.—
i. Susannah, b. Dec. 31, 1825 ; d. Feb. 27, 1850.
ii. Sarah C., b. Dec. 19, 1831 ; m. Oct. 8, 1850, Edward M. Clark, b. Oct. 15, 1812, d. April 26, 1884. Res. Graves, Cloud Co., Kansas. Ch.—John J., b. July 25, 1851, res. Maxwell, Cal.; Clara F., b. March 25, 1853, d. Oct. 19, 1853 ; Fanny J., b. July 3, 1854, d. Sept 15, 1854 ; Eugene F., b. Feb. 20, 1857 ; Duane M., b. M., b. Jun. 19, 1866 ; Herbert E., b. Oct. 28, 1868 ; Nathaniel J., b. Feb. 10, 1874, d. Sept. 5, 1874 ; Mamey F., b. Oct. 19, 1876.
190. iii. A. Simmons, b. Feb. 2, 1837 ; m. Clara A. Hall.
iv. Martha C., b. Feb. 26, 1827 ; unm.
191. v. Nathaniel, b. Nov. 22, 1829 ; m. Lydia E. White.
vi Mary E., b. Jan. 20, 1842, m. Aug. 9, 1841 ; Alonzo Krom, b. Aug. 9, 1841, div. Jan., 1871 ; m. 2nd, Aug. 5, 1877, Wm. S. Hitchcock, b. Aug. 18, 1823, res. Lebanon, Madison Co., N. Y. Ch.—Louise, b. March 28, 1868 ; Eunice C., b. July 20, 1878 ; Nathaniel J., b. Dec. 11, 1879.
vii. Emma, b. June 26, 1846 ; unm.
192. viii. J. Oscar, b. Oct. 27, 1827 ; m. Hannah M. Randall.

117 Val[6] Pearce (Ezekiel[5], James[4], James[3], George[2], Richard[1]), b. Jan. 28, 1791 ; m. Feb. 4, 1815, Mercy Simmons, b. Oct. 22, 1793, d. Nov. 23, 1819 ; m. 2nd, July , 1820, Catherine Boss, b. July 29, 1794, d. Aug. , 1845 ; m. 3rd, Sept. 26, 1846, Antrice Pearce, b. May 3, 1804. He d. May 29, 1879. Res. Cassville, N. Y. Ch.—

i. Angeline, b. May 7, 1817 ; m. Aug. 21, 1836, Joshua P. Tompkins, b. Dec. 22, 1814. Res. Cassville, N. Y. Ch.—Mary L., b. Jan. 20, 1838, m. July 12, 1861, d. June 18, 1862 ; Mary S., b. Apr. 25, 1842, m. Chas. Chapman, Dec. 25, 1860, res. Cassville, N. Y.; Nancy M., b. Nov. 7, 1843 ; Clara B. b. Dec. 12, 1850, d. Jan. 24, 1852 ; Herbert A., b. June 27, 1853, d. Nov. 11, 1854 ; Chas. H., b. Feb. 24, 1856, res. Cassville.
ii. Mercy S., b. Oct. 29, 1819 ; m. Apr. 3, 1844, Thomas Bosworth, b. May 29, 1823. Res. Cortland, N. Y. Ch.—Francis L., b. June 24, 1845 ; Adelbert D., b. July 29,

1848; Maria D., b. Aug. 26, 1850; Ella J., b. Apr. 7, 1853, m. ——— Jones, res. Waterville, N. Y.; Lillian A., b. June 7, 1855; Byron J., b. Nov. 15, 1857, d. Mar. 27, 1880; Hubert E., b. Apr. 15, 1860, res. Cortland, N. Y.; Clara P., b. Oct. 19, 1862, res. Cortland, N. Y.

iii. SARAH, b. Oct. 28, 1821; m. Dec. 3, 1838, James Tompkins; b. May 7, 1819. Res. Appleton, Wis. Ch.—Jane A., b. Feb. 3, 1839, m. ——— Mills, Feb. 21, 1860, res. Hortonville, Wis.; Maria L., b. June 30, 1846, m. ——— Babcock, Apr. 7, 1868, res. Appleton, Wis.; Loretta C., b. May 3, 1849, m. ——— Babcock, Nov. 13, 1867, res. Appleton, Wis.; Helen P., b. Sept. 7, 1851, m. ——— Clark, Dec. 4, 1879, res. White Lake, Dak.; Sarah A., b. ———, 1850, d. ———, 1860; Henrietta E., b. Mar. 6, 1855, m. ——— Usher, Dec. 13, 1871, 2nd, E. E. Thompson; Cornelia I., b. July 28, 1858, d. Aug. 13, 1881; Nabby O., b. June 5, 1863, m. ——— Thompson, June 28, 1882, res. White Lake, Dak.

iv. PAULINA, b. Mar. 24, 1828; m. Oct. 1, 1862, Forbes Head, b. Feb. 17, 1828; d. Jan. 1, 1883; m. 2nd, Mar. 12, 1884, Wm. Hadcock, b. May 12, 1818. Res. New Hartford, N. Y.

v. CATHERINE, b. Nov. 9, 1833; unm. Res. Cassville, N. Y.

118 PARDON S.[6] PEARCE (Ichabod[5], James[4], James[3], George[2] Richard[1]), b. Dec. 3, 1792, m. June 11, 1818, Mary Gray Boyd, b. Feb. 9, 1798, d. Mar. 21, 1878. Res. Providence, R. I. He was a pattern maker by trade, attended the universalist church and was a republican in politics. He d. Mar. 24, 1875. Ch.—

i. SARAH G. b. 1819.
ii. PHEBE A., b. 1820, m. Samuel M. Willard.
193. iii. WILLIAM J. b. 1822, d. 1871.
194. iv. SAMUEL B. b. 1826, m. Susan J. Anthony.
v. JOHN S. b. 1828, d. 1868.
195. vi. EDMUND S., b. ———, 1832; m. Jan. 16, 1874, Mary A. Mossey, b. ———, 1851. He d. s. p. July 13, 1877. Res. Providence, R. I.
vii. MARY E., b. ———, 1836.
viii. CLARENCE H., b. Oct. , 1840; d. Feb. , 1885.

119 WILLIAM[6] PEARCE (James[5], James[4], James[3], George[2], Richard[1]), b. June 7, 1766; m. July , 1790, Eleanor Pearce [ ], b. Jan. 5, 1769; d. Jan. 22, 1834. He d. May 15, 1846. Res. Little Compton, R. I. He served in the Revolutionary army through that war and at its close was a corporal of a Rhode Island company. Ch.—

i. JONATHAN E., b. May 28, 1791; d. June 7, 1814.
196. ii. HENRY L., b. Apr. 30, 1793; m. Haity T. Pearce.
197. iii. PARKER H., b. Dec. 11, 1794; m. Hannah Withington.

iv. HARRIETT, b. June 14, 1799 ; m. ——— Brownell. She d. Sept. 7, 1864, leaving one son, Homer, who res. in Battle Creek, Mich.

198. v. BENJAMIN F. b. July 2, 1801 ; m. Rowena Hills.

vi. CYRUS E., b. Feb. 24, 1809. Went to Chili, S. A. ; m. and d. leaving quite a family. He d. at sea, enrote to France in 1864.

120 BENJAMIN[6] PEARCE, (James[5] James[4], James[3], George[2], Richard[1]), b. May 19, 1784, m. Aug. 19, 1810, Sarah Pearce [ ] b. Apr. 27, 1788, d Jan. 7, 1866. He d. Aug. 10 1869. Res. Little Compton, R. I. Ch.—

i. WRIGHT, b. Feb. 9, 1818. Has a son James E, res. Little Compton.

199. ii. JAMES P. b. May 4, 1819, m. Lucy Blake and Margaret J. Palmer.

200 iii. ROUSE b. June 18, 1826, m. Comfort M. ——— and Deborah Bower.

iv. BENJAMIN, b. May, , 1822. Res. Little Compton, R. I.

v. PHEBE, b. May 22, 1813, m. Joseph Pearce [ ].

vi. SOPHIA, b. Aug. 14, 1811, res. Portsmouth, R. I.

vii. SARAH, b. Nov. 3, 1820.

viii. BENJAMIN, b. Nov. 18, 1815, d. Dec. 4, 1815.

ix. MARY, b. Aug. 20, 1824, d. Oct. 3, 1824.

121 GILES[6] PEARCE, (James[5], James[4], James[3], George[2], Richard[1]), b. Feb. 2, 1778, m. Dec. 22, 1799, Sarah Champlin. Res. Newport, R. I. Ch.—

i. BARTON, b. Sept. 1, 1800.

ii. MARY, A. b. Jan. 26, 1804.

iii. PHEBE, b. Mar 11, 1805.

iv. SUSAN, b, Mar. 8, 1811.

122 GILES[6], PEARCE, (James[5], Giles[4], James[3], George[2], Richard[1],) b. Apr. 1, 1794, m. Nov. 20, 1817, Content Hall, b. Jan. 26, 1799, d. Sept. 22, 1871. ' He d. July 30, 1858, res. Berea and Scipio, Ohio. Ch.—

i. JOHN O. b. Nov. 9, 1818, res. Endicott, Neb.

201 ii. JAMES B. b. Feb. 20, 1822, m. Jane A. Thompson.

iii. LUCIUS, b. Mar. 17, 1824, d. Dec. 12, 1848.

iv. AMANDA, b. Jan. 16, 1826, m. Nov. 1, 1851, Aaron Schuyler, res. Berea, Ohio.

v. CLARA H. b. July 1, 1829, unm. res. Berea, Ohio.

vi. WM. H. b. July 20, 1833, m. June. 17, 1873, Sarah A. Watson, b, Aug. 29, 1836, res., s. p. Oberlin, Ohio.

202. vii. ORLANDO, b. Aug. 11, 1836, m. Susan Dwire aud Mary A. Dwire.

viii. LYDIA M. b. Oct. 30, 1836, d. Mar. 17, 1842.

ix. GEO. B, b. June 17, 1842, d. Dec. 27, 1842.

123 ABEL[6] S. PEARCE, (James[5], Giles[4], James[3], George[2], Richard[1]), b. Feb. 7, 1805, m. Apr. 3, 1833, Samuel Herring, b. June 30, 1810. He d. Apr. 1, 1872. Res. Auburn, Ind. Ch.—

i. CHARLES W. b. Sept. 20, 1833, res. Auburn, Ind.
ii. ANN M., b. May 4, 1836, m. July 3, 1851, Simson Brooks. He d. Feb. 1881, res. Centralia, Wis.
iii. JAMES E. b. June 2, 1839, m. Mar. 17, 1870, Ada C. Ruth. He d. Feb. 25, 1880, res. Auburn, Ind.
iv. LINDON J. b. May 15, 1846.
v. SARAH C. b. Nov. 9, 1842, m. July 4, 1859 Nelson D. Gregg, b. Apr. 4, 1837, res. Defiance Ohio. Ch.— Sylvester J. b. July 15, 1861; Ida L. b. June 16, 1867; John A. b. Jan. 6, 1871; Ora L. b. Oct. 17, 1874; Addie L. b. Feb. 3, 1877.
vi. HARRIET C. b Mar. 4, 1839, d. June 3, 1868.
vii. GEORGE W. b. Aug. 22, 1843, d. Dec. 23, 1845.

124 SANFORD[6] PEARCE, (Samuel[5], Samuel[4], James[3], George[2], Richard[1]), b. Apr. 23, 1789, m. Oct. 1811, Lydia Sherman, d. June 1819. He d. Dec. 1818. Res. Plainfield, Ct. Sanford the second of Samuel and Ruth (Martin) Pearce was born in Little Compton, R. I. in 1789. Like his father he was a builder and contractor. His wife was a daughter of Job Sherman a member of the Society of Friends. In 1816, he moved to Plainfield, Conn., his family at that time consisting of his mother, wife one sister and two children. Ch.—

203. i. ALLEN S. b. Sept. 2, 1816, m. Almina Wright.
204. ii. GEO. W. b, Oct. 23, 1812, m. Emeline Porter.
iii. ALLEN H. b. , 1815, d. , 1816.

125 DR. JOSEPH[6], PEARCE, (Jeremiah[5], Samuel[4], James[3], George[2], Richard[1]), b. July 31, 1785, m. 2nd. Mary Carey. In 1815, he res. in Ashtabula, Ohio. He d. Nov. 24, 1840 in Angola, Ind. Dr. Joseph was born in Fairfield, New York, was educated at the public schools of his native town and the Fairfield Academy. He graduated at the Medical School and after receiving his diploma removed to Indiana where he settled, lived and died. Ch.—

i. NARCISSA m. ———, Eliot, res. Cleveland, Ohio.
ii. MARY A. m. ———, Gabe, res. Angola, Ind.
iii. SARAH m. Dr. Slosser. She and her husband died in the Hospital service during the war.
iv. LAURA.

126 GEORGE[6] PEARCE, (Jeremiah[5], Samuel[4], James[3], George[2], Richard[1]), b. May 14, 1803, m. May 27, 1828, Sophronia Haskins, b. Feb. 10, 1806, d. Oct. 20, 1871. He d. June 24, 1878. Res. Little Falls, N. Y. George was born in Fairfield, New York where he was educated and raised. He lived on the old homestead and continued raising grain and stock, also making butter and cheese until his working energies began to fail, when he disposed of his farm and moved to Little Falls, where he built a fine house, in which he lived, and died in 1877, about 75 years of age. George Pearce aside from his home business held several town offices as well as in church, and was universally respected by all who knew him, Ch—

205. i. JAMES B., b. Aug. 31, 1829 ; m. Charlotte White.
ii. MARIA, b. Feb. 12, 1832; m. June 23, 1861, Irving W. Haskins, b. Aug. 1332, s. p., res. Little Falls, N. Y.
iii. LAURA H. b. Mar. 27, 1834, d. Aug. 31, 1852.

127 JOHN[6] PEARCE (John[5], Samuel[4], James[3], George[2], Richard[1]), b. May 28, 1802 ; m. Oct. 2, 1825, Mary T. Hale, b. ——, 1806, d. Sept. 11, 1871 ; m. 2nd, June 22, 1873, Mary H. Jones. Res. Warren, R. I. He d. Apr. 7, 1876. Ch.—

i. MARY L., b. ——, 1827 ; unm. Res. Warren, R. I.
ii. ANNIE, b. Sept. 14, 1833 ; m. Samuel Fales. She d. Dec. 7, 1871. Res. Warren.
206. JOHN H., b. Dec. 6, 1837 ; m. Henrietta S. Simmons.
iv. GEORGE, b. Sept. 30, 1840 ; d. Aug. 5, 1847.

128 COL. SAMUEL[6] PEARCE (John[5], Samuel[4], James[4], George[2] Richard[1]), b. Dec. 20, 1810 ; m. Oct. 27, 1833, Elizabeth H. Chase. Res. Warren, R. I. Ch.—

i. ELIZABETH H., b. Aug. 1, 1834 ; unm. Res. Warren.
ii. LAURA, b. Aug. 6, 1836 ; unm. Res. Warren.
iii. JAMES, b. ——, 1838 ; d. Dec. 17, 1868.
iv. SARAH, b. ——, 1841 ; d. Aug. 3, 1857.
v. ANNIE ; m. Wm. Burgess.

129 GEORGE A.[7] PEARCE (Nathaniel[6], Richard[5], Nathaniel[4], Richard[3], Richard[2], Richard[1]), b. Oct. 19, 1788 ; m. Jan. 1, 1809, Lucretia Carpenter, b. Sept. 15, 1789, d. May 3, 1874. Res. Rehoboth and Monson, Mass.

207. i. NATHANIEL, b. Feb. 25, 1817 ; m. Sylvia W. Bates.
208. ii. SANFORD R., b. Oct. 4, 1819 ; m. Betsey Fairbrother.
iii. MARY R., b. June 18, 1815. Res. Pawtucket, R. I.
iv. WM. H., b. Sept. 27, 1812. Res. 8 Melrose street, Providence, R. I.
v. AUGUSTUS F., b. Dec. 15, 1809. Res. 119 East 72nd st., New York city, N. Y.

130 ALBERT S.[7] PEARCE (Nathaniel[6], Richard[5], Nathaniel[4], Richard[3], Richard[2], Richard[1]), b. Apr. 1, 1804 ; m. Sept 1, 1831, Mary S. Bradford, b. June 29, 1813. He d. Aug. 20, 1878. Res. Bristol, R. I.

From a brief obituary notice of Albert S. Pearce, Sr., published in the BRISTOL PHŒNIX, 1873, I extract the following : "In the death of Albert S. Pearce (which occurred on Monday, August 20), aged 74 years, Bristol la ments the loss of one of her old and most estimable citizens. Descended from a distinguished and pious ancestry, having as his maternal grandfather Rev. Robert Rogerson,* (Harvard University, A. M. 1765) of Rehoboth, Mass., and connected by marriage with the lineal descendeuts of Governors Bradford of Plymouth Colony, and of R. I. (the former of whom came over in the Mayflower), he attaches no undue importance to this family distinction, but was eminently a self-made man, and the architect† *literally* of his own fortune. Above all he was a sincere and consistent Christian, an office-bearer in the Congregational church, at one time superintendent of the Sabbath school and leader of the choir, for which service he was well adapted, having a decided musical taste and ability, the latter position he occupied when working at his trade, as a young man, in Cincinnati, what was then the far west. Here he was the first among his fellow workmen to sign the temperance pledge, and advocate the temperance cause, when to do so subjected the individual to opposition and ridicule. He was especially fond of Dr. Watts' version of Psalms and Hymns, which he often quoted and sang, and which he considered next to inspired ; these he was many times heard repeating in his sickness, and which were undoubtedly a solace in his hours of suffering. He had a rich vein of humor, which exhibited itself in anecdote, always apt, and at the same time evinced the possession of peculiarly fine and tender feelings when the occasion called for them. He was a dutiful son (losing his parents at an early age, he was brought up by an uncle), an affectionate husband, father, brother (though his constitution was never robust, outliving his family of brothers and sisters by many years), a kind neighbor and friend.

The immediate cause of Mr. Pearce's decease was a painful accident (requiring a severe surgical operation, which, however, proved unsuccessful in saving his life), and accompanied with great suffering, protracted for several months, borne with Christian patience and submission, and alleviated by the untiring attentions of relatives, neighbors and friends. His end was calm and peaceful. To his bereaved widow and children, and the large circle of kindred, he has left the best legacy—his own pious example. His funeral was attended by his pastor, Rev. Mr. Lane. His former pastor, the venerable Dr. Shepard, also, though feeble, was able to be present on the occasion. (Mr. Pearce was born in Rehoboth, Mass., April 1, 1804. A portion of his married life was spent in Erie, Pa.)."

---

* Born in Great Britain, and pastor of the Cong. Ch. in Rehoboth, Mass. about forty-two years.

† Mr. P. was for several years a house carpenter.

Ch.—

i. Marian R., b. Mar. 5, 1837 ; m. Oct. 23, 1872, Prof. Edward W. Robbins, b. May 17, 1822, s. p. Res. Kensington, Ct.

From a genealogical chart of this branch of the "Robbins Family," compiled by the late Dr. Daniel P. Holton of N. Y. city, published a year two since, and dedicated to the subject's grandfather—Capt. Elisha Robbins of Wethersfield, Conn., I extract the following :*

"Edward Wright Robbins oldest son of the late Rev. Royal and Martha (Wright) Robbins, b. May 17, 1822, at (Kensington) Berlin, Conn., m. Bristol, R. I., Oct. 23, 1872, Marian Rogerson Pearce, b. March 5, 1837, Bristol, dau. Albert S. Pearce and Mary S. (Bradford) of B. Mr. R. grad. (Yale, 1843, A. M., 1846), studied law, but owing to delicate health was not admitted to the bar ; has been engaged in teaching in private and boarding schools, and as Prof. in Conn. State Normal and High School, also in various literary pursuits, contributor to several periodicals and magazines, in prose and verse--of the latter has a volume (in print and ms.) designed for publication. In 1870–71 he made an extensive tour abroad, visiting many of the countries of Europe, Lower Egypt (including the pyramids of Gheeseh), Suez, Palestine, Syria, Damascus, Baalbek, and other places and objects of historical interest, with a visit to Constantinople and Athens, and an excursion through a portion of the Pelopennesus. The results of his observations, during this fourteen months tour, revised from notes taken on the spot, he has prepared for the press. Mr. R. has been president of the Linonian Society, and editor of the Yale Lit. Magazine, is a member of the "Psi Upsilon Fraternity," the "Scroll and Key," and other societies, and a contributor to the "New Englander," and the "Songs of Yale." He is still living in the place of his birth, and is occupied in rural, educational and literary pursuits.*

209. ii. J. Russell, b. Dec. 30, 1850 ; m. Isabella Kirkwood.

iii. Wm. B., b. Sept. 30, 1832 ; d Sept. 2, 1845.

iv. Marion, b. Nov. 11, 1834 ; d. Dec. 11, 1835.

---

* I have changed or added a paragraph for the sake of making the sketch more complete.

* Mr. R.'s latest publication is a pamphlet entitled "Historical Sketch of (Kensington)," Berlin, Conn. During the last one hundred years an address delivered by request at the Congregational church in that place July 4, 1876, by Edward W. Robbins; A. M., (first published by request in the Kensington "Church Record," vol. 1, 1885–6) New Britain, Conn., Press of Wm. A. House, 1886." Mr. R. has delivered, among others, an illustrated lecture on the "Egyptian Campaign, including Reminiscences of an American Traveler in Egypt.' This also he has in Ms. A lecture on "Greece, Old and New." He is a member of the Connecticut Historical Society.

v. ALBERT S., b. May 15, 1840 ; unm. Res. Bristol, R. I.
vi. FRED'K P., b. Aug. 11, 1848 ; m. July 19, 1873, Ellen F. Wilson, b. Dec. 15, 1851. He d. s. p. Bristol, R. I., Dec. 30, 1881.
210. vii. EDWARD B., b. Feb. 1, 1843 ; m. Mary J. Coffin.

131 GILES D.[7] PEARCE (Robert[6], Richard[5], Nathaniel[4], Richard[3], Richard[2], Richard[1]), b. Dec. 16, 1809 ; m. Mar. 28, 1847, Eliza Wheaton, b. Mar. 11, 1825, d. Aug. 4, 1877. He. d. Apr. 13, 1882. Res. Rehoboth, Mass. Ch.—

i. SARAH F., b. Sept. 20, 1848 ; d. July 14, 1877.
ii. WILLIAM P., b. Dec. 29, 1851 ; d. Nov. 21, 1878.
211. iii. EDWIN S., b. May 26, 1856 ; m. Charlotte C. Apt.
iv. GEORGE W., b. Feb. 14, 1857 ; d. Oct. 20, 1858.
v. FANNIE B., b. July 19, 1860.
vi. GEORGE W.. b. Nov. 10, 1862 ; d. Aug. 20, 1871.

132 JAMES HENRY[7] PEARCE (Robert[6], Richard[5], Nathaniel[4], Richard[3], Richard[2], Richard[1]), b. May 29, 1818 ; m. Jan. 10, 1843, Mary A. Brown, b. Jan. 4, 1825. Res. De Witt, Iowa. Ch.—

i. ELIZABETH A., b. June 26, 1844.
ii. JAMES G., b. Jan. 9, 1846.
iii. WILLIAM C., b. Oct. 22, 1848. Res. N. Y. city.
iv. WALTER E., b. Sept. 13, 1858.

133 ROBERT M.[7] PEARCE (Robert[6], Richard[5], Nathaniel[4], Richard[3], Richard[2], Richard[1]), b. Oct. 27, 1803 ; m. Lucy C. Blanding, b. May 23, 1813. Res. 399 Pine street, Providence, R. I. Ch.—

i. MARY B., b. Dec. 21, 1839 ; m. Sept. 25, 1872, Francis L. Hill, b. Nov. 26, 1841. She d. Mar. 26, 1873, s. p. Res. Rehoboth, Mass.
ii. ROBERT R., b. Dec. 14, 1841 ; m. Ruth A. Kent.
iii. ELIZA P., b. Jan. 10, 1844.
212. iv. CHRISTOPHER B., b. Apr. 30, 1847.

134 HON. GEORGE[7] PEARCE (William[6], George[5], William[4], Richard[3], Richard[2], Richard[1]), b. Nov. 14, 1787 ; m. Sept. 12, 1812, Elizabeth T. Childs, b. Mar. 31, 1792, d. Dec. 16, 1854. He d. May 12, 1862. Res. Swansea, Mass.

Died, in Swansea, Mass., May 12th, 1862, at the residence of his son, William H. Pearce, George Pearce, of this town (Bristol, R. I.), in the 74th year of his age.

OBITUARY—DEATH OF A PROMINENT CITIZEN.

We are again called upon to announce the death of another aged and valuable citizen, Hon. George Pearce, who died at the residence of his son, William Henry Pearce, in Swansea, Mass., on Monday last (May 12th, 1862), in the 75th year of his age.

Mr. Pearce was known to the public as the proprietor of the Bristol ferry (from the mainland to the Island of R. I.) for nearly thirty years past, having succeeded his father, the late William Pearce, Esq., in that place.

He took a prominent part in the affairs of town and state, and was for many years a very useful member of the Town Council, and also represented this town in both branches of the State Legislature. He was a leading member of the Episcopal church, having become a communicant as an early age, and ever continued to adorn his profession by a well-ordered life Godly conversation. His seat was seldom vacant in the sanctuary and his voice was often heard in prayer and exhortation in the conference room. Mr. Pearce, in consequence of failing health, disposed of his interest in the ferry estate a bout three years since, subsequently residing with his children in different parts of the State. On Wednesday afternoon last the funeral services of the deceased were held at St. Michael's church, Rev. Mr. Stowe conducting the exercises. His remains were intered in Juniper Hill Cemetery.—From Bristol *Pheonix* of May 17, 1862.

BRISTOL, R. I., *May* 14, 1862.

At a meeting of the Wardens and Vestry of St. Michael's Church, held in St. Michael's Chapel, this day at 12 o'clock, the following preamble and resolutions submitted by a committee appointed at a previous meeting of the Vestry were received and unanimously adopted.

It having pleased Almighty God in His wise Providence to take from us to his reward in Heaven, Mr. George Pearce who for eighteen years filled the office of Warden in St. Michael's Church, we the Wardens and Vestry of said Church, unanimously adopt the following resolutions, as expressions of our appreciation of his worth and respect for his memory.

Resolved, That we recognize in this event the hand of our Father in Heaven, and bow in humble submission to His holy will.

Resolved, That we bear testimony to the strong affection for the Church manifested by our deceased brother, the fidelity with which he discharged the various trusts committed to him, and the humble piety for which he was so distinguished.

Resolved, That we tender to the family of the deceased, our heartfelt sympathy in this their season of sorrow, and commend them to that God, who alone can sustain and comfort them.

Resolved, That as a token of respect we attend the funeral of our departed brother, and walk in procession to the grave.

Resolved, That these resolutions be communicated to the family of our deceased brother and published in the Bristol *Pheonix*, and *Christian Witness*.—[From Bristol *Pheonix* of May 17, 1862.

Died at Bristol Ferry, on Saturday, 16th inst. (Dec. 1854), Mrs. Elizabeth Tripp Pearce, wife of Hon. Geo. Pearce, in the 63d year of her age.

The memory of the deceased will be affectionately cherished by a large circle of friends who sympathize with the bereaved husband and family in their affliction. Mrs. Pearce had been for about forty years a worthy communicant of the Protestant Episcopal church, having been baptized and confirmed by the late venerable Bishop Griswold, then the beloved rector of St. Michael's church, Bristol. She has ever since adorned her profession by a consistent and exemplary Christain life, abounding in those meek and quiet virtues which though less observed constitute so much to the honor of the Gospel and the happiness of social life. She was an affectionate and devoted wife and mother, an amiable, confiding and faithful friend, charitable to the poor, and liberal in every good work. Her decline was gradual and lingering, but she was patient and unmurmuring. Although aware of her situation, death had for her no terrors. She said but little on the subject of a separation, being apparently sustained by a tender regard for the feelings of her afflicted family. Unaffected by disease, her death seemed the result of a premature decay of the physical system ; and when at last exhausted nature ceased to act she breathed her life out, as she had always lived, quietly and peacefully falling asleep in Jesus : " Blessed are the dead who die in the Lord ; even so saith the Spirit, for they rest from their labors."—Rev. Geo. W. Hathway in *Christian Witness*. Ch.—

213. i. WILLIAM H. b. June 15, 1813, m. Roseamey H. Gardner.

ii. ELIZABETH A. b. Mar. 19, 1815, m. Nov. 2, 1835, William A. Richmond, b May 4, 1810, d. Mar. 16, 1879. Ch.— Anna A. b. Aug. 7, 1836, m. Capt. Charles H. Norris; Ruth P. b. Oct. 31, 1831, d. Feb. 2, 1840, res. Fresno, California.

iii. MARY, b. Apr. 10, 1819, m. Nov. 3, 1835, Dr. Charles Gardner, b. Apr. 10, 1812, d. May 1, 1882. She d. Nov. 28, 1878, res. Dixon Ill. Ch.— Mary Augusta, b. Jan. 6, 1837, m. June 20, 1855, Jas. A. Hawley, res. Dixon, Ill.; Elizabeth Pathima b. June 26, 1840, d. May 29, 1845; George Henry b. Sept. 20, 1842, d. Oct. 3, 1843 ; Seraphine Francis b. Jan. 14, 1846, m. Eli C. Smith, res. Dixon, Ill.; George Pearce b. Jan. 30, 1848, d. Mar. 24, 1865; Hannah Elizabeth b. Feb. 19, 1852, d. Aug. 8, 1872; Charles Henry b. Apr. 16, 1854, m. Virginia Heaton, res. Dixon, Ill.; William Francis b.

Apr. 7, 1856, m. Margaret Sheffield, res. Dixon, Ill.; Joseph Henry, b. May 3, 1858, d. Aug. 26, 1858.

Mrs. Mary Pearce Gardner, wife of Dr. Charles Gardner who resides about six miles east of this city died Thursday, Nov. 28, 1878, aged sixty-two years. Mrs. Gardner has not enjoyed good health for a year or more, but still her death was a shock to the community, especially old residents of this vicinity, who have known her so long and respected her so highly. With her husband, Dr. Gardner, the deceased settled upon the farm in South Nachusa in 1833, removing from Bristol, Rhode Island. Her children, Mrs. Jas. A. Hawley, Mrs. E. C. Smith and Charles Gardner, of this city, as well as her husband, all have the heartfelt sympathy of our people in this their sad bereavment.—[Dixon, Ill. *Telegraph.*

Dr. Charles Gardner died at his residence near Chamberlin, Dakota, May 1, 1882. Deceased was born in Swansea, Mass., Apr. 10, 1812, and was therefore a little more than seventy years of age. Though born on the shores of the Atlantic, and dying on the banks of the Missouri, just one year from the date of his settling there, Dr. Gardner belonged to Dixon, Ill., and there will his memory be cherished for generations to come.

He went to Dixon a young man, only 26 years of age when the country was new and wild, and to him is due much of the change which has given to our broad treeless prairie, the tree embroidered homes that dot and crown its beauty.

Public spirited, generous, intelligent and warm hearted, Dr. Gardner sought earnestly for the general good in every way. He was always ready, too, to lend a helping hand to every needy individual. The "blessed physician" to countless numbers, the almost father to homeless, friendless ones, the kindly gentleman and the deep conscientious Christian friend to all. He will be sadly missed, and deeply mourned.

iv. Joseph C. b. Aug. 19, 1819, d. unm. Mar. 1857.

v. Hannah, b. June 23, 1821, m. Oct. 22, 1844, Albert Robinson, b. July 8, 1812, d. Nov. 30, 1856, m. 2nd, Sept. 1859, William G. Kenyon, res. Wakefield, R. I. Ch.—Albert C. b. Aug. 5, 1854, m. Aug. 7, 1886. Maria B. Blackington, res. Wakefield, R. I.; George P. b. Sept. 15, 1856.

vi. Frances C. b. Apr. 6, 1826, m. Oct 16, 1855, Charles Chase, b. Feb. 2, 1824, res. Bristol, R. I. Ch.— Charles F. b. Oct, 23, 1856, res. 65 Westminster St., Providence, R. I.; Geo. C. b. Aug. 16, 1859, res. Kingston, Grant county, New Mexico; William P. b. Feb. 17, 1864, d. Sept. 27, 1864.

vii. REBECCA C. b. June 26, 1832, m. Feb.. 13, 1855, Daniel Gorham, b. June 14, 1825, d. Feb. 14, 1861; m. 2nd, Apr. 16, 1873, Eliza Watson, b. Oct. 8, 1808, d. May 31, 1877, s. p. res. Wakefield, R. I. Ch.— Anginette E. b. May 20, 1857; Elizabeth C. b. Aug. 18, 1859, d. July 24, 1868; Rebecca, b. May 27, 1861.

214. viii. GEORGE E. b. Jan. 25, 1824, m. Mary N. Robinson.

135 WILLIAM⁷ PEARCE, (William⁶, George⁵, William⁴, Richard³, Richard², Richard¹), b. Mar. 8, 1798, m. Mary Coit. Res. Swansea, Mass. He d. Nov. 2, 1865. Ch.—

215. i. WILLIAM, b. , m. Harriet F. Cook.

136 GEORGE T.⁷ PEARCE, (Richard S.⁶, William⁵, Thomas⁴, Jeremiah³, Richard², Richard¹), b. Feb. 7, 1837, m. Nov. 6, 1866, Martha Moor, b. Oct. 25, 1850, d. Oct. 7, 1869, m. 2nd, Dec. 22, 1870, Sarah J. Pearce, b. July 14, 1841. Res. 2, Elm St. Worcester, Mass. Ch.—

i. NELLIE M. b. Oct. 25, 1868.
ii. NELLIE F. b. Sept. 19, 1871.

137 RICHARD S.⁷ PEARCE JR., (Richard S.⁶, William⁵, Thomas⁴, Jeremiah³, Richard², Richard¹), b. Apr. 2, 1839, m. Oct. 20, 1872, Addie F. Sweet, b. Nov. 30, 1849. Res. 2633, Pleasant Avenue, Minneapolis, Minn. Ch.—

i. RAY, b. Feb. 8, 1874.
ii. MAYBELL, b. Dec 12, 1879.
iii. ADDIE, b. Aug. 23, 1878.

138 OLIVER C.⁷ PEARCE, (Richard S.⁶, William⁵, Thomas⁴, Jeremiah³, Richard², Richard¹), b. Apr. 10, 1848, m. Sept. 19, 1871, Mary T. Fowler, b. Oct. 29, 1856. Res. Bristol, R. I. Ch.—

i. HATTIE E. b. Oct. 18, 1873.
ii. LYDIA F. b. Dec. 1, 1882.
iii. LEVI, b. July 6, 1876.

139 WILLIAM T.⁷ PEARCE, (Thomas⁶, William⁵, Thomas⁴, Jeremiah³, Richard², Richard¹), b. Apr. 20, 1846, m. Sept. 27, 1871, Hannah B. Briggs. Res. Bristol, R. I. Ch.—

i. WILLIAM E. b. July 16, 1872.

140 MARTIN⁷ PEARCE, (Jeremiah⁶, Jeremiah⁵, Giles⁴, Jeremiah³, Giles², Richard¹), b. Apr. 12, 1784, m. Feb. 13, 1814, Freelove Boyd, d. Aug. 16, 1840. He d. , 1829. Res. East Greenwich, R. I. Ch.—

216. i. THOMAS A. b. Sept. 2, 1815, m. Thankful G. Crandall.
ii. WILLIAM M. b. Nov. 5, 1820, d. Aug. 1876.
iii. FREELOVE A. b. , 1817, m. ——— Marsey, removed to Illinois.

iv. MARY E. b. Feb. 27, 1826, m. June 15, 1845, Milton Cady, d. 1856, m. 2nd, Jan. 27, 1870, Caleb Young, b. Oct. 25, 1818, res. Yansevoort, Saratoga Co., N. Y. Ch.— Lucy A. b. May 17, 1847, m. Nov. 2, 1871, Almond Freeman, res. Saratoga Springs, N. Y.

141 GEORGE[7] PEARCE, (Giles[6], George[5], Giles[4], Jeremiah[3], Giles[2], Richard[1]), b. Mar. 5, 1786, m. Sept. 10, 1812, Lydia Littlefield, b. May 3, 1794, d. Sept. 28, 1873. He d. Feb. 11, 1872. Res. New Troy, Mich. Ch.—

217. i. WILLIAM S. b. Oct. 16, 1814, m. Almyra Hill.
218. ii. PITT J. b. Nov. 10, 1816, m. Mary Hill.
iii. DOUGLASS, b. Sept. 20, 1820, d. unm
iv. SANDERS, b. Oct. 14, 1818, d. unm.
v. LYDIA, b. Sept. 18, 1824, d. unm.
vi. PIZZARO, b. Aug. 25, 1828, d. unm.
219. vii. GEORGE, b. Aug. 19, 1822, m. Cordelia A. Stetson.

142 JOSEPH A.[7] PEARCE (Giles[6], George[5], Giles[4], Jeremiah[3], Giles[2], Richard[1]), b. Jan. 15, 1805 ; m. June 10, 1827, Rachel C. Morse, b. June 28, 1808. He d. Mar. 30, 1885. Res. Hamburg, N. Y. Ch.—

i. MARY A. b. May 29, 1828, unm. Res. Hamburg, N. Y.
ii. WM. H. b. Feb. 28, 1830, m. Oct. 7, 1849. Res. Hamburg, N. Y.
iii. LUCIA M. b. Jan. 1, 1832, m. Aug. 7, 1855, William Hoag. She d. Oct. 27, 1863. Ch.— Allen K. b. Jan. 12, 1857, res. Eden Center, N. Y.; Sarah E. b. Nov. 12, 1858, d. Oct. 7, 1863.
iv. SUSAN M. b. Mar. 1, 1834, m. Mar. 13, 1861, Charles Freeman, b. Jan. 22, 1831, res. Derby, N. Y. Ch.— Carrie F. b. Aug. 22, 1864; Lillie E. b. June 8, 1870.
220. v. GEORGE M. b. Mar. 3, 1836, m. Sarah Jane Hickox.
vi. SANFORD W. b. June 14, 1839, m. Dec. 8, 1869, Phebe Bartholomew b. July 20, 1829, res. s. p. Hamburg, N. Y.
221. vii. FRANCIS G. b. May 2, 1846, m. Louise A. Meyer.
viii. SARAH E. b. Feb. 5, 1850, m. Oct. 28, 1868, ——— Bartholomew, res. Canaseraga, N. Y.
222. ix. CHARLES M. b. Jan. 5, 1842, m. Martha J. Smith.

143 OLIVER S.[7] PEARCE, (Giles[6], George[5], Giles[4], Jeremiah[3], Giles[2], Richard[1]), b. Feb. 11, 1791, m. 1812, Susan Hammond, b. Dec. 6, 1794, d. Sept. 21, 1866. He d. July 22, 1874. Res. Hamburg, N. Y. Oliver settled in Hamburg in 1816, going to that place overland in a lumber wagon. The following year he purchased a farm of 175 acres, on which he always resided. Ch.—

223. i. ARNOLD D., b. June 1, 1816 ; m. Mary J. Ills.
224. ii. WINSLOW S., b. Aug. 20, 1818 ; m. Rozelia S. Titus.
225. iii. AARON, b. Dec. 10, 1820 ; m. Helen Chitaker.

226. iv. GEORGE M., Feb. 18, 1823 ; m. Harriett Dwight.
v. HANNAH, b. July 16, 1825 ; m. , 1846, Richard Caldwell. Res. West Seneca, N. Y. She d. Sept. 15, 1868, leaving John, Lillie, Sarah, George, William, Hannah, Frank.
vi. OLIVER C., b. May 24, 1827 ; m. Helen M. Comstock.
227. vii. SARAH, b. , 1829 ; m. John B. Salisbury. Res. Blasdell, N. Y. Ch.—John W. Res. Goddard, Kansas ; R. C., Geo. B., Smith, and Oliver C.

144 CHARLES[7] PEARCE (Job[6], Job[5], John[4], Jeremiah[3], Giles[2], Richard[1]), b. June 7, 1806 ; m. Aug. 1, 1830, Ruby W. Gorton, b. Aug. 13, 1807, d. July 29, 1879. Res. East Greenwich, R. I. Ch.—

i. HENRY A., b. Feb. 25, 1836 ; d. Aug. 10, 1841.
ii. ELIZABETH D., b. July 17, 1838 ; d. Dec. 20, 1842.
iii. EDWARD, b. Nov. 25, 1840 ; d. Aug. 15, 1841.
iv. MARY E., b. Mar. 20, 1845 ; m. Apr. 15, 1867, M. W. Weld.
v. OCEANA, b. Feb. 25, 1848.

145. JOB[7] PEARCE, JR. (Job[6], Job[5], John[4], Jeremiah[3], Giles[2], Richard[1]), b. Mar. 30, 1811 ; m. June 10, 1831, Maria A. Briggs, b. June 1, 1813. He d. Jan. 8, 1885, Res. Warwick, R. I. Ch.—

i. CHARLES E., b. June 28, 1832 ; m. Aug. 16, 1858, Ida S. J. Trafton, b. Apr. 14, 1834, s. p. Res. 31 Brighton st., Providence, R. I.
228. ii. JOB A., b. Feb. 27, 1834 ; m. Sarah S. Bird.
229. iii. PRESERVED R., b. Dec. 6., 1835 ; m. Harriett A. Fairbanks.
iv. VERNON R., b. Jan. 6, 1838 ; d. Jan. 8, 1841.
v. MARIA M., b. July 5, 1840 ; m. Oct. 8, 1882, Charles T. Carpenter, b. Aug. 4, 1826, s. p. Res. Compton, R. I.
230. vi. VERNON R, b. May 31, 1844 ; m. Mariana H. Marshall.

146 CHARLES[7] PEARCE (Stephen M.[6], Phillip[5], John[4], Jeremiah[3], Giles[2], Richard[1]), b. Sept. 29, 1811 ; m. Nov. 13, 1831, Mariah Atwood, b. Aug. 4, 1810. Res. 25 Central street, Providence, R. I. Ch.—

i. SARAH M., b. Feb. 4, 1839.
ii. ELLEN A., b. Dec. 1, 1848.

147 SAMUEL W.[7] PEARCE (Phillip[6], Phillip[5], John[4], Jeremiah[3], Giles[2], Richard[1]), b. May 11, 1818 ; m. Nov. 19, 1837, Caroline Sherman, b. May 11, 1815, d. May 2, 1879. He d. July 1, 1885. Res. East Greenwich, R. I. Ch.—

i. AARON, b. Mar. 13, 1838 ; m. Sept. 29, 1862, Arte F. Warner, b. Sept. 27, 1838. They had two ch. but both d. young. Res. East Greenwich, R. I., and Spring Lake, Mich.

148 WILLIAM R.[7] PEARCE (Robinson[6], Phillip[5], John[4], Jeremiah[3], Giles[2], Richard[1]), b. Aug. 11, 1827; m. June 7, 1855, Hannah M. Sheridan, b. Apr. 18, 1829, d. Dec. 1, 1871; m. 2nd, Apr. 22, 1875, Sarah I. Rand, b. Apr. 6, 1845. Res. 34½ Knight st., Providence, R. I. Ch.—

i. FRANK S., b. Jan. 20, 1861. Res. Auburn, Me.
ii. MARY B., b. Dec. 19, 1862. Res. 34½ Knight st., Prov.

149 ROBINSON[7] PEARCE JR. (Robinson[6], Phillip[5], John[4], Jeremiah[3], Giles[2], Richard[1]), b. Aug. 10, 1822, m. May 22, 1848, Roby W. Brown, b. Dec. 17, 1818, d. Apr. 18, 1864, m. 2nd, Dec. 5, 1870, Sarah Dening b. June 28, 1847. Res. 172 Prospect St., Providence, R. I. Ch.—

i. ELISHA C. b. Sept. 7, 1849.
ii. FRED F. b. Apr. 10, 1854.
iii. DANIEL B. b. Aug. 26, 1858.
iv. MORRIS D. b. Dec. 8, 1872.
v. ROBINSON, b July 6, 1878.
vi. MAUDE, b, Apr. 24, 1881.

150 JAMES L.[7] PEARCE, (James B.[6], Daniel[5], Thomas[4], John[3], Giles , Richard[1]), b. Mar. 25, 1830, m. June 22, 1853, Lucretia Foster, b. Apr. 6, 1831. Res. 18 So. Water St. Providence, R. I. Ch.—

i. ANNIE T. b. Aug. 21, 1866.

151 DANIEL A.[7] PEARCE, (James B.[6], Daniel[5], Thomas[4], John[3], Giles[2], Richard[1]), b. May 9, 1838, m. June 5, 1866, Emily G. Vaughn, b. Aug. 19, 1845. Ad. 70 Weybossett St., Providence, R. I. Ch.—

i. ADELINE V. b. July 15, 1872, d. Mar. 28, 1881.

152 CHRISTOPHER A.[7] PEARCE, (Christopher B[6]., Daniel[5], Thomas[4], John[3], Giles[2], Richard[1]), b. Feb. 10, 1835, m. Sept. 25, 1861, Clara Fisher, b. Aug. 23, 1834. Ad. 37 Weybossett St., Provinence, R. I. Ch.—

i. CLARA A. b. June 29, 1862.
ii. CHARLES H. b. June 15, 1864, d. Apr. 24, 1873.
iii. LOUISE, F. b. July 24, 1868.
iv. WALTER P., b. Apr. 10, 1870.
v. HOWARD L. b. Jan. 28, 1874.

153 EDWARD H.[7] PEARCE, (Christopher B.[6] Daniel[5], Thomas[4], John[3], Giles[2], Richard[1]), b. Aug. 4, 1838, m. Nov. 27, 1861, Kate L. Anthony, b. June 16, 1841. He d. Jan. 16, 1866. Res. Providence, R. I. Ch.—

i. AMEY W. b. Nov. 9. 1865, d. June 6, 1878.
ii. AUGUSTUS R. b. Nov. 11, 1862.

154 Rt. Rev. Henry Niles[7] Pearce, (Benjamin B.[6], Moses[5], Thomas[4], John[3], Giles[2], Richard[1]), b. Oct. 19, 1820, m. Apr. 18, 1854, Nancy H. Sheppard, b. Mar. 6, 1830. Res. Little Rock, Ark.

Rt. Rev. Henry Niles Pearce, DD. LL.D, fourth Bishop of Arkansas, was born in Pawtucket, R. I., Oct. 19, 1820, m. Apr. 18, 1854, Nannie Haywood Sheppard, daughter of Abraham and Eleanor of Matagorda, Texas, and was born near Selma, Ala., Mar. 6, 1830. He was fitted for College at Portsmouth High School, and entered the Sophomore class of 1839, and graduated in 1842. His theological studies were chiefly under the direction of Dr. Francis Vinton, then of Newport, and Rev. Geo. W. Hathaway, then of Warren, R. I. In the fall of 1846, he went to Florida and in 1848, removed to Matagorda, Texas, where Apr. 23, 1848, he was made a deacon of the Episcopal Church and was admitted to the priesthood Jan. 3, 1849. He began his ministry in Washington county where he founded the churches of St. Peter, Brenham and St. Paul's Washington. He became rector of Christ's church, Matagorda, in June, 1854, he took charge temporarily of the church of the Holy Trinity in New Orleans. On Easter 1856, he became rector of St. Paul's church, Rahway, New Jersey. Oct. 1867, he became rector of St. John's church, Mobile, Alabama. Nov. 1868, he became rector of St. Paul's church, Springfield, Ill. Jan. 25, (St. Paul's day) 1870, he was consecrated Bishop of Arkansas and the Indian Territory, in Christ church, Mobile, Alabama. Ch.—

- i. Abraham W. b. May 28, 1855. Priest in charge of the church of the Good Shepherd, at Mobile, Ala., m. and B. A.
- ii. Henry W. b. Feb. 3, 1857, m. May 6, 1880, Maria Moffatt, res. Vera Cruz, Mexico.
- iii. Elizabeth P. b. Apr. 17, 1859.
- iv. Susan S. b. Sept. 18, 1862, m. Oct. 12, 1882, Wm. C. Stevens, res. Little Rock, Arkansas, s. p.

155 Moses[7] Pearce (Benjamin B.[6], Moses[5], Thomas[4], John[3], Giles[2], Richard[1]), b. July 3, 1808, m. Nov. 24, 1831, Harriet G. Hathaway, b. Apr. 13, 1813, d. May, 1870.

Moses is a member of the Norwich Bleaching and Calendering Co., in Norwich, Ct. He has been a representative to the State Legislature and trustee of the State Reform School. Res. 24 Broad St., Norwich, Ct. Ch.—

- i. Edwin M. b. Apr. 22, 1833, d. Feb., 1861.
- ii. Harriet A. b. Apr. 10, 1836.
- iii. Sarah W. b. Dec. 3, 1838, d. May, 1873.
- iv. George L. b. Mar. 8, 1841, d. Sept. 7, 1852.
- v. Henry A. b. July 2, 1845, d. Jan. 1, 1846.
- vi. Emily G. b. Dec. 4, 1847.

156 GEORGE^{7} PEARCE (Benjamin B.^{6}, Moses^{5}, Thomas^{4}, John^{3}, Giles^{2}, Richard^{1}), b. Apr. 27, 1810 ; m. May 9, 1837, Harriett N. Brown, b. July 27, 1817. Res. 116 Union st., Norwich, Ct. Ch.—

i. HARRIET A., b. Apr. 5, 1838 d. Jan. , 1861.
ii. GEORGE F., b. , 1845 ; d. , 1848.
iii. WILLIAM B., b. Jan. 30, 1848 ; m. Jan. 20, 1878. Res. 50 White st., New York, N. Y.

157 WILLIAM B.^{7} PEARCE (Benjamin B.^{6}, Moses^{5}, Thomas^{4}, John^{3}, Giles^{2}, Richard^{1}), b. Aug. 12, 1818 ; m. , 1838, Amanda Peet, b. Aug. 11, 1817, d. Jan. 1886 ; m. 2nd, Feb. , 1844, Catherine Roath, d. Feb. , 1866 ; m. 3rd, Sept. , 1866, Martha Freeman, b. 1846. Res. 8 Melrose st., Providence, R. I. Ch.—

231. i. ZEPHENIAH G., b. ——— ; m. Susan F. Smith.
ii. SUSAN E., b. Nov. 14, 1844. Res. 8 Melrose st.

158 THOMAS J.^{7} PEARCE (John B.^{6}, John^{5}, Giles^{4}, John^{3}, Giles^{2}, Richard^{1}), b. June 20, 1857 ; m. Oct. 12, 1880, Sarah M. Wrightman, b. May 18, 1860. Res. Wickford, R. I. Ch.—

i. MARY J., b. Sept. 14, 1881.
ii. JOHN P. B., b. Feb. 5, 1883.

159 JOHN F.^{7} PEARCE (Thomas C.^{6}, John^{5}, Giles^{4}, John^{3}, Giles^{2}, Richard^{1}), b. Aug. 17, 1852 ; m. Dec. 19, 1876, Emma F. Sprink. Res. Wickford, R. I. Ch.—

i. JOSEPH F. b. Sept. 24, 1877.
ii. EDITH E., b. Feb. 12, 1879.
iii. ELIZABETH B., b. Sept. 22. 1880.
iv. EMMA G., b. Feb. 23, 1882.

160 THOMAS W^{7}. PEARCE (Thomas C.^{6}, John^{5}, Giles^{4}, John^{3}, Giles^{2}, Richard^{1}), b. Mar. 21, 1859 ; m. Apr. 6, 1881, Hattie A. Sunderland, b. Jan. 18, 1861. Res. Wickford, R. I. Ch—

i. LYDIA M., b. Nov. 24, 1882.

161 WILLIAM E.^{7} PEARCE (William^{6}, Giles^{5}, Giles^{4}, John^{3}, Giles^{2}, Richard^{1}, b. Aug. 15, 1819 ; m. Oct. 4, 1841, Phebe A. Rodman, Res. Allinton, R I, Ch.—

i. ALVIRA R., b May 15, 1843 ; m. Philogen Nichols.
ii. MERVIN R., b. Aug. 15, 1846 ; d. young,
iii. CARRIE E., b. Sept. 19, 1849 ; m. Frank L. Gay.
iv. FLORENCE W., b. Sept. 1, 1852 ; m. June 24, 1885, Thomas M. Pearce. Res. Hamilton, R. I.
v. PHEBE E., b. ———, 1858.

162 EBSON S.^{7} PEARCE (William^{6}, Giles^{5}, Giles^{4}, John^{3}, Giles^{2}, Richard^{1}), b. Feb. 1, 1827 ; m. Mar. 28, 1853, Elizabeth Hall, Res. Hamilton, R. I, Ch.—

i. HERBERT L., b. Dec. 14, 1857.

163 Albert C.^{7} Pearce (William^{6}, Giles^{5}, Giles^{4}, John^{3}, Giles^{2}, Richard^{1}), b. Oct. 8, 1829; m. May 25, 1852, Caroline F. Gardiner. Res. Wickford, R. I. Ch.—

- i. Mervin H., b. Oct. 20, 1854; m. Sept. 16, 1885. Res. Wickford, R. I.
- ii. William A., b. Oct. 14, 1856; m. Aug. 23, 1882, Merian Hazard. Res. Wickford, R. I.

164 Peleg F.^{7} Pearce (William^{6}, Giles^{5}, Giles^{4}, John^{3}, Giles^{2}, Richard^{1}), b. Mar. 15, 1835; m. Nov. 23, 1863, Harriett N. Rodman. Res. Wickford, R. I. Ch.—

- i. Frank H., b. Oct. 16, 1866; d. Feb. 25, 1871.
- ii. Hannah M., b. Aug. 26, 1874; d. Sept. 5, 1874.
- iii. Walter R., b. Aug. 24, 1876.
- iv. Harriett S., b. Mar. 2, 1878.

165 Edward^{7} Pearce (Giles^{6}, Giles^{5}, Giles^{4}, John^{3}, Giles^{2}, Richard^{1}), b. Apr. 29, 1819; m. Jan. 25, 1846, Frances M. Clark. Ch.—

- i. Edward, b. May 16, 1847; d. May 24, 1847.
- ii. Mary F., b Aug. 20, 1848.
- 232. iii. Edward M., b. Jan. 13, 1850; m. Minnie Hervey.
- iv. Julia A., b. Aug. 2, 1852; d. Jan. 27, 1854.
- v. Susan B., b. Jan. 4, 1854.
- vi. Julia A., b. Jan. 14, 1857; m. May 1, 1876, Walter H. Gardiner. Ch.—Ida M., b. Oct. 26, 1877; Mary P., b. Nov. 26, 1878; Julia A., b. July 30, 1880; George A., b. July 23, 1882.

166 Samuel^{7} Pearce (William L.^{6}, Samuel^{5}, Michael^{4}, Samuel^{3}, Samuel^{2}, Richard^{1}), b. Feb. 9, 1848; m. Jan. 10, 1869, Mary E. Clark. Res. Joliet, Ill. Ch.—

- i. William E., b. Oct. 3, 1869.
- ii. Edward S., b. Apr. 12, 1875; d. Oct. 1. 1877.
- iii. Van S., b. Jan. 19, 1877.
- iv. Francis M, b. Aug. 25, 1881.

167 John F.^{7} Pearce (Daniel C.^{6}, John^{5}, Michael^{4}, Samuel^{3}, Samuel^{2}, Richard^{1}), b. Nov. 12, 1841; m Jan. 18, 1865, Lucy B. Green, b. Sept. 1, 1834. Res. Rushville, N. Y. Ch.—

- i. Nellie C., b. Nov. 2, 1865.
- ii. William F. b. Apr. 1, 1868.
- iii. Samuel G, b. Dec. 21, 1872.
- iv. Graty M., b. June 1, 1878.

168 Edwin^{7} Pearce (Nathaniel^{6}, Isaac^{5}, Jeptha^{4}, George^{3}, George^{2}, Richard^{1}), b. Jan 17, 1815; m. Mar. 14, 1839, Eliza Winchester, b. Feb. 23, 1819, d. Sept. 16, 1872. Res. Adamsville, R. I. Ch.—

- i. Harrison H., b. Mar. ——, 1840; d. Nov. ———, 1842.

169 WILLIAM S.[7] PEARCE (Nathaniel[6], Isaac[5], Jeptha[4], George[3], George[2], Richard[1]), b. June 25, 1824; m. Oct. 16, 1853, Amelia McDonald, b. Feb. 26, 1830. Res. Greene, R. I. Ch.—

i. FRANKLIN A., b. Oct. 4, 1854; d. Oct. 29, 1854.
ii. MARY S., b. Aug. 24, 1857; d. Dec. 19, 1858.
iii. JESSIE A., b. Aug. 15, 1860. Res. Coventry Centre, R. I.
iv. JANE S., b. Dec. 5, 1864. Res. Howard, R. I.
v. WM. J., b. Jan. 3, 1866; d. Jan. 11, 1874.

170 ABEL H.[7] PEARCE (Jonathan D.[6], Isaac[5], Jeptha[4], George[3], George[2], Richard[1]), b. June 29, 1834; m. Sept. 27, 1865, Fanny Lacy, b. Feb. 5, 1839, d. Dec. —, 1870; m. 2nd, Oct. —, 1875, Harriett James. Res. Pierce Station, P. O., B. N. Ranch, Texas.

He was born in Little Compton, R. I., and left there Aug. 4, 1847. For six years he resided in Petersburg, Va., then removed to Lone Star State in 1853. Since that time, with the exception of four years he served the Southern Confederacy, he has resided in Texas. Is an extensive stock raiser. Ch.—

i. MAMIE F., b. July 19, 1867.

171 JONATHAN E.[7] PEARCE (Jonathan D.[6], Isaac[5], Jeptha[4], George[3], George[2], Richard[1]), b. Dec. 6, 1839; m. May 2, 1866, Nannie Lacy, b. Aug. 11, 1845. He is a large land-owner and stock raiser like his brother. Res. Denning's Bridge, Metagoda county, Texas. Ch.—

i. JONATHAN P., b. Nov. 5, 1868.
ii. PEARL, b. Dec. 26, 1873.
iii. ABEL B., b. Dec. 4, 1875.
iv. GRACE, b. Sept. 1, 1879.

172 JOHN S.[7] PEARCE,) John[6], John[5], Nathaniel[4], George[3], George[2], Richard[1], b. Dec. 18, 1828, m. July 15, 1853, Rose A. Cragle, b. 1834, d. Oct. 11, 1854, m. 2nd, Oct. 15, 1857, Margaret E. Campbell, b. Feb. 28, 1838. Res. Baton Rouge, La.

John S. Pearce is the oldest son of John Pearce and Lucinda Carter Trout. Owing to the early death of his father, he had to go to work at an early age to assist in in supporting the family. Worked for quite a while as boy-of-all-work in the publishing house of J. B. Lippincott. Afterwards learned the machinist's trade. Left Philadelphia about 1850, and traveled and worked as a "journeyman" through the eastern and southern part of the Union. Reached Baton Rouge, in 1852, where he became foreman of the local machine shop, in which position he remained until the outbreak of the war of secession. At this juncture he became an engineer in Farragut's west Gulf

Blockading squadron, where he remained until the close of the war. In June 1866, he removed his family to his native town (Philadelphia), where he worked at his trade till 1869 when he again came to Baton Rouge to take charge of the machine shop. His family followed about nine months after.

For the past three years he has been running a rented machine shop, but is now establishing one of his own.

A man of a high order of intelligence, a good citizen, and a useful man in any community. He has never held office nor sought it. Ch.—

i. John H. b. Oct. 16, 1854, d. Jan. 7, 1855.
233. ii. John W. b. July 16, 1858, m. Nellie M. Endt.
iii. Mary C. b. Feb. 23, 1860, m. Dec. 25, 1883, Thomas F. Maher. She d. Sept. 4, 1885. Res. New Orleans, La. Ch.— Geo. O., b. Oct. 1884.
iv. Jessie E. b. May 19, 1862.
v. Margaret A., b. Sept. 16, 1866.
vi. Eli H. b. Mar. 29, 1869.
vii. Locke C. b. Mar. 19, 1872, d. Mar. 25, 1872.
viii. Lucretia K. b. Aug. 6, 1873.
ix. Barney, b. Feb. 6, 1875.

173 William K.[7] Pearce, (John[6], John[5], Nathaniel[4], George[3], George[2], Richard[1]), b. Sept. 19, 1832, m. June 18, 1863, Elizabeth G. Miller, b, Oct. 13, 1839. Res. 1823, South street, Philadelphia, Penn. Ch.—

i. Catherine D. b. June 2, 1864, d. July 25, 1864.
234. ii. Martin C. b. Aug. 13, 1865, m. Emma C. Kenney.
iii. Caroline O. b. Dec. 11, 1870, d. Aug. 24, 1872.

174 Alexander S.[7] Pearce, (Peleg[6], John[5], Nathaniel[4] George[3], George[2], Richard[1]), b. July 17, 1826, m. Apr. 27, 1851, Anna W. Hambly, b. May 11 1831. Res. Tiverton Four Corners, R. I. Ch.—

i. Alexander F. b. Apr. 4, 1852, d. Mar. 14, 1871.
ii. Sarah P. b. May 15, 1858, res. Madison Ave., Baltimore, Md.
iii. Edward R. b. Jan. 13, 1866, res. Providence, R. I.
iv. Emily R. b. July 29, 1873.

175 Benjamin S.[7] Pearce, (Val[6], Joseph[5], Nathaniel[4], George[3], George[2], Richard[1]), b. Aug. 30, 1827, m. Nov. 27, 1851, Phebe A. Brayton, b. Feb. 12, 1833. Res. Little Compton, R. I. Ch.—

i. Annie B. b. Oct. 5, 1864.
ii. Philander R. b. Aug. 10, 1866.
iii. Hubert W. b. Sept. 7, 1870.

176 Henry C.[7] Pearce, (Joseph[6], Joseph[5], Nathaniel[4], George[3], George[2], Richard[1]), b. Jan. 11, 1834, m. Aug. 16, 1866, Catharine C. Chester, b. Sept. 17, 1834, d. Sept. 1886. He d. Sept. 19, 1874. Res. 17, Colfax St., Providence R. I. Ch.—

i. Katie C. b. Apr. 19, 1869.
ii. Alice M. b. Oct. 6, 1871.

177 Elery A.[7] Pearce, (Joseph[6], Joseph[5], Nathaniel[4], George[3], George[2], Richard[1]), b. July 18, 1846, m. Nov. 18, 1868, Leah M. Freeborn, b. Nov. 22, 1846. Res. 50 Orange St., Providence, R. I. Ch.—

i. Mary E. b. Sept. 15, 1869.
ii. Ada A. b. June 2, 1872, d. Sept. 8, 1872.
iii. Josie F. b. June 14, 1875.
iv. Ernest G. b. Nov. 7, 1882.

178 Nathaniel A.[7] Pearce, (Nathaniel[6], Joseph[5], Nathaniel[4], George[3], George[2], Richard[1]), b. Aug. 24, 1839, m. Jan. 8, 1862, Mary T. Davis. Res. Fall River, Mass. Ch.—

i. George E. b. 1862, d. Sept. 7, 1863.
ii. Hattie B. b. Nov. 2, 1863.
iii. Orrin A. b. Feb. 19, 1865.
iv. Lizzie D. b. Aug. 23, 1868.
v. Lillie M. b. Oct. 1, 1871.
vi. Harry C. b. Aug. 17, 1873.
vii. Nathaniel b. Aug. 10, 1876.
viii. Frank P. b. Aug. 23, 1882.

179 Orrin F.[7] Pearce, (Nathaniel[6], Joseph[5], Nathaniel[4], George[3], George[2], Richard[1]), b. June 26, 1847, m. Feb. 23, 1882, Mary E. Blair. Res. 8 Wellington St., Providence, R. I. Ch.—

Bethena B. b. June 3, 1883.

180 James[7] Pearce, (Godfrey[6], Wright[5], James[4], James[3], George[2], Richard[1]), b. July 6, 1802, m. Dec. 12, 1822, Nancy Pearce, [ ] b. May 16, 1802, d. July 28, 1856. Res. Little Compton, R. I. Ch.—

i. Sarah A. b. May 28, 1831, d. Nov. 13, 1845.
ii. Harriett A. b. Dec 13, 1832, m. July 1, 1862, Horatio Richmond. Ch.— Harriett P. b. June 1, 1863, d. June 1, 1863. She d. June 1, 1863. He d. May 1876. Res. Fairhaven, Mass.

181 Abner T.[7] Pearce, (Thomas[6], Wright[5], James[4], James[3], George[2], Richard[1]), b. Oct. 4, 1811, m. Sept. 1, 1831, Sarah R. Briggs, b. Aug. 27, 1810, He d. Dec. 3, 1864. Res Little Compton, R. I. Ch.—

235. i. CHAS F. b. Apr. 29, 1835, m. Sarah H. Smith.
ii. PELEG T. b. Feb. 5, 1833, d. unm. Sept. 12, 1866.
236. iii. WALDO A. b. Mar. 14, 1837, m. Emma C. Webster.
iv. RUBY A. b. Sept. 7, 1839, m. May 1860, Capt. Richard G. Shaw, 1st Lieut. U. S. A., Alcatroz, California.
v. SARAH L. b. July 12, 1841, m. Nov. 22, 1864, Willliam Glenny. She d. June 2, 1867.
vi. FRANK I. b. May 18, 1844, m, Oct. 11, 1866, res. 752 West Madison St., Chicago, Ill.
vii. MARY G. b. Nov. 28, 1846, m. Nov. 20, 1866, John M. Dean, res. Fall River, Mass.
viii. EUGENE T. b. Feb. 9, 1851, m. Feb. 1, 1868, d. June 17, 1875.

182 FRANKLIN[7] PEARCE, (Thomas[6], Wright[5], James[4], James[3], George[2], Richard[1]), b. June 20, 1820, m. Oct. 12, 1847, Elizabeth Najac, b. Nov. 7, 1823. Res. 10 Lane St., Providence, R. I. Ch.—

237. i. FRANK T. b. Nov. 13, 1848, m. Annie R Gardiner.
ii. ANNA E. b. Sept. 2, 1850, m. George H. Richardson. She d. Nov. 5. 1877, leaving Ann E. res. New York. N. Y.
iii. ELEANOR B. b. Jan. 3, 1852, d. June 6, 1856.
iv. NELLIE B. b. Mar. 19, 1857, unm.

183 ADDISON L.[7] PEARCE (George T.[6], Stephen[5], James[4], James[3], George[2], Richard[1]), b. Apr. 3, 1807 ; m. Feb. 19, 1836, Sarah Stillwell, b. May 22, 1811. Res. Waterburgh, Tompkins Co., N. Y. Ch.—

i. WM. H., b. May 30, 1837. Res. Canona, N. Y.
ii. STEPHEN B., b. Aug. 11, 1841. Res. Ovid Centre, N. Y.
238. iii. SAMUEL, b. May 30, 1843 ; m. Bessie Carberry.
iv. ELIAS, b. Sept. 2, 1847 ; unm. Res. Waterburgh, N. Y.
v. EMMA F., b. Jan. 1, 1858 ; m. ——— Whipple. Res. Union Springs, N. Y.
239. vi. GEORGE W., b. Oct. 7, 1852 ; m. Elnora Clark.
vii FRANK, b. June 14, 1854 ; unm.
viii. M'ARY P., b. Aug. 6, 1855 ; m. Nov. 27, 1872, Cornelius J. Hamilton, b. Nov. 25, 1849. Res. Waterburgh, N. Y. Ch.—Willie C. b. Feb. 20, 1874 ; d. May 2, 1874 ; Fred. W.. b. July 8, 1875 ; Henry E., b. May 2, 1879 ; Mary, b. Sept. 18, 1881, d. Jan. 28, 1883 ; Bertie, b. Feb. 5, 1885.

184 GAMELIEL[7] PEARCE (George T.[6], Stephen[5], James[4], James[3], George[2], Richard[1]), b. Aug. 27. 1808 ; m. Nov. 1, 1841, Polly Brown, b. Apr. 12, 1810, d. Oct. 24, 1875. He d. June 5, 1881. Res. North Hartford, Cortland County N. Y. Ch.—

i. CALISTA, b. Sept. 2, 1842 ; m. Dec. 16, 1859, Alonzo Carpenter, b. Feb. 10, 1837. Res. Dryden, N. Y. Ch.—Carrie J., b. Apr. 6, 1860, d. Jan. 2, 1861 ; Charlie A., b. Oct. 20, 1861 ; Libbie L., b. Dec. 7, 1865 ; Bertie B., b. May 10, 1878, d. Jan. 7, 1879 ; Maggie M., b. Nov. 17, 1880. Charlie Carpenter and Hattie Westfall married Dec. 22. 1885, at Newark Valley, Tioga Co.

ii. CLARISSA A., b. Nov. 4, 1845 ; m. Aug. 12, 1859, Andrew J. Carpenter, b. Apr. 27, 1834. Res. Hartford, N. Y. Ch.—Cora B., b. Jan. 4, 1872 ; Jay M., b. June 26, 1878; Lee, b. Jan. 7, 1881.

240. iii. ANSEL, b. Nov. 27, 1852 ; m. Sarah L. Shevalier.

185 JUDGE JAMES O.[7] PEARCE (James[6], Stephen[5], James[4], James[3], George[2], Richard[1]). b. Feb. 3, 1836 ; m. Sept. 14, 1862, Ada Butterfield, b. Oct. 12, 1844. Res. Memphis, Tenn., Minneapolis, Minn.

Hon. James O. Pearce is a descendant of the Pearce family of Rhode Island, and his grandfather, Stephen Pearce, was a soldier in the Rhode Island line during the Revolutionary war. Judge Pearce was born in Oneida county, New York, and was reared and educated at Syracuse. He commenced business life as a book-keeper and accountant in the public works in Central New York. In 1857 he removed to Wisconsin, where he studied law and was admitted to the bar. At the outbreak of the late war he enlisted as a private soldier in the Federal army, and saw his first field service in the army of General Robert Patterson, on the Potomac. Afterwards, as a commissioned officer, he was transferred to the Mississippi department, where he was advanced to the rank of major and assistant adjutant general. In this capacity he was attached to the staff of Gen. B. M. Prentiss. Later, he served as a staff officer with Generals Hurlburt, Washburn and Dana, in the Inspector-General's Department and the Judge Advocate's Department. In the last named department his legal education was brought under requisition, and frequent opportunities were afforded him to mitigate some of the severities of the state of civil war. When first placed on duty as Judge Advocate at Memphis, he found many prisoners who had been in confinement a long time without trial and took immediate measures to correct the abuse, securing the immediate discharge of many who were unjustly confined for semi-political offenses. At the close of the war, Major Pearce being then judge advocate for the department and State of Mississippi, proposed and published a novel plan for the gradual but early rehabilitation of the States whose governments had been displaced by the war, which he still believes would, if it had been adopted, have facilitated the settlement of the vexed political questions which the war left as a legacy, and proved itself a readier and smoother plan than any which was adopted. Maj. Pearce tendered his resignation upon the cessation of hostilities, but was detained in the service till the fall of 1865, preparing work for the military courts.

Having previously selected Memphis as his home he commenced the practice of the law there upon his retirement from the army. After the death of the lamented Judge Thomas G. Smith, in the fall of 1867, Governor Brownlow tendered to Mr. Pearce a commission as judge of the law court of Memphis, which, however, he declined to accept until requested to do so by nearly the entire bar of Memphis. Judge Pearce resigned this position in the summer of 1868, and practiced his profession closely and assiduously for ten years. In the election of 1878 he was tendered the nomination for circuit judge by the combined republican and national parties, which he reluctantly accepted, and was elected by a majority of 3,300. His judicial term of eight years is now about closing. At its commencement the epidemic of 1878 detained him in Wisconsin, where he devoted his vacation to the work of editing and carrying through the press, the treatise on the "Laws of Carriers," which his late competitor, Judge Robert Hutchinson, who had died of yellow fever, had left unfinished. His labors on this book Judge Pearce gave to the children of his late competitor. At the dedication of the National Cemetery, near Memphis, in 1868, Judge Pearce officiated as president of the day, and he has since delivered addresses on memorial day on one or two occasions. In 1875 the first formal and studied attempt at a union of the blue and the gray for memorial exercises occurred at Memphis, when Judge Pearce, as the orator of the day for the Federal side, was introduced by the late Gen. Gideon J. Pillow, and spoke earnestly in favor of a more complete fraternization between the soldiers of the two late armies. Gen. Luke E. Wright on the same occasion spoke in a like fraternal vein for the Confederate veterans.

Judge Pearce is a member of two organizations of veteran soldiers, the military order of the Loyal Legion, (an order in imitation of the Cincinnati), and the Grand Army of the Republic, both of which are purely fraternal and non political organizations. He has been for several years an active member of the benevolent order of the Knights of Honor, in which he now holds the position of Grand Vice-Dictator for Tennessee, and chairman of committee of appeals in the Supreme Lodge, this being the central judicial tribunal of the whole order. He is also an active member of the order of Knights and Ladies of Honor, in which he has been advanced to the degree of

Past Grand Protector. Since 1876, he has been continuously honored with the position of President of the Eclectic Club, one of the most active and thorough literary clubs in this city.—[*Memphis, Tenn., Paper.*

Ch.—

i. CARRIE, b. Nov. 1, 1867.

ii. ROBERT C. b. Dec. 17, 1871.

186 WELLINGTON C.[7] PEARCE (Andrew T.[6], Stephen[5], James[4] James[3], George[2], Richard[1]), b. Aug. 12, 1825; m. Mar. 16, 1853, Sarah Crandall. Res. Franklin and Alba, Pa. Ch.—

i. CLARENCE D., b. May 10, 1854 ; d. Dec. 28, 1862.

ii. HARRIETT J., b. Mar. 6, 1857 ; m. Sept. 18, 1876, T. Waldo Stevens. Res. Oneonta, N. Y. Ch.—Clara M., b. June 12, 1879 ; Charles F., b. Jan. 21, 1886.

iii. ALBERT A., b. Nov. 12, 1860 ; m. Mar. 9, 1882, Lillie Wetherell. Res. Alba, Pa. Have a son, Wellington, J.

187 ALBERT A.[7] PEARCE (Andrew T.[6], Stephen[5], James[4], James[3], George[2], Richard[1]), b. Apr. 1, 1833 ; m. Jan. 13, 1864, Lucinda R. Mott. He d. July 22, 1883. Res. Utica and Hamilton, N. Y. Ch.—

i. RICHARD M., b. May 8, 1865 ; d. Sept. 16, 1865.

ii. FRANK W., } twins ; b. Apr. 2, 1868.
iii. FRED. M., }

188 DR. BENJAMIN[7] PEARCE (Benjamin[6], John[5], James[4], James[3], George[2], Richard[1]), b. Feb. 17, 1813 ; m. Aug. 13, 1836, Sarah P. Nickerson, b. Aug. 17, 1814, d. June 22, 1880. Res. 1197 Euclid ave. Cleveland, O. Ch.—

i. JOHN M., b. Sept. 10, 1837 ; m. Dec. 25, 1860, Mary E. Whitney. Res. Kenton, O.

ii. WALTER B., b. ——, 1841 ; d. ——, 1842.

iii. SARAH, b. —— ; d. young.

189 GEORGE H.[7] PEARCE (Benjamin[6], John[5], James[4], James[3], George[2], Richard[1]), b. ——, 1809 ; m. Abby S. Pearce of Bristol, R. I. He d. Dec. 28, 1832. Res. Bristol, R. I. Ch.—

i. MARY A., b. —— ; m. Manton E. Hoard. Res. Providence, R. I.

ii. WALTER, b. —— ; m. Rose Benet. Res. Hartford, Conn.

190 A. SIMMONS[7] PEARCE (Nathaniel[6], Ezekiel[5], James[4], James[3], George[2], Richard[1]), b. Feb. 2, 1837 ; m. Apr. 17, 1870, Clara A. Hall, b. Nov. 3, 1850. Res, Rushford, Minn. Ch.—

i. GUY H., b. Feb. 27, 1871.

ii. Clara, b. Nov. 16, 1872.
iii. Jennie, b. Feb. 25, 1877.
iv. Ole F. J., b. Feb. 11, 1883.

191 Nathaniel^7, Pearce (Nathaniel^6, Ezekiel^5, James^4, James^3, George^2 Richard^1), b. Nov. 22, 1829 ; m. Feb. 10, 1869, Lydia E. White, b. Feb. 22, 1844. Res. Dartford Green, Wis. Ch.—

i. Clinton J., b. June 6, 1871.

192 J. Oscar^7 Pearce (Nathaniel^6, Ezekiel^5, James^4, James^3, George^2, Richard^1), b. Oct. 27, 1827 ; m. July 4, 1853, Hannah M. Randall, b. Sept. 6, .1832. Res. Wonenoc, Wis. Ch.—

i. Annie D., b. Apr. 3, 1854 ; d. Sept. 16, 1870.
ii. Geo. O., b. Mar. 25, 1856 ; drowned July 21, 1868.
241. iii. M. E., b. Mar. 15, 1861 ; m. Nellie Sherwood.
iv. Harry S., b. June 7, 1866 ; d. Dec. 14, 1868.
v. Bertie D., b. Apr. 28, 1871.
vi. Ruby L., b. May 22, 1874 ; d. Mar. 9. 1880.
vii. Lilian M., b. July 1878.

194 Samuel B.^{7} Pearce (Pardon G.^{6}, Ichabod^5, James^4, James^3, George^2, Richard^1), b, ———, 1826 ; m. May 6; 1857, Susan J. Anthony, b. ———, 1838, d. May 30, 1870 ; m. 2d, Jan. 30, 1871, Abby F. Sherburne, b, 1830. Res 124 Chestnut st., Providence, R. I. Ch.—

i. Jennie E., b.Aug. 15, 1858 ; d. Mar. 15, 1861.
ii. Mary L., b. Jan. 27, 1864 ; June 1, 1887, Dr. Earl Palmer Hawes. Res. Providence, R. I.

196 Henry L.^{7} Pearce (William^6, James^5, James^4, James^3, George^2, Richard^1), b. Apr. 30, 1793 ; m. Hailey T. Pearce, b. Dec. 17, 1792, d. Dec. 30, 1851. He d. June 13 1681, at Athens, Mich. Res. Naples, N. Y. Ch.—

i. Eleanor D., b. Oct. 12, 1813 ; d. Mich.
ii. Jonathan E., b. Dec. 16, 1814 ; d. Mich.
iii. Rosinda H., b. Sept. 4, 1816.
iv. Wm. H., b. Jan. 3, 1818 ; m. Rowena ———. Res. Bristol, N. Y.
v. Hannah H., b. Feb. 2, 1820.
242. vi. Oliver P., b. Feb 4, 1822 ; m. Waitey A. West.
vii. John A., b. Oct. 11, 1824.
viii. Anne E., b. Jan. 29. 1827.
ix. Cyrus M., b. Apr. 20, 1831 ; d. Mich.
x. James H., b. Aug. 20, 1833 ; d. Mich.
xi. Henry L., b. Oct. 15, 1837 ; d. July 5, 1854.

197 Capt. Parker H.^{7} Pearce, (William^6, James^5, Sames^4, James^3, George^2, Richard^1), b. Dec. 11, 1794, m. Feb. 23, 1818, Hannah Wittington, b. Mov. 24, 1797, d.

Mar. 31, 1878. He d. June 25, 1875. Res. Boston, Mass., and Springwater, N. Y.

Capt. Parker H. Pearce was born in Little Compton, R. I. He went to Boston Mass., at the age of 15, and for several years was a clerk in a store there. Later he was admitted a member of the firm of Humphrey and Pearce which continued business until its dissolution in 1830. Mr. Pearce then took the presidency of the Commercial Bank and also of the United States Insurance Company. At the same time he was always interested in shipping and mercantile pursuits. In the panic of 1836–7–8, he lost all his property which at one time had amounted to a large sum. In 1838, he moved with his family to Springwater, Livingston County, New York, where he conducted quite a large farm.

Capt. Pearce took a great interest in military affairs. He joined the Boston Light Infantry in 1817, the crack company of Boston, in 1824 he was chosen Captain and had the honor of doing sort duty to General Lafayette who visited Boston that year. In 1826, the Boston Light Infantry went to New York, the first military visit between the two cities. They were very highly complimented by the press of New York on their drill and appearance. In April 1827, Capt. Pearce resigned. In 1830, the two hundredth anniversary of the settlement of Boston was celebrated, and that year he was chosen as Captain of the Ancient and Honorable Artillery Company, which company lacked but a few years of the same age as the city and is the oldest military organization in this country. It is composed exclusively of officers and ex-officers of other companies. It was a great celebration. The company did escort duty to the Governor and city authorities. June 17, 1825, the corner stone of Bunker Hill monument was laid, Hon. Daniel Webster making the address, the Boston Light Infantry with Capt. Pearce commanding, again doing escort duty. He was connected with this company ten years and never missed a drill.

Ch.—

243. i. Parker H. b. Feb. 8, 1819, m. Jane E. Blamdar.

ii. Hannah E. b. Apr. 4, 1821, m. Jan. 1, 1839, Daniel B. Woods, res. St. Louis, Mo.

iii. Francis M. b. May 26, 1824, d. Nov. 29, 1824.

iv. Wm. H. b. Dec. 27, 1825, unm., res. Springwater, N. Y.

Wm. H. Pearce was a sickly child, but grew stronger as he grew older, and held his own with those of his age. He was kept in a boarding school mostly until he was thirteen years old. His father lost his property in 1838, and moved to Springwater, he worked on the farm with him till 1845. Wm. went to Boston and was engaged in keeping books there till 1849, he afterwards went to St. Louis and was a book-keeper there some time. In January 1857, he went into the hardware trade with his brother-in-law, Robert McCarthy and Charles T. Redfield, in Syracuse, N. Y., where he remained till Aug. 1869, when he retired from business. The concern is still in business, Robert McCarthy & son and is one of the largest and most successful houses in that state. Mr. Pearce takes pride in having helped to build it up. Since he left Syracuse he has been living in Springwater, and being fond of sailing, shooting and fishing he spends about half the year at his cottage on Hemlock Lake (near Springwater), and the winter at that village. His business life was a very active one and now he is taking his rest.

244. v. Geo. A. b. July 2, 1828, m. Joseph Hopkins.
vi. Eliza J. b. Oct. 23, 1831, m. Sept. 15, 1852, Robert McCarthy, res. Syracuse, N. Y.
vii. Sarah W. b. Apr. 15, 1836, m. Marcus O. Austin, m. June 9, 1858, d. Dec. 16, 1859, in Springwater, N. Y.

198 Benjamin F.[7], Pearce, (William[6], James[5], James[4], James[3], George[2], Richard[1]), b. July 2, 1801, m. Dec. 10, 1822, Rowena Hills, b. Feb. 9, 1803. Res. North Cape, Wis. Ch.—

i. Asa W. b. Sept. 8, 1833, m. Aug. 22, 1849, d. Apr. 5. 1881, in Fon du Lac, Wis.
245. ii. Alvin A. b. July 3, 1827, m. Elizabeth Sproot.
iii. Calvin L. b. July 3, 1827, m. Nov. 27, 1858, res. Fon du Lac, Wis.
246. iv. Benjamin F. Jr. b. Nov. 24, 1829, m. Mary Cameron.
v. Rowena H. b. July 6, 1837, m. Oct. 25, 1856, Carlisle Waite, b. May 19, 1835, res. s. p. North Cape, Wis.

199 James P.[7] Pearce, (Benjamin[6], James[5], James[4], James[3], George[2], Richard[1]), b. May 4, 1819, m. Jan. 8, 1848, Lucy Blake, b. 1822, d. Jan. 1, 1861, m. 2nd, Nov. 4, 1862, Margaret J. Palmer, b. June 14, 1833. Res. Cranston. R. I. Ch.—

i. Emma C. b. June 8, 1853, m. Mar. 28, 1876, a Mr. Cook, and d. Oct. 19, 1878.
ii. Milton E. b. Apr. 12, 1866, Res. Cranston, R. I.

200 Rouse[7] Pearce (Benjamin[6], James[5], James[4], James[3], George[2], Richard[1]), b. June 18, 1826, m. Comfort M. ——— b. , 1832, d. Oct. 19, 1862, m. 2nd, Jan. 2, 1865, Deborah Bower, b. Aug. 22, 1839. Res. Little Compton, R. I. Ch.—

i. FRANK A. b. Mar. 1851, d. June 27, 1857.
ii. ANN E. b , 1852, d. Nov. 29, 1853.
iii. ESTELLE, b. June 27, 1858, m. June 2, 1878, Charles R. Wilbour, b. Oct. 3, 1838. Ch — Antem C. b. Sept. 18, 1879. She d. Aug. 27, 1884, res. Little Compton, R. I.

201 JAMES B.[7] PEARCE, (Giles[6], James[5], Giles[4], James[3]. George[2], Richard[1]), b. Feb. 20, 1822 ; m. May 10, 1855, James A. Thompson, b. Apr. 25, 1827. Res. Mt. Pleasant, Iowa. Ch.—

i. LOVLILIA W., b. Apr. 6, 1856 ; m. Dec. 25, 1875, James N. Tolley, b. Dec. 27. 1852. She d. at Mt. Pleasant, Iowa, Feb. 17, 1884, leaving Clarence L., b. Sept. 25, 1876 ; Frank E., b. June 25, 1879 ; James K., b. July 3, 1881 ; Netta R., b. July 26, 1883.
ii. CLARA B., b. Aug. 28, 1860 ; d. Aug. 20, 1881.
iii. GEORGIA, b. Aug. 2, 1866.

202 ORLANDO[7] PEARCE (Giles[6], James[5], Giles[4], James[3], George[2], Richard[1]), b. Aug. 11, 1836; m. April 13, 1858, Susan Dwire, b. Oct. 30, 1835, d. Aug. 5, 1871 ; m. 2nd, Mary A. Dwire, b. Mar. 20, 1841. Res. Clyde, O. Ch.—

i. EMMA A., b. Feb. 17, 1867 ; d. Mar. 29, 1869.
ii. WILLIAM D., b. May 1876.

203 ALLEN S.[7] PEARCE (Sanford[6], Samuel[5], Samuel[4], James[3], George[2], Richard[1]), b. Sept. 2, 1816 ; m. June 18, 1838, Almira Wright, b. July 1, 1815, d. July 21, 1854. Res. Scituate, R. I., and Hebron, Ct. Ch.—

i. JASON S., b. June 11, 1839 ; m. Nov. 10, 1869, Ellen S. Greene, b. July 4, 1839. He d. s. p. Sept. 3, 1886. Res. Hills' Wharf, Providence, R. I.
247. ii. MILLARD A., b. Apr. 11, 1841 ; m. Mrs. Mary Richardson.
iii. HENRY B., b. Oct. 16, 1842 , d. July 29, 1865.
iv. LYDIA O., b. Feb. 16, 1846 ; m. Oct. 30, 1871, Roscoe O. Wood, b. Feb, 22. 1850. Res. 69 Laura st., Providence, R. I. Ch.—Elizabeth Hill, b. Aug. 23, 1872 ; Arthur Pearce, b. June 2, 1874 ; Henry Allen, b. Oct. 31, 1875, d. Sept. 9, 1876 ; Mabel Emma, b. Mar. 12, 1877, d. July 3, 1881 ; Lydia Almira, b. Apr. 6, 1880 ; Ellen Stella, b. July 9, 1883 ; Annie Thornton, b. Sept, 19, 1884,
v. IVANHOE G., b. July, 3 1850 ; m. Littie Briggs. Res. Joy, near Col. st., Providence, R. I.
vi. HEMAN S., b. Oct. 20, 1851 ; m. Oct. 17, 1882, Cynthia Burke, b. Feb. 7, 1852, s. p. Res. East Providence, R. I.

204 GEORGE W.[7] PEARCE (Sanford[6], Samuel[5], Samuel[4], James[3], George[2], Richard[1]), b. Oct. 23, 1812 ; m. July 3, 1839, Emeline Porter, b. Nov. 21, 1813, d. Mar. 19, 1866. Res. Geneva, N. Y.

He was born in Plainfield, Ct. On the death of his father, when but five years of age, he went to live with a farmer. George worked on the farm and attended the district school a short time each year. Entering a newspaper office he served his time as printer on a county paper. Later he was employed on book work in an office in New York city. subsequently he was editor of a paper. After a few years he became weary of the work and purchasing a farm followed husbandry. He was extensively engaged in stock raising and the manufacture of butter and cheese, which he conducted for twenty years. About the time he engaged in agricultural pursuits, in 1839, he was united in marriage to Miss Emeline Porter, an estimable young lady, and a native of Connecticut. She was a cousin of the late Elihu Buriett, the learned blacksmith. In 1860 he disposed of his farm in Phelps, where his sons and daughters had attended a union classical school, and located in Geneva. His son entered Hobart College, where he pursued a full four years' course, while his sister had the advantages of a young ladies' high school. After another series of years in a newspaper office as assistant and editor, George W. again turned his attention to agricultural pursuits, in which he is at present engaged. Ch.—

248. i. George B., b. Mar. 3, 1843 ; m. Kate M. Cross.
ii. Emma B., b. Mar. 4, 1846 ; m. Mar. 11, 1885, Cornelius L. Vosburgh, b. Oct. 5, 1843, s. p. Res. Geneva, N. Y.

205 James B.[7] Pearce (George[6], Jeremiah[5], Samuel[4], James[3], George[2], Richard[1]), b. Aug 31, 1829 ; m. May 4, 1859, Charlotte White. He d. Dec. 18, 1884.

James Brown Pearce, born in Fairfield, N. Y., removing while young, with parents, to Little Falls, N. Y. At first he conducted a large farm but after several years he abandoned that, and after engaging in numerous business ventures, and the death of his wife, he removed to California. He was respected by all who knew him and with those who had business with him he enjoyed their confidence. Res. Santa Barbara, Cal. Ch—

i George, b. ———, 1867.

206 John H.[7] Pearce (John[6], John[5]. Samuel[4], James[3], George[2], Richard[1]), b. Dec. 6, 1837 ; m. Nov. 23, 1864, Henrietta S. Simmons. Res. Warren, R. I. Ch.—

i. Cora L., b. Dec. 2, 1869.
ii. Fannie H., b. Oct. 6, 1873.

207 NATHANIEL[8] PEARCE (George A.[7], Nathaniel[6], Richard[5], Nathaniel[4], Richard[3], Richard[2], Richard[1]), b. Feb. 25, 1817; m. Apr. 6, 1840. Sylvia W. Bates, b. Dec. 18, 1818. He d. Dec. 18, 1854. Res. Cumberland, R. I. Ch.—

249\. i. WM. H., b. May 14, 1848; m. Emily J. Arnold.

ii. ELLEN T., b. Sept. 28, 1843; d. Apr. 29, 1876.

250\. iii. CHAS. F., b. June 4, 1846; m. Harriett L. Howland.

251\. iv. NATH'L W., b. Mar. 20, 1851; m. Alice E. Butts.

252\. v. THEO. B., b. May 4. 1854; m. Kate M. Woods.

208 SANFORD R.[8] PEARCE (George A.[7], Nathaniel[6], Richard[5], Nathaniel[4], Richard[3], Richard[2], Richard[1]), b. Oct. 4, 1819; m. Mar. 21, 1842, Betsey Fairbrother, b. Aug. 11, 1816. Res. Main st. North Providence, R. I. Ch.—

i. HENRY A., b. Mar. 12, 1846; unm. Clerk U. S. Senate, Wash., D. C.

Henry A. Pearce, second son of Sanford R. and Betsey (Fairbrother) Pearce, born March 12, 1846, in the town of North Providence (now city of Pawtucket), county of Providence, State of Rhode Island. Educated in the common and high schools of his native town, supplemented by a course in a commercial college at Providence. Enlisted at the age of sixteen in the Ninth Rhode Island (infantry) as a private in Co. H., in May, 1862, and served with his regiment until expiration of term of service. Was appointed, upon his return to Rhode Island, commissary sergeant of the Pawtucket Light Guard Battalion. Was appointed in May, 1871, aid-de-camp to the brigade commander of the Second Brigade, R. I. M., with the rank of captain, and served as such until his appointment, April, 1874, as aid-de-camp to the division commander R. I. M., with the rank of major, in which capacity he served five years. Was appointed, May, 1880, chief of staff, to the governor of Rhode Island, with the rank of colonel, and served three terms. Was elected town auditor of the town of Pawtucket, for the year 1877–8. Elected to the board of assessors of taxes for the town of Pawtucket in 1883, and re-elected in the following May for a term of three years, and served as chairman of the board until duties elsewhere compelled him to resign his home office. Was treasurer of St. Paul's church from 1878 to 1885. Elected master of Union Lodge No. 10, A. F. and A. M., in 1872, and re-elected in the following year. Was elected Commander of Holy Sepulchre Commandery, K. T., in 1876 and again in 1877. Was appointed assistant financial clerk of the United States

Senate in 1884. Though temporarily residing at Washington, D. C., his home is retained at Pawtucket, R. I.

ii. CLARA R., b. June 10, 1848 ; m. ———, 1871, Wellington Burlingame. Ch.—Anna S. and Harry W. Res. 6 Mulbury st., Pawtucket, R. I.

iv. ELIZABETH F., b. Feb. 26, 1850 ; d. ———, ———.

v. ANNA L., b. Apr. 22, 1855 ; d. ———. ———.

209 J. RUSSELL[8] PEARCE (Albert S[7]., Nathaniel[6], Richard[5], Nathaniel[4], Richard[3], Richard[2], Richard[1]), b. Dec. 30, 1850 ; m. May 23, 1878, Isabella Kirkwood, b. June 15, 1855. Res. Bristol, R. I. Ch.—

i. WILLIAM B., b. May 14, 1880.
ii. MABEL R., b. Aug. 18, 1882.
iii. FRED'K J., b. May 18, 1885.

210 EDWARD B[8]. PEARCE (Albert S[7]., Nathaniel[6], Richard[5], Nathaniel[4], Richard[3], Richard[2], Richard[1]), b. Feb. 1, 1843 ; m. May 16, 1867, Mary J. Coffin, b. Oct. 29, 1846. Res. Bristol, R. I. Ch.—

i. NETTIE P., b. June 10, 1869.
ii. FRED'K B., b. Dec. 12, 1873 ; d. Nov. 3, 1874.

211 EDWIN S[8]., PEARCE (Gilbert D[7]., Robert[6], Richard[5], Nathaniel[4], Richard[3], Richard[2], Richard[1]), b. May 26, 1856 ; m. Sept. 19, 1880, Charlotte C. Apt, b. Nov. 22, 1856. Res. Attleboro, Mass. Ch.—

i. ELIZABETH C., b. Apr. 7, 1881.

212 ROBERT R[8]., PEARCE (Robert M[7]., Robert[6], Richard[5], Nathaniel[5], Richard[3], Richard[2], Richard[1]), b. Dec. 14, 1841 ; m. June 3, 1869, Ruth A. Kent, b. Aug. 4, 1843. Res. Rumford, R. I. Ch.—

i. ANNIE R., b Apr. 1, 1870.
ii. MARY B., b. June 11, 1875.

213 WILLIAM H[8]. PEARCE (George[7], William[6], George[5], William[4], Richard[3], Richard[2], Richard[1]), b. June 15, 1813 ; m. Oct. 3, 1836, Roseamey M. Gardner. Res. Swansey, Mass., p. o. Warren, R. I. Ch.—

i. HENRY B., b. Oct. 4, 1858.

214 GEORGE G[8]. PEARCE (George[7], William[6], George[5], William[4], Richard[3], Richard[2], Richard[1]), b. Jan. 25, 1824 ; m. Oct. 15, 1849, Mary N. Robinson, b. Apr. 2, 1827. Res. Wakefield, R. I. Ch.—

253. i. GEO. R., b. July 14, 1850 ; m. Nellie F. Morse.
ii. JEREMIAH N., b. Mar. 9, 1855. Res. Dolores, Col.
iii. MARY N., b. July 7, 1852 ; d. Dec. 23, 1859.

iv. JAS. C., b. July 27, 1857. Res. N. Y. City, p. o. box 3241.
v. MARY F., b. Jan 26, 1864; d. Aug. 16, 1874.
vi. ELIZABETH E., b. July 9, 1866.

215 WILLIAM[8] PEARCE (William[7], William[6], George[5], William[4], Richard[3], Richard[2], Richard[1]), b. ——— ; m. Aug. 17, 1852, Harriett F. Cook. Res. Bristol, R. I. Ch.—

i. SON, b. July 12, 1853.
ii. " b. Jan. 6, 1856.
iii. LIZZIE C., b. Mar, 20, 1857; d. Mar. 26, 1857.
iv. WM. C., b. , 1862; d. Feb. 9, 1865.
v. MARY L., b. Apr. 1, 1866.
vi. JAS. E., b. Jan 19, 1875.

216 THOMAS A[8]. PEARCE (Martin[7], Jeremiah[6], Jeremiah[5], Giles[4] Jeremiah[3], Giles[2], Richard[1]), b. Sept. 2, 1815; m. Nov. 7, 1841, Thankful G. Crandall, b. Sept. 19, 1847. He d. June 13, 1880. Res. Charlestown, R. I.

Thomas Arnold Pearce, son of Martin Pearce and Elizabeth A., his wife, was born in East Greenwich, R. I., Sept. 2,1815. Received his early education in the public schools of his native town. Was married to Thankful Green Crandall, of Charlestown, R. I., Nov. 7, 1841. Was an officer in command of the Kentish Guards during a portion of the "Dorr War," in 1842. In 1845 removed to Charlestown, R. I. In 1848–9, during the gold excitement, went to California, but health failing remained only about a year and returned to Charlestown, R. I., where he established a cigar manufactory. He represented Charlestown in the State legislature for a number of years. In 1860 was engaged with the A. & W. Sprague Manufacting Company, and for a number of years had charge of their business at Baltic, Ct. In 1866 was appointed agent of the New York, Providence & Boston R. R. Co., at New London, Ct., which position he continued to hold at the time of his death, which occurred at Charlestown, R. I., June 13, 1880. Ch.—

i. CARRIE G., b. Sept. 11, 1842; m. Apr. 20, 1868, Isaac Crandall, b. Feb. 4, 1841. Ch.—Carrie T., b. Oct. 13, 1869. Res. Mystic, Ct.
ii. HANNAH M., b. Aug. 23, 1845; m. Aug. 23, 1871, Michael Craven, b. May, 1, 1845. Ch.—Maud E., b. Sept. 26, 1872. Grace G., b. Aug. 30, 1876; d. Jan. 20, 1877. Frances A., b. Dec. 25, 1879; d. May 16, 1881; res. North Adams, Mass.
iii. THOS. A. Jr., b. Sept. 2, 1847. Res. East Greenwich, R. I.

Thomas Arnold Pearce, Jr., son of Thomas A. Pearce and Thankful G., his wife, was born at Charlestown, R. I., Sept.

2, 1847. Received his early education in the public schools of his native town, and where he was engaged in various pursuits. In 1868 was appointed agent of the New York, Providence & Boston R. R. Co., at East Greenwich, R. I., which position he continues to hold. In 1876–77 and 78 he represented East Greenwich in the State legislature.

iv. Henry A., b. Nov. 5, 1851. Res. Holyoke, Mass.

217 William S[8]., Pearce (George[7], Giles[6], George[5], Giles[4], Jeremiah[3], Giles[2], Richard[1]), b. Oct. 16, 1814; m. May 3, 1838, Almyra Hill. He d. Feb. 19, 1873. Res. New Troy, Mich. Ch.—

254. i. William, b. Feb. 1, 1848; m. Anna J. Lein.
255. ii. Albert D., b. July 18, 1851; m. Maggie Clark and Myrtle Tiffney.

218 Pitt J[8], Pearce (George[7], Giles[6], George[5], Giles[4], Jeremiah[3], Giles[2], Richard[1]), b. Nov. 10, 1816; m. Apr. 9, 1839, Mary Hill, b. Feb. 28, 1818; Res. New Troy, Mich. Ch.—

i. Arnold W., b. Mar. 14, 1840; m. Mar. 24, 1865. Res. New Troy, Mich.
ii. Lucinda M., b. Aug. 29, 1842; m. —— Jennings. Res. New Troy, Mich.

219 George[8] Pearce (George[7], Giles[6], George[5], Giles[4], Jeremiah[3], Giles[2], Richard[1]), b. Aug. 19, 1822; m. June 21, 1849, Cordelia A. Stetson. Res. New Troy. Mich. Ch.—

256. i. Frank M., b. June 13, 1850; m. Jane C. Mann.
ii. Nora, b. July 14, 1854; m. Dec. 24, 1873. —— Pyle., Res. Galien, Mich.
iii. Mary S., b. Dec. 25, 1858; d. June 5, 1873.

220 George M.[8] Pearce (Joseph A.[7], Giles[6], George[5], Giles[4], Jeremiah[3], Giles[2], Richard[1]), b. Mar. 3, 1836; m. May 22, 1861, Sarah Jane Hickox, b. Oct. 25, 1836. Res. Hamburg, N. Y. Ch.—

i. Stella T., b. Mar. 16, 1862.
ii. May E., b. May 20, 1866.

221 Francis G.[8] Pearce (Joseph A.[7], Giles[6], George[5], Giles[4], Jeremiah[3], Giles[2], Richard[1]), b. May 2, 1846; m. June 29, 1871, Louisa A. Meyer, b. Nov. 29, 1855. Res. Hamburg, N. Y. Ch.—

i. Everette L., b. June 17, 1878.
ii. Orville F., b. Apr. 25, 1882.

222 Charles M.[8] Pearce (Joseph A.[7], Giles[6], George[5], Giles[4], Jeremiah[3], Giles[2], Richard[1]), b. Jan. 5, 1842; m. Mar. 4, 1863, ——; m. 2d, June 1, 1871, Martha J. Smith, b. Sept. 12, 1849. Res. Big Tree Corners, Erie Co., N. Y. Ch.—

i. CROMWELL C., b. Sept. 2, 1873.
ii. MAUD E., b. Mar. 7, 1875.
iii. ADDIE M., b. July 24, 1885.

223 ARNOLD D.[8] PEARCE (Oliver S.[7], Giles[6], George[5], Giles[4], Jeremiah[3], Giles[2], Richard[1]), b. June. 1, 1816; m. Mary J. Ills. Res. West Seneca, N. Y. Ch.—

i. LAURA, m. Mr. Partridge.
ii. SUSIA, d.
iii. HERBERT B., May 2, 1863.

224 WINSLOW S.[8] PEARCE (Oliver S.[7], Giles[6], George[5], Giles[4], Jeremiah[3], Giles[2], Richard[1]), b. Aug. 20, 1818; m. Feb. 8, 1848, Rozelia S. Titus. Res. Abbott's Corners, Hamburgh, N. Y. Ch.—

257. i. JEROME W., b. Dec. 17, 1849; m. Mary S. Deuel.
258. ii. PERRY D., b. Aug. 8, 1854; m. Jennie M. Deuel.
iii. EVA S. b. Apr. 2. 1857; m. Jan. 23, 1878, Frank P. Titus. Ch.—Toodles H. A., b. May 11, 1880, res. Hamburg, N. Y.
259. iv. HIRAM A., b. Oct. 24, 1864; m. Isa Kilgore.

225 AARON[8] PEARCE (Oliver S.[7], Giles[6], George[5], Giles[4], Jeremiah[3], Giles[2], Richard[1]), b. Dec. 10, 1820; m. Helen Chita, ker, b. Aug. 10, 1828. He d. May 16, 1875. Res. Hamburgh, N. Y. Ch.—

i. EDWARD, b. Dec. 10, 1864 (adopted).

226 GEORGE M.[8] PEARCE (Oliver S.[7], Giles[6], George[5], Giles[4], Jeremiah[3], Giles[2], Richard[1]), b. Feb. 18. 1823; m. Dec. 30, 1858, Harriett Dwight, b. June 21, 1840. Res. Hamburgh, N. Y. Ch.—

i. SARAH L., b. Aug. 6, 1859; m. Feb. 17, 1880, Wm. Kronenberg.
ii. GEO. M. Jr., b. May 23, 1861; d. Oct. 7, 1862.
iii. HENRY D., b. Apr. 25, 1863; d. Mar. 24, 1864.
iv. CARRY M., b. Sept. 22, 1865; m. June 15, 1886, F. S. Martin.
v. DANIEL C., b. May 2, 1874.
vi. BESSIE E., b. June 22, 1877.
vii. GEO. M. Jr., b. Jan. 6, 1869; d. Sept. 28, 1872.

227 OLIVER C.[8] PEARCE (Oliver S.[7], Giles[6], George[5], Giles[4], Jeremiah[3], Giles[2], Richard[1]), b. May 24, 1827; m. Sept. 29, 1851, Helen M. Cumstock, b. June, 2, 1837. Res. Hamburg, N. Y. Ch.—

260. i. FRANK O., b. July 7, 1853; m. Jennie Williston.
ii. LYMAN, b. May 17, 1858; m. Jan. 10, 1882, Mamie Keeler.
iii WILBER E., b. Oct. 24, 1869.

228 JOB A.[8] PEARCE (Job[7], Job[6], Job[5], John[4], Jeremiah[3], Giles[2], Richard[1]), b. Feb 27, 1834; m. Nov. 23, 1864, Sarah S. Bird, b. Oct. 9, 1839. Res. 10 Appleton St., Boston, Mass. Ch.—

i. GRACE, b. Aug. 29, 1869.
ii. CHARLES A., b. June 24, 1870.

229 PRESEVED R.[8] PEARCE (Job[7], Job[6], Job[5]. John[4], Jeremiah[3], Giles[2], Richard[1]), b. Dec. 6, 1835; m. Nov. 23, 1864, Harriett A. Fairbanks, b. Mar. 22, 1842. Res. Crompton, R. I. Ch.—

i. EDWIN A., b. Dec. 19, 1865.

230 VERNON R.[8] PEARCE (Job[7], Job[6], Job[5], John[4]. Jeremiah[3], Giles[2], Richard[1]), b. May 31, 1844; m. Dec. 26, 1871, Mariana H. Marshall, b. June 21, 1849. Res. No. 169, West Newton street, Boston, Mass. Ch.—

i. MARION G., b. Nov. 27, 1873.
ii. VERNON M., b. Oct. 4, 1875.

231 ZEPHENIAH G.[8] PEARCE (Willliam B.[7], Benjamin B.[6], Moses[5], Thomas[4], John[3], Giles[2], Richard[1]), b. ———; m. Dec. 6, 1867, Susan F. Smith, b. April 1, 1842. Res. 32 Wilson st., Providence, R. I. Ch.—

i. EDWARD E., b. June 27, 1869.
ii. FRED'K L., b. May 15, 1873.

232 EDWARD M.[8] PEARCE (Edward[7], Giles[6], Giles[5], Giles[4], John[3], Giles[2], Richard[1]), b. Jan. 13, 1850; m. May 6, 1874, Minnie Harvey. Ch —

i. FRANK E., b. Dec. 13, 1875.
ii. LEVIN M., b. May 3, 1877.
iii. GEORGE E., b. Oct. 4, 1880.
iv. CHARLES L, b. Dec. 3, 1882.

233 PROF. JOHN W.[8] PEARCE (John S.[7], John[6], John[5], Nathaniel[4], George[3], George[2], Richard[1]), b. July 16, 1858; m. Mar. 9, 1881, Nellie M. Endt, b. May 1, 1859. Res. Baton Rogue, La.

John W. Pearce educated himself by working with his father during six months of the year, and attending the Louisiana State university during the other six months. Left the university in 1879, without graduation; married Mar. 9, 1881. On Oct. 2, 1881, took charge of a large academy in North Louisiana. Since that time he has almost constantly followed the teachers' calling as principal of several of the chief schools of Louisiana, and as assistant professor in the State University, from which he received the degree of B. A., in 1883, and of M. A. in 1884; said to be a young man of unusual promise and ability.

Ch.—

i. JOHN S., b. June 5, 1882.
ii. WILLIAM M., b. July 2, 1884.

234 MARTIN C.[8] PEARCE (William K.[7], John[6], John[5], Nathaniel[4], George[3], George[2], Richard[1]), b. Aug. 13, 1865 ; m. Sept. 15, 1884, Emma C. Kenney, b. Mar. 23, 1866. Res. 215 Madison st., Philadeiphia Pa. Ch.—

i. MABEL E., b. June 8, 1885.

235 CHARLES F.[8] PEARCE (Abner T.[7], Thomas[6], Wright[5], James[4], James[3], George[2], Richard[1]), b. April 29, 1835 ; m. Jan. 12, 1860, Sarah H. Smith, b. Dec. 14, 1835. He d. Oct. 8, 1884. Res. Santiago, Chili, South America. Ch.—

i. EARL F., b. July 17, 1863. Res. 14 South Main st., Fall River, Mass.

ii. HELEN A. E., b. Mar. 19, 1866. Res. 14 South Main st., Fall River, Mass.

236 WALDO A.[8] PEARCE (Abner T.[7], Thomas[6], Wright[5], James[4], James[3], George[2], Richard[1]), b. Mar. 14, 1837 ; m. Nov. 29, 1864, Emma C. Webster, b. Mar. 31, 1847. Res. Boston, Mass., office 228 Washington st. Ch.—

i. EMMA L., b. Sept. 8, 1865.

237 FRANK T.[8] PEARCE (Franklin[7], Thomas[6], Wright[5], James[4], James[3], George[2], Richard[1]) b. Nov. 13, 1848 ; m. May 14, 1873, Annie R. Gardner, b. May 29, 1855. Res. 79 Greenwich st., Providence, R. I. Ch.—

i. ALDRIDGE G., b. April 2, 1875.
ii. WILLIAM H., b. Feb. 4, 1882 ; d. Mar. 23, 1882.
iii. ANN E., b Dec 14, 1886.

238 SAMUEL[8] PEARCE (Addison L.[7], George T.[6], Stephen[5], James[4], James[3], George[2], Richard[1]), b. May 30, 1845 ; m. Mar. 20, 1870, Bessie Carburry. Res. Trumansburg, N. Y. Ch.—

i. EDWARD, b. Oct. 16, 1871.
ii. WILLIAM, b. Mar. 26, 1873.
iii. ANNIE, b. Jan. 19, 1876.
iv. CATHERINÈ, b. Feb. 4, 1880.
v. MARGARET, b. May 13, 1883.

239 GEORGE W.[8] PEARCE (Addison L.[7], George T.[6], Stephen[5], James[4], James[3], George[2], Richard[1]), b. Oct. 7, 1857 ; m. Nov. 3, 1874 ; Elnora Clark, b. June 30, 1853. Res. Lodi, N. Y. Ch.—

i. CLARK, b. Feb. 25, 1876.
ii. HELEN, b. May 20, 1883.
iii. GROVER C., b. May 11, 1886.

240 ANSEL[8] PEARCE (Gameliel[7], George T.[6], Stephen[5], James[4], James[3], George[2], Richard[1]), b, Nov. 27, 1852 ; m. June 15, 1875, Sarah L. Chevalier, b. Apr. 25, 1860. Res. Harford, N. Y. Ch.—

i. FREDIE A., b. June 12, 1876.

241 Tho. E.^{8} Pearce (J. Oscar^{7}, Nathaniel^{6}, Ezekiel^{5}, James^{4}, James^{3}, George^{2}, Richard^{1}), b. Mar. 15, 1861 ; m Nov. 12, 1882, Nellie Sherwood, b. Nov. 19, 1865. Res. 323 Vleit st., Milwaukee, Wis. Ch.—

i. Archie, b. Sept. 27, 1883.
ii. Bessie L., b. Sept. 11, 1884.

242 Oliver P.^{8} Pearce (Henry L,^{7}, William^{6}, James^{5}, James^{4}, James^{3}, George^{2}, Richard^{1}), b. Feb. 4, 1822 ; m. Mar. 16, 1845, Waitey A. West, b. April 3, 1824. Res. Naples, N. Y. Ch.—

261. i. William M., b. Oct. 26, 1845 ; m. Chloe Knapp, and——
ii. Lucy A., b. Feb. 12, 1851 ; m. Feb. 22, 1867 ; Charles M. Struble, b. July 1, 1845. Res. Honeoye, N. Y. Ch.—Nettie, b. Mar. 1, 1868 ; Ettie b. June 26, 1870 ; Ella, b. Feb. 16, 1872 ; Amos b. Nov. 2, 1877, d. Jan. 6, 1879 ; Bert, b. Feb. 19, 1880.
262. iii. Francis M., b. Jan. 2, 1855 ; m Carrie Simmons.
263. iv. Warren L., b. Sept. 14, 1860, m. Ettie S. Ingraham.

243 Parker H.^{8} Pearce, Jr. (Parker H.^{7}, William^{6}, James^{5}. James^{4}, James^{3}, George^{2}, Richard^{1}), b. Feb. 8, 1819 ; m, Sept. 15, 1853, Jane E. Blancher.

He was born in Boston, Mass., and at one time was a member of the Boston Light Infantry, and later of the Boston Cadets. He died Aug. 26, 1872. Ch.—

i. Parker H., b. ——, ——, } both. Res. St. Louis, Mo.
ii. William G., b.——, }

244 George A.^{8} Pearce (Parker H.^{7}, William^{6}, James^{5}, James^{4}, James^{3}, George^{2}, Richard^{1}), b July 2, 1828; m. Oct. 22, 1866, Josephine Hopkins, b. 1836. Res. Springwater, N. Y. Ch.—

i. George A., b. Nov. 11, 1867.

245 Alvin A.^{8} Pearce (Benjamin F.^{7}, William^{6}, James^{5}, James^{4}, James^{3}, George^{2}, Richard^{1}), b. July 3, 1827 ; m. Nov. 27, 1855, Elizabeth Sprout, b. June 13, 1840. Res. Waterford, Wis. Ch.—

i. Calvin L., b. July 4, 1857 ; m. Dec. 18, 1879. Res. North Cape, Wis.
ii. Sarah R., b. Feb. 25, 1860 ; m. Dec. 25, 1879, James Hankerson. Res. Rochester, Wis.
iii. Edward C. b. Nov. 23, 1869.
iv. Delia, b. Jan. 15, 1879.

246 Benjamin F.^{8} Pearce (Benjamin F.^{7}, William^{6}, James^{5}, James^{4}, James^{3}, George^{2}, Richard^{1}), b. Nov. 24, 1829 ; m. Nov. 5, 1856, Mary Cameron, b. June 14, 1834. Res. North Cape, Wis. Ch.—

i. Ellen, b. Nov. 22, 1857 ; m. Jan. 15, 1879, Wm. Beatty.
iii. Kittie L., b. May 26, 1860 ; d. Jan. 3, 1861.
iii. Henry C., b. Aug. 28, 1862.
iv. Laura H., b. July 11, 1867.
v. Albert L., b. Jan. 8, 1872.
vi. Frank L., b. April 18, 1874.

247 Willard A.[8] Pearce (Allen S.[7], Sanford[6], Samuel[5], Samuel[4], James[3], George[2], Richard[1]), b. April 11, 1841 ; m. June 6, 1870, Mrs. Mary E. Richardson *nee* Collins, b. Mar. 27, 1840. Res. No. 56 West 132d street, New York, N. Y.

Willard Allen Pearce, Thrice Potent Grand Master of the Lodge of Perfection of New York City.

"There's proud modesty in merit."—*Dryden.*

It is a pleasing novelty in our experiences in this mundane sphere to meet occasionally with those whose unobtrusive merit commend them to our admiration and regard, whose distrust of their own ability but adds an additional charm to the performance of pleasing and self-imposed duties.

Of this class are those who without ostentation extend the hand of charity to the suffering and needy, and quietly perform unnumbered acts of kindness and of love, whose peerless recompense is the consciousness of duty performed, with the glad realization that

"'Tis better to give than to receive."

These reflections are induced by a contemplation of the characteristics which distinguish the living life of the subject of our sketch.

Brother Pearce is a native of Providence, in the State of Rhode Island, and is now about forty years of age. His father is a prominent and distinguished scientist, and for the last forty years has been known as a popular lecturer on electricity and astronomy. His opinions are recognized as authority in scientific circles, and his erudition marks him as a tireless and indefatigable student.

The subject of our notice, who inherits the virtues of the father, had all the educational advantages which his early surroundings permitted, and early gave promise of untiring industry and persistent zeal which has marked his course in every relation in life. By quiet perseverence his mind was enriched, and he soon acquired that self-confidence which enabled him successfully to encounter the vicissitudes of life. His business avocations called him to the city of New York in 1870, where he has since been permantly located, and in business circles possesses and commands that confidence and appreciation which ever follows an upright and honorable man.

In masonry our friend has been no less successful. Soon after his advént in New York he received the symbolic degrees in Manhattan Lodge, No. 489, and subsequently served as Senior Deacon and Senior Warden. He was elected Worshipful Master for two consecutive terms, 1876–7; in December 1872, he was exalted in Zerubabel Chapter, R. A. M., wherein he was elected Royal Arch Captain the following year and served with great acceptability. Subsequently he received the Cryptic Degress in Columbian Council, No. 1, R & S. Masters, wherein he served one year as Deputy Master, afterwards declining the office of Thrice Illustrious Master, to which he had been unanimously chosen.

The Orders of Masonic Knighthood were conferred upon Companion Pearce in Ivanhoe Commandery, No. 36, July, 1873, and subsequently during the same year he was initiated in, and completed the Ineffable grades of the Ancient Accepted Scottish Rite in Garabaldi (afterward styled "Ancient") Lodge of Perfection, and after attaining the Philosophical and Historical degrees in Templar Council and Templar Chapter Rose Croix, respectively, he was, in 1874, conducted through the Sublime grades, culminating with the thirty-second S. P. R. S., in Aurora Grata Consistory.

Our Ill. Bro. was elected presiding officer in Ancient Lodge of Perfection in 1874, and was annually rechosen until 1879, when he declined a re-election. During all his administration this body was eminently successfull and prosperous, and the energy which he infused into his *personnel* has lost nothing of its vitalizing influence.

In Templar Council 16°, he was elected and served as Senior Grand Warden in the years 1875, 76, and 77; also, as Junior Grand Warden of TemplarChapter Rose Croix in 1878.

This brief and imperfect recapitulation of the masonic history and services of our distinguished Bro. can scarcely give the reader an idea of the extent of the self-sacrificing labor and zeal which has marked his modest course; and it is with great pleasure that we are privileged to add the latest and best evidence of appreciation by his fellows, in his unanimous election during the present season as the presiding officer of The Lodge of Perfection of the City of New York, this body having been formed by the consolidation of New York Ancient and Templar Lodges of Perfection.

This distinguished honor was unexpectedly thrust upon its modest recipient, and it is sufficient to say that he and the station are alike worthy of each other, and that he will bring to the discharge of his newly-assumed duties an energy an devotion which will subserve the highest interest of the united body, and fully realize the best wishes and hopes of its enlarged membership.

In social life the subject of our notice is genial, and companionable, never encouraging excess, and in all things affable and courteous ; scarcely yet in the meridian of life, his walk and conversation evidences a deep study of mankind and men.

May we not indulge the hope that in the not far distant future, still higher honors await him with the craft, and that he will long remain to serve them, whether in station or ortherwise, and thus establish the proud fact that during his day and generation he

"Lived not in vain."

(From a Masonic paper). Ch.—

i. May E. b. Dec. 29, 1867.
ii. Willard J. b. July 29, 1869.
iii. Trelis, A. b. May 21, 1871.
iv. Emma A. b. June 28, 1874.

248 George B.^{8} Pearce (George W^{7}, Sanford^{6}, Samuel^{5}, Samuel^{4}, James^{3}, George^{2}, Richard^{1}), b. Mar. 3, 1843 ; m. Jan 20, 1885, Kate M. Cross, b. Dec. 17, 1846. Res. Geneva, N. Y. Ch.—

i. George F., b. Mar. 9, 1886.

249 William H.^{9} Pearce (Nathaniel^{8}, George A^{7}., Nathaniel^{6}, Richard^{5}, Nathaniel^{4}, Richard^{3}, Richard , Richard^{1}), b. May 14, 1848 ; m. Mar. 1, 1867, Emily J. Arnold. Res. Olneyville. R. I. Ch.—

i. Mabel H,. b. Sept. 17, 1867 ; m. Feb. 10, 1885, Lowell B. Sherman. Res. Olneyville, R I.

250 Charles F.^{9} Pearce (Nathaniel^{8}, George A^{7}., Nathaniel^{6}, Richard^{5}, Nathaniel^{4}, Richard^{3}, Richard^{2}, Richard^{1}),b. June 4, 1846; m. June 1, 1868, Harriett L. Howland. Res 21 Hudson st., Providence, R. I. Ch —

i. Jesse H., b. Mar. 19, 1869.
ii. Hattie, b. Aug. —, 1870.
iii. Alice R., b. April —, 1874.

251 Nathaniel W ^{9} Pearce (Nathaniel^{8}, George A^{7}., Nathaniel^{6}, Richard^{5}, Nathaniel^{4}, Richard^{3}, Richard^{2}, Richard^{1}), b. Mar. 20, 1851 ; m. Sept. 20, 1871, Alice E. Butts, b Nov. 7, 1853. Res. 21 Allen ave., Pautucket, R. I. Ch.—

i. Minnie D., b April 13, 1872, d. June 9, 1873.
ii. Nathaniel W., b. July 8, 1873.
iii. Ellen T., b. Dec. 11, 1875 ; d. April 7, 1876.
iv. Albert D., b. Feb. 22, 1877.
v. Frank, b. May 4, 1879.
vi. Chester A., b. July 23, 1881.

252 THEODORE B.[9] PEARCE (Nathaniel W[8]., George A[7]., Nathaniel[6], Richard[5], Nathaniel[4], Richard[3], Richard[2], Richard[1]), b. May 4, 1854; m. Nov. 28, 1875, Kate M. Woods, b. Mar. —, 1853. He d. June 29, 1876. Res. Pautucket, R. I. Ch.—

i. THEODORE B., b. Nov. 12, 1873.

253 GEORGE R.[9] PEARCE (George G[8]., George[7], William[6], George[5], Willliam[4], Richard[3], Richard[2], Richard[1]), b. July 14, 1850; m. Oct. 14, 1880, Nellie F. Morse, b. Jan. 27, 1860. Res. Wakefield, R. I. Ch.—

i. LE BARON, b. May 14, 1881; d. Aug. 27, 1881.
ii. GEORGE M., b. May 17, 1882.
iii. MARY F., Feb. 1, 1884.
iv. RUTH LE B., b. Mar. 6, 1886.

254 WILLIAM[9] PEARCE (William S.[8], George[7] Giles[6], George[5], Giles[4], Jeremiah[3], Giles[2], Richard[1]), b. Feb. 1, 1848; m. Dec. 25, 1871, Ann J. Levin. Res. New Troy, Mich. Ch.—

i. DAISY A., b Dec. 12, 1876; d. Oct. 15, 1880.
ii. OLLA W., b. Sept. 21, 1880.

255 ALBERT D.[9] PEARCE (same as above), b. July 18, 1851; m. Oct. 25, 1875, Maggie Clark, b. Sept. 10, 1851; d. Sept. 25, 1876; m. 2d, Feb. 17, 1881, Myrtle Tiffney. Res. New Troy, Mich. Ch.—

i. CLARK A., b. Sept. 24, 1876; d. young.
ii. GUY A. b. July 17, 1882.

256 FRANK M.[9] PEARCE (George[8], George[7], Giles[6], George[5], Giles[4], Jeremiah[3], Giles[2], Richard[1]), b. June 13, 1850; m. Dec. 24, 1873, Jane C. Mann. Res. Galien, Mich. Ch.—

i. MAY S., b. Nov. 30, 1881.
ii. Delbert, b. Aug. 30, 1883.

257 JEROME W.[9] PEARCE (Winslow S.[8], Oliver S.[7], Giles[6], George[5], Giles[4], Jeremiah[3], Giles[2], Richard[1]), b. Dec. 17, 1849; m. Oct. 9, 1873, Mary S. Deuel, b. July 31, 1854. Res. Hamburg, N. Y. Ch.—

i. CLARENCE A., ——— ———.

258 PERRY D.[9] PEARCE (Winslow S.[8], Oliver S[7]., Giles[6], George[5], Giles[4], Jeremiah[3], Giles[2], Richard[1]), b. Aug. 8, 1854; m. Dec. 19, 1877, Jennie M. Deuel, b. Aug. 25, 1859. Res. Hamburg, N. Y. Ch.—

i. EVERETT D., b. Aug. 13, 1883.

259 HIRAM A.[9] PEARCE (same as above), b. Oct. 24, 1864; m. Jan. 26, 1887, Isa Kilgore, b. Dec. 3, 1863. Res. Hamburg, N. Y. Of their wedding the Pecatoniea (Ill.) *News*, said: At the residence of Mrs. Sarah Kilgore, last Wednes-

day evening, Jan. 26th, about fifty of the relatives and intimate friends assembled to witness the marriage ceremony which made Hiram A. Pierce and Miss Isa Kilgore husband and wife. The ceremony was performed by Rev. W. F. Cooley, of Seward, and after the usual season of congratulations an elaborate wedding feast was partaken of. The presents were numerous and beautiful combining utility and ornamentation. The groom is of Hamburg, N. Y., a young man of pleasing address and excellent reputation, while the bride is well known and highly respected in this vicinity in which she has lived all her life Mr. and Mrs. Pierce expect to leave this morning for their future home in New York state, where they go accompanied by the best wishes of a host of warm friends.

260 FRANK O.^{9} PEARCE (Oliver C.^{8}, Oliver S^{7}., Giles^{6}, George^{5}, Giles^{4}, Jeremiah^{3}, Giles^{2}, Richard^{1}) b. July 7, 1853; m. Oct. 20, 1874, Jennie L. Williston, b. Feb. 4, 1856. Res. Water Valley, N. Y. Ch.—

i. GLEN W., b. Oct. 27, 1875; d. Dec. 24, 1875.
ii. ARTHUR L., b. Dec. 22, 1876.
iii. WALLACE R., b. Mar. 12, 1882; d. April 1, 1882.

261 WILLIAM M.^{9} PEARCE (Oliver P.^{8}, Henry L.^{7}, William^{6}, James^{5}, James^{4}, James^{3}, George^{2}, Richard^{1}), b. Oct. 26, 1845; m. Mar. 10, 1867, Charles Knapp, d. ——; m. 2d. Res. Athens, Mich. Ch.—

i. OLIVER J., b. Dec. 23, 1867.
ii LELAND, ——— ———.

262 FRANCIS M.^{9} PEARCE (same as above), b. Jan. 2, 1855; m. Oct. 6, 1878, Carrie Simmons, b. Aug. 13, 1861. Res. Bristol Centre, N. Y. Ch.—

i. LEVIN O., b. April 16, 1882.
ii. MARK G., b. June 6, 1887.

263 WARREN L.^{9} PEARCE (same as above), b. Sept. 14, 1860; m. Feb. 21, 1883, Ettie S. Ingraham, b. April 13, 1864. Res. Naples, N. Y. Ch.—

i. EARLE A., b. Oct. 13, 1884.

INDEX TO PEARCES.

DESCENDANTS OF RICHARD PEARCE.

INDEX TO NAMES OTHER THAN PEARCE.

DESCENDANTS OF RICHARD PEARCE.

www.ingramcontent.com/pod-product-compliance
Lightning Source LLC
Chambersburg PA
CBHW031532260326
41914CB00026B/1660

9781596413351